*Resistance, Revolt, and Gender Justice in Egypt*

**Gender, Culture, and Politics in the Middle East**
miriam cooke, Simona Sharoni, and Suad Joseph, *Series Editors*

Other titles in Gender, Culture, and Politics in the Middle East

# Resistance, Revolt, and Gender Justice in Egypt

## MARIZ TADROS

SYRACUSE UNIVERSITY PRESS

Copyright © 2016 by Syracuse University Press
Syracuse, New York 13244-5290

All Rights Reserved

First Edition 2016

16  17  18  19  20  21        6  5  4  3  2  1

Material in chapter 2 of this book draws heavily on a chapter that was published in an edited book called *Voicing Demands: Feminist Activism in Transitional Contexts*, edited by Sohela Nazneen and Maheen Sultan (Zed 2014). I am grateful for authorization to reprint.

Material in chapters 4 and 5 draws on research undertaken for the Developmental Leadership Programme and published in a research paper titled "Working Politically behind Red Lines: Structure and Agency in a Comparative Study of Women's Coalitions in Egypt and Jordan" in 2011.

∞ The paper used in this publication meets the minimum requirements of the American National Standard for Information Sciences—Permanence of Paper for Printed Library Materials, ANSI Z39.48-1992.

For a listing of books published and distributed by Syracuse University Press, visit www .SyracuseUniversityPress.syr.edu.

ISBN: 978-0-8156-3461-4 (cloth)          978-0-8156-3450-8 (paperback)
                                          978-0-8156-5375-2 (e-book)

**Library of Congress Cataloging-in-Publication Data**
Names: Tadros, Mariz, 1975– author.
Title: Resistance, revolt, and gender justice in Egypt / Mariz Tadros.
Description: First edition. | Syracuse, New York : Syracuse University Press, [2016] | Series: Gender, culture, and politics in the Middle East | Includes bibliographical references and index.
Identifiers: LCCN 2016003696| ISBN 9780815634614 (cloth : alk. paper) | ISBN 9780815634508 (pbk. : alk. paper) | ISBN 9780815653752 (e-book)
Subjects: LCSH: Feminism—Egypt. | Women's rights—Egypt. | Women—Egypt—Social conditions. | Egypt—Politics and government—1981–
Classification: LCC HQ1793 .T327 2016 | DDC 305.420962–dc23 LC record available at http://lccn.loc.gov/2016003696

*Manufactured in the United States of America*

*To my daughters Mariam and Merit and to all the Egyptian women and men who have struggled for a humane, gender-just world*

# CONTENTS

# TABLES

# NOTE ON TRANSLITERATION

Arabic words have not been fully transliterated in this book. An apostrophe (') has been used to render the letter "hamza," and a reverse apostrophe (') has been used to render the letter "'ayn." Names have been transliterated without apostrophes or reverse apostrophes. Neither macrons nor dots have been used with letters unique to Arabic.

# ACKNOWLEDGMENTS

This book is the culmination of twenty years of researching, participating in, and writing about collective action in relation to gender equality. I owe a great deal to colleagues, friends, family, and members of the community who shared their lives, insights, and experiences with me along this journey.

I could not have embarked on this book without the mentoring support of Andrea Cornwall, Rosalind Eyben, and Deniz Kandiyoti, who are living examples not only of "lift while you climb," but of "never stop lifting others even after you have reached the apex." They have set the bar very high for academic integrity, humility, generosity, and magnanimity.

I am grateful for many helpful conversations with leading feminist scholar-activists in Egypt, whose commitment to gender and social justice is exceptional, and I am thankful for members of my "tribe" at the Institute of Development Studies (IDS), former and existing, who have been a constant source of nurturing and encouragement over the years. I am indebted to many individuals and organizations for the interviews, focus groups, conversations, and debates, and for the wealth of knowledge and insights that I gained from these processes.

This book would not have been possible without the critical contributions of Egyptian researchers. I am especially grateful for the capable and incisive research assistance of Dr. Hind Mahmoud, whose devotion to gender justice and deep respect for all voices and perspectives are exemplary.

I would like to thank writer and human rights expert Mohamed Hussein el Naggar for the interviews he did in April and May 2012 and then again in July 2012. Mohamed Hussein, known to many as Sheikh el Arab of the human rights community in Egypt, had a repertoire of goodwill and trust among a broad spectrum of activists in Egypt.

I would also like to thank leading journalist and author Robeir el Fares for his critical interviews with members of the constituent assembly who were tasked with writing the constitution in 2012. He was careful to interview people from all political orientations and to offer insights not only on the spoken but also on the unspoken.

Chapter 9 benefited from empirical research involving dozens of interviews, the production of a video by Andrea and Khokha, and a workshop and life histories from November 2011 to April 2013.

I would like to express my heartiest gratitude to those whose identities I could not reveal but who have been quoted in this manuscript. In accordance with Syracuse University Press publishing protocol, I could not quote people without their written permission to be featured in the book even if they had consented to the interviews and such consent was tape-recorded. This meant that two groups appear "faceless," particularly in chapters 6–8: members of the Muslim Brotherhood and women youth revolutionaries. Due to the highly securitized context and the incarceration of many interviewed members of the Muslim Brotherhood, I had to withdraw their names. I never intended to conceal the identities of members of the Muslim Brotherhood and the women revolutionaries while revealing the identities of others. This action in no way represents a double standard in representing people of different political orientations; it is simply because there were serious accessibility issues by the time I was seeking permissions.

I am immensely grateful to Hania Sholkamy for her joint collaborative research initiative with the Social Research Center (SRC), which she supported tirelessly even in the midst of her one thousand and one other obligations. Many thanks go to Shaza Abd el Latif, whose encyclopaedic knowledge of youth-based activism on gender and social justice is unparalleled. She brought passion and great insights to the work. I would also like to thank Rasha Habib, one of Egypt's most brilliant anthropologists, who is able to make anyone feel at ease in seconds and whose life histories with men in gender-based movements were extremely powerful for this research.

I am indebted to the women and men of the informal youth-based initiatives who patiently shared visions, strategies, and techniques with me. Their openness, sacrificial giving of their time, and energy have been sources of hope for me and many others. I am grateful for the leaders and practitioners of the local development organizations who undertook focus groups and case studies in Cairo, Alexandria, Fayoum, Minya, Beni Suef, and Qena in 2012–15. Their skills, rigor, and integrity are unparalleled; they are my great instructors to whom I will be indebted all my life. Many of the insights and perspectives shared in chapter 10 emanate from the focus group discussions held in the eighteen months after the regime change of July 2013.

I would like to thank the British Academy for their Mid-Career Fellowship, which provided me this unique opportunity to think, reflect, and write. Without this fellowship, it would have been impossible to have the time to write this book. I would also like to thank the Institute of Development Studies for a three-month sabbatical that I used to write the proposal for this book. I cannot thank enough Andrea Cornwall and Jenny Edwards of Pathways of Women's Empowerment for funding the writing of chapters 3 and 4 and for providing critical feedback on both chapters. A different version of chapter 2 appeared in *Voicing Demands: Feminist Activism in Transitional Contexts* (2014), edited by Sohela Nazneen and Maheen Sultan, to whom I am grateful for feedback on earlier work.

The support and intellectual energy of the late Adrian Leftwich, together with that of Chris Roche and Steve Hogg, provided the enabling environment for me to pursue the research that informed chapters 3 and 4. Earlier versions of this work appeared in "Working Politically behind Red Lines: Structure and Agency in a Comparative Study of Women's Coalitions in Egypt and Jordan" (2011). I am thankful to the SRC office in Egypt for funding some of the research that appears in chapters 5 and 6. I am also grateful for the Department for International Development's Accountable Grant, which funded the field research presented in chapters 7–9. Thank you to Dr. Yousry Mustapha at the German International Development Agency (GIZ) for funding the writing of my paper, "The Politics of Mobilising for Gender Justice in Egypt from Mubarak to Morsi and Beyond" (2014). I would also like to thank the European Council for

Foreign Relations for funding interviews in July and August 2012. All disqualifiers apply.

I am deeply indebted to my daughters Mariam and Merit, who have discussed, debated, and challenged me on justice, fairness, and inequality. This manuscript would never have been written had it not been for the consistent, unbounded, unconditional support of my husband, Akram, the greatest feminist I have ever known. He spent many weekends and nights being there for Mariam and Merit while I hid away to work.

This manuscript benefited beyond words from the feedback of two blind peer reviewers. Thanks also to Professor Diane Singerman for her meticulous and constructive feedback. Professor Singerman has set the bar very high for academic congeniality and generosity.

I cannot find the words to express how grateful I am to Professor Suad Joseph, one of the series editors of Gender, Culture, and Politics in the Middle East at Syracuse University Press. Professor Joseph is a paragon of what it is to live every word you preach. Her commitment to supporting generations of women academics working on justice issues in the Middle East has been unparalleled. She has challenged us to be probing while remaining unreservedly nurturing and encouraging. May we find the strength to walk in her footsteps.

Sincere thanks are due to Suzanne Guiod, editor-in-chief of Syracuse University Press, who never tired of sending me kind and assuring messages and updates. Many thanks also to Kelly Balenske, assistant editor at Syracuse University Press, who tirelessly put the manuscript together for production. I owe a great deal to Sara Cleary, who copyedited the document with extraordinary professionalism and commitment. Many thanks also go to Judith Acevedo for kindly compiling the index.

*Resistance, Revolt, and Gender Justice in Egypt*

# INTRODUCTION

## *Women and Men Defying Red Lines*

*B*anat misr khat ahmar!" ("The girls[1] of Egypt are a red line!") was the catchcry of the protesters on December 20, 2011. That day marked the largest women-led uprising that the country had witnessed since 1919 when women staged demonstrations against British colonial rule. The 2011 protests erupted days after soldiers had stripped a woman protester in Tahrir Square. They had ripped her long black 'abayya (a thick, loose, and often black robe that covers the entire body down to one's ankles), dragging her by her hair across the street. From the video footage she became known internationally as "the blue bra woman" (on account of the exposure of her undergarments). The video of her assault went viral, and it showed another soldier about to stomp on her bare stomach as she lay on the ground.[2]

Although hundreds of thousands of women participated in what became known as the 25th of January Revolution, and millions joined in the revolts of June 30, 2013, the protest on December 20, 2011, was different because it was based on identity. Women had gathered not only as *citizens* but also as *women* who were claiming a new moral order and setting their own red lines between what would and would not be tolerated. Women of

1. The word *banat* can mean the female sex or daughter. In translating it to "girls" it means both girls and women and is not meant in the derogatory sense of the word "girl" when applied to women.

2. See Amina Al-Masriya's "Not Your Booty" video for individual accounts, http://www.youtube.com/watch?v=0DkdYPs_qfE.

all ages, nonveiled, with head cover, in a full *niqab* (covering face), urban, rural, working-class, and upper-class women were present in Tahrir Square that night. One estimate puts the turnout at 100,000, whereas the calls for women and men to congregate in Tahrir to mark International Women's Day in March 2011 attracted less than 100 demonstrators.

Unlike past and future uprisings, during this protest it was the women who shouted the slogans and the men who tagged along. It was the women who led and the men who followed. Though most of the women present were unlikely to identify themselves as feminists, their narrative was "raise your head high; you are more honorable than those who tread on you." This slogan was chanted over and over again, sending a clear message to the women who were stripped and assaulted that they need not bow their heads in shame. The protesters recognized the survivors of assault not as defiled or disgraced but as heroines: they were turning middle-class respectability on its head and giving new meaning to the concept of dignity. For the army, the protesters had a different message. "Instead of protecting us, you strip us!" chanted the women. In a show of defiance, they continued, "Is this manliness? Come and strip us all, we are here in Tahrir Square." For the nation, the women protesters also bore a message: "Here are the men," they said, pointing to the cordon comprised of men who had formed a chain in solidarity and in defense of possible assaults. "Where are the rest of you?" they challenged their countrymen. The message was clear to the commander of the ruling Supreme Council of Armed Forces (SCAF), *Mosheer* (Field Marshal) Mohamed Tantawy: "O, you *Mosheer*, just you wait, the women of Egypt will dig your grave!" One man asked the person next to him in Tahrir Square, "Do you think these women will lead the next revolution in this country?" (Tadros 2011b).

### Shifting Red Lines

Egypt presents a particularly good case study for examining the interface of citizen–state–society relations under shifting red lines. The country has experienced four dramatic changes in political leaderships within the space of four years. President Hosni Mubarak, who reigned for thirty years (1981–2011), was overthrown by a popular revolution that brought the country under the leadership of the army. Field Marshal Mohamed Tantawy, who presided over the Supreme Council of Armed Forces, was in charge from February 2011 to June 2012. After presidential elections were held, Mohamed Morsi from the Muslim Brotherhood became Egypt's first post-Mubarak president (July 2012 to June 2013). His first anniversary in office was marked by a popular uprising followed by intervention from the military, which announced his overthrow and put in place an interim government headed by the former Supreme Constitutional Court judge, Adly Mansour (July 2013 to May 2014).

Shifting red lines is a metaphor for the visible, hidden, and invisible demarcations of power that signal to people what rules, restrictions, and controls they are required to comply with, be subjugated to, and ultimately not cross. But the lines are not simply determined by the authorities; they are negotiated. Sometimes they are drawn by citizens' slow and subtle encroachments, sometimes more radically by multitudes' revolts that lead to revolutions, and sometimes by ruptures to the status quo. This book examines the collective struggles of women and men who challenge the red lines around gender equality and broader social justice issues through conventional pathways of political engagement as well as through revolts and mass protests. It does so through a historicized, contextualized, and relational approach that examines organized activism around gender equality issues from the mid-1990s up to the end of 2014, a period of almost twenty years. This period offers an opportunity to examine gendered struggles during Mubarak's last years and how they have affected collective engagements in between Egypt's two ruptures of the status quo (2011–13) and beyond.

*Amoebic Red Lines under Mubarak*

For many decades it was the authorities, those who govern and preside over maintaining the status quo, who played a hegemonic role in determining the red lines that citizens should never transgress. Mubarak ruled Egypt with what I call *amoebic governance*, a term indicating a fluid, dynamic form of rule that, like an amoeba that alters its shape, extends and retracts projections/spheres of control as it deems fit for its preservation and sustenance.[3] I use this term in contradistinction to the notion of a hybrid regime, which in its various definitions refers to authoritarian regimes that allow limited freedoms and elections (Gilbert and Mohseni 2011). Conceptions of hybrid regimes tend to suggest a mix of methods that are simultaneously pursued by any single regime, whereas amoebic governance suggests a mode of rule in which the deployment of liberalization and repression can never be taken as a given. Amoebic styles of governance are subject to change, sometimes unpredictably, according to the interface among local, national, and international contextual factors. In some instances, spaces are open for certain actors; in others, they are closed or deeply circumscribed.

In the case of Mubarak's Egypt, amoebic governance was employed on a micro and a macro level. From above, the Mubarak regime used pluralist and corporatist strategies of engaging elites and coalitions in its first decade. From below, it kept contracting and expanding spaces for citizen and civil society agency, assuming both could be sufficiently controlled by the state security investigation apparatus so as not to threaten the status quo. During the last ten years of Mubarak's reign, however, amoebic governance strategies faltered. The political rise of "Mubarak Junior" (Gamal Mubarak) and his grooming for the inheritance of the presidency alienated many Egyptians. Gamal Mubarak and his entourage broke ranks with the intricate, corporatist style of governance maintained by his father within and outside the ruling party. Plans for his inheritance of the presidency, widespread corruption, economic deprivation, and a host of other factors culminated in the emergence of a countercoalition that drew together different forces from within the opposition. During its last ten years, Mubarak's reign was also characterized by a rising tide of protests, not only around political leadership but also around bread-and-butter issues (Ali 2012).

3. According to *The American Heritage Student Science Dictionary* (2014), an amoeba is "a one-celled microscopic organism that constantly changes shape by forming pseudopods, temporary projections that are used for movement and for the ingestion of food. Amoebas are members of the group of organisms called protozoans."

On January 25th, ironically known as Police Force Day (celebrates one of the central pillars of preserving Mubarak's reign), protests began against the regime. The protests were no doubt deeply affected by the people's overthrow of another authoritarian regime in the region, that of Ben Ali in Tunisia, only a few weeks earlier. The protests in Egypt, which lasted for eighteen days, brought to the streets and squares millions of citizens. The popular uprising culminated in the overthrow of the Mubarak regime in what is now referred to in Egypt as the "25th of January Revolution." The military stepped in and announced that the Supreme Council of Armed Forces would run the country in the interim until a democratically elected parliament and president were put in power.

*Revolutionary Red Lines*

By rebelling against Hosni Mubarak's nearly thirty-year reign (1981–2011), Egyptians were breaking the fear barrier that had been cultivated by the political police, the security forces, and the president's entourage. Symbolically, the crossing of the red line represented the tipping point at which people overcame internalized restraints and rose en masse. In the hundreds of protests that took place between February 2011 and June 2013 one of the most popular catchcries was *"Ehna shaab elkhat al ahmar"* ("We are the red line people!"). This slogan represented a clear expression of the pulse of a citizenry who readily resorted to the streets to claim rights and express anger at injustices.

Though SCAF had come to power with the blessings of the revolutionaries, in terms of its role in siding with the people rather than the president, the next phase did not witness the emergence of a new revolutionary order. Field Marshal Tantawy, the former minister of defense, presided over the Supreme Council of Armed Forces and governed the country until June 2012. SCAF's time in power was a period of almost daily protests against military rule and poor governance, leading to the emergence of the slogan, "Down down with military rule!" This slogan ultimately replaced the revolutionary slogan, "The people, the army, one hand!" which was chanted in Tahrir Square during the eighteen days before Mubarak's ousting.

But the slogan of Egyptian women, "The girls of Egypt are a red line!" remained distinct from these other slogans. It turned the tables on a highly authoritarian and patriarchal status quo: rather than the authorities, or the powers that be, setting the rules of the political game, it was the women citizens who were laying new demarcations and new rules for political engagement. Some have criticized the slogan as a reductionist sexist slogan. Does it imply that Egyptian men who are violated, tortured, and killed are not a red line? The context of this critique is important: the slogan emerged shortly after the blue bra woman was assaulted by the military police. The military police had embarked on an operation to clear Tahrir Square of the revolutionary protesters and their tents, and in the process many men and women were brutally attacked (Longbottom and Gye 2011). The case of the blue bra woman provided a harsh human face to the military deployment of brutal tactics of oppression.

Moreover, some wonder if the slogan intended to speak to patriarchal conceptions of women's honor being prized above all else, such that its violation represents the intolerable? Is this the right way to capture the nation's empathy with the cause of liberation? No doubt popular conceptions of honor have something to do with it, but not in simplistic terms. The women protesters were reclaiming the meanings of honor and dignity by celebrating the assaulted woman as a heroine rather than one who was humiliated because her nakedness was "exposed" worldwide via the media. This tactic represents an important rupture with the mainstream narrative, which tends to blame women victims for any exposure to sexual violence. But Egyptians' reactions to the blue bra woman incident were not always sympathetic. Even some middle-class, educated women reacted by saying, "Isn't it suspicious that under her *'abayya* this woman was not wearing any other clothing? Had she been wearing more clothing underneath, this would not have happened."

The protests did manage to challenge one of the country's most important red lines: the army. Feminist activists in Egypt had, over the course of many months, sought to influence the Supreme Council of Armed Force's agenda on gender equality to no avail; their pleas largely fell on deaf ears. Yet the mass mobilization of the citizenry in Tahrir in December 2011 produced an instantaneous result: Field Marshal Tantawy issued a formal apology to Egyptian women for "the violation" that occurred. When faced with a highly masculinist and hierarchical establishment such as the army

(Kandeel 2014), the opportunities for holding it accountable are virtually nonexistent. Tantawy's apology suggests that SCAF felt sufficiently threatened by the women's protest to make such an uncharacteristic political gesture. The fact that this women's protest delivered on sending a strong signal to the ruling regime is commensurate with evidence from across the globe suggesting that political demands for gender equality made through collective mobilization can at times compel the ruling class to respond in one way or another. Hence, when, why, and how this form of collective action occurs are important questions to ask, especially in a context in which women's rights issues are not high on most Egyptian citizens' lists of concerns.

When examining the vignette of the blue bra woman, it is also worth considering why women and men were compelled to join a women's protest collectively with such passion when subsequent and ensuing calls to join in women-led protests in Tahrir Square in the same year failed to attract even a small fraction of the crowds that had gathered on that day. Though Egyptian women had not stopped mobilizing in the period between the two ruptures (January 2011 and June 2013), the blue bra woman incident captures some of the underlying dynamics influencing Egyptian politics at the time, and it raises important questions about gendered politics and revolutionary activism at a critical juncture when the nation's identity was being reimagined in all directions.

*Challenging the Brothers' Red Lines*

In the case of the blue bra woman, it is pertinent to reference who was *not* there in the protests against SCAF in December 2012: the women belonging to the Muslim Brotherhood and the ultraradical Salafis.[4] The Muslim Brotherhood is one of the oldest, most well established international religious movements. Its goal is to reinstate a state governed fully according to the Shari'a (Islamic canonical law). Hassan el Banna, who established the movement in 1928, provided the most comprehensive, holistic definition of the Muslim Brothers:

4. Some of these women may have been there as individuals, not representing their movements.

1. A Salafi call (*da'wa*): because they call for returning Islam to its purist meaning from God's Book and the Sunnah of his Prophet.

2. A Sunni way (*tariqa*): because they take it upon themselves to work according to the pure Sunnah in all things, especially in beliefs ('*badat*), whenever they find a way for that.

3. A Sufi truth: because they know the essence of goodness is purity of soul and purity of heart and persistence in work.

4. A political entity: because they call for the reform of internal government, and the revision of the Islamic *ummah*'s relations with other nations.

5. A sports group: because they care about their bodies and believe that a strong believer is better than a weak one.

6. A scientific, cultural solidarity: because Islam makes the quest for knowledge a *farida* (ordinance from God) for every Muslim man and woman and because the Muslim Brotherhood clubs are in reality schools for education and enculturation and institutes for pedagogy for the body, mind, and spirit.

7. A commercial company.

8. A social idea: because they are concerned with the ills of Islamic society and they try to reach ways of remedying and healing the *ummah* from them. (quoted in Tadros 2012e)

The Muslim Brotherhood is an international movement with a decentralized system that allows each national organization to govern itself. However, within each country, the movement has a deeply hierarchical and intricate organizational structure. Women members of the Muslim Brothers have their own organizational umbrella but are embedded within the overall structure as opposed to being a parallel movement. Hence, most women members identify themselves as members of the Muslim Brothers rather than as Muslim Sisters.

The movement has had an ebb-and-flow trajectory in terms of its political position and influence. It experienced a phase of flourishing (1930s–1950) followed by a phase of repression (1950–70) and then another phase of flourishing (late 1970s to early 1980s). Under Mubarak's reign, the movement experienced periods of tolerated existence with moments of informal but significant political inclusion and spates of repression

(1990s–2000s). After the Egyptian revolution of 2011, the Brotherhood reached the apex of its power (2011–13), which was quickly followed by its demise and repression (July 2013–present).

It is difficult to talk about the Salafis in the same terms as the Muslim Brothers, that is, as an organization with a clearly defined leader, mandate, self-description, and organizational structure. Salafis do not have this unitary leadership or organizational structure. There is such a thing as traditional Salafi thought or a common set of references and sources that Salafi leaders share (to varying extents). To provide a generic definition of Salafi thought, it is important to refer back to the traditional Salafi thinkers who are regarded as common reference sources for the different Salafi organized entities.[5] The Salafis believe in *Al Salaf al Saleh*, which refers to the righteous path that was lived and prescribed by the Prophet and his companions *only* in the first century of Muslim society (Abasi 2002; Bakr 2011; M. F. Othman 1981). Salafis reject all forms of *ijetehad* (revisionist interpretation of the text). According to the late Dr. Mustapha Al Shak'a (1994), one of the most authoritative sources of Salafi thinking, Salafism rejects all political thinking that emerged after the Prophet and his companions. Another authoritative source on Salafism, Dr. Mustapha Helmy, defines Salafism as underpinned by three foundations. The first is to follow *Al Salaf al Saleh*. The second is to reject modern *tafsir* (interpretation). The third is to follow the ways of thinking mentioned in the Qur'an and to reject philosophy, logic, and other ways of thinking (Helmy 1976, 35–46).

For more than a century, Salafi thought thrived in Egypt.[6] However, organizationally, Salafis belong to a multitude of different entities. Each

---

5. Ibn Hanbal formed one of the four schools in Islamic jurisprudence and is considered the most conservative and rigid of the main sources of Salafi thinking. The other sources include Imam Ibn Taymeyah and Mohamed Abd el Wahab, who founded the Wahabi school of thought in Saudi Arabia.

6. Salafi organizations have been active for a long time, and many of their founders occupied leading or prominent positions in Al-Azhar University, the pinnacle of Sunni learning. Sheikh Mohamed el Khedr Hussein, who became Sheikh el Azhar in 1952, established one of the three most important Salafi organizations in Egypt, Gam'yet al Hedaya al Islammiyya, in 1928. Ansar Al Sunna Al Muhammadiyya was founded in

*tanzeem* (group/entity) follows a different leader, and this structure is also reflected in how they define themselves, each other, and the *fiqh* (jurisprudence) and political thinking that they follow. The first organized group (*tanzeem*) of Salafis in Egypt emerged between 1972 and 1977 in Alexandria; the founders announced the formation of *al madrasah al salafiyyah* (Salafi school) in 1977. The Muslim Brothers tried to bring them into their fold but the Salafis refused to join. In 1980 the Salafis announced that they would not give their endorsement to Omar el Telmesani, then Supreme Guide of the Muslim Brothers. This refusal became a source of enduring contention between the Muslim Brothers and the various Salafi entities in terms of their ability to achieving a unified organizational leadership (Abd el 'Al 2012, 25–31). During the 1980s, the Salafi *tanzeem* established an institute for the preparation of proselytizers (*ma'had 'edad al dou'ah*), which served as a springboard for organized outreach. During Mubarak's era, they rejected engagement in formal politics as anathema to their mission and operated through the mosques and media. However, following the demise of the Mubarak regime, they became a powerful political force and one of their groups, Al Da'wa al Salafiyya, established the Al-Nour political party. Al-Nour at times supported and at times clashed with the Muslim Brotherhood. The party endorsed the July 3, 2013, roadmap announced by General Abdel Fattah el-Sisi, though many of the Salafi followers sided with the Muslim Brothers and joined ranks in their struggle against the new regime.

In 2011, following the Egyptian revolution, the Muslim Sisters and Salafi women's activism flourished as inhibition to public activism relaxed. The women belonging to the Muslim Brothers and the Salafi movements played an instrumental role in transforming the social base of

---

1926 by a group of Al Azhar *'ulama* (scholars) and Salafi proselytizers and led by Sheikh Mohamed Hamed Al Fekki, a leading Azhar figure who was also a prominent writer and editor of Salafi publications such as *Al Huda al Nabawi*. The third most prominent organization, Al Gam'iyya Al Shar'iyya leta'awon al 'ameleen bel Kettab wal Sunna al Muhamadiyya, was established in 1912 by Sheikh Mahmoud Khattab Al Sobky, one of the leading Al-Azhar scholars.

support of their respective movements into political constituencies for the movements' newly established political parties. Though Islamist political organizations such as the Muslim Brotherhood and Salafis have ardently campaigned to cover women up, the incident of the blue bra woman did not stir any qualms from these respective movements. The day after the protests over the blue bra assault, leading members of the Muslim Brotherhood suggested that women should not be out protesting in the first place, and they denounced the protests. Manal Abou Hassan, one of the sisters of the Muslim Brotherhood and a leading political figure who served as head of the women's committee of the Freedom and Justice Party, expressed her own distaste for the women who went out to protest: "It is disrespectful for a woman's dignity when she has to take to the streets to defend her rights. . . . Does she not have a husband, a brother or a son to defend her?" (Fleishman 2012)

But despite the objections of some, women continued to play a part in the revolutionary fervor as it was sustained against all odds during the thirty months between the first and second rupture (January 2011 and June 2013). The revolts that erupted from June 26th onward and reached their apex June 30–July 3, 2013, have yet to be researched with the attention and detail that they merit. The revolts of 2013 saw a broader base of citizen participation than those of 2011 (Tadros 2013c), and it was clear from the video footage[7] that many of those citizens were women. As discussed in chapter 9, the revolts would have failed if women had not gone out in the streets in the numbers that they did on June 30, 2013.

When pro-Morsi supporters sought to deter Egyptians from joining the call for protests on that day, their catchcry was *"al shar'yya khat ahmar"* ("legitimacy is a red line"). Their choice of words perhaps reflects an attempt to instate new rules of the game based on the limits of what citizens can and cannot contest. In one sense, it is a reproduction of the

7. See, for example, YouTube videos of the predominantly workers' town of Al Mahalla al Kobra, https://www.youtube.com/watch?v=Qh_vSCpcfEY; Fayoum, a traditionally Islamist stronghold, https://www.youtube.com/watch?v=-bPOvR1Zaos; and, in front of the presidential palace in Cairo, https://www.youtube.com/watch?v=mUZS09bpAwE.

Mubarak administration's speeches in 2011 to the people, warning them of not venturing beyond the red lines. It is also a clever pun: the word *shar'yya* (legitimacy) sounds very close to Shari'a (Islamic law). The slogan was intended to resonate among Muslims the sacrosanct nature of Islamic law, which should be upheld, defended, and never transgressed.

Women belonging to the Muslim Brothers as well as other Islamist groups, including some Salafi groups, played a leading role in mobilizing citizens to join counterprotests. However, the pro-Morsi protesters were dramatically smaller in number than those who revolted against the regime. The military intervened on July 3, 2013, under the leadership of General Abdel Fattah el-Sisi, minister of defense in Morsi's government. El-Sisi announced that the political forces (see chapter 9) had agreed to the formation of an interim civilian government led by Adly Mansour, head of the Supreme Constitutional Court. The country became deeply divided, with pro-Morsi supporters denouncing the overthrow as a coup and pro-revolution supporters celebrating the end of Muslim Brotherhood rule.

Many of the anti-Morsi protesters (though not all) attributed the success of the overthrow and the aversion of civil war to the minister of defense's intervention. The question in present-day Egypt is whether the demise of the Muslim Brotherhood will open new political opportunities for claiming women's rights.

**Gendered Collective Mobilizations**

Studying the ebbs and flows of collective action around gender equality matters provides invaluable insights on broader macro struggles over power, governance, and authority that go well beyond "the woman question." Egypt has a long history of collective mobilization for claiming equal rights for women paralleled by countermovements that have pressed against reform. A feminist conscience developed in the nineteenth century in Egypt, although the formation of a collective women's front to defend the rights of women is often associated with the establishment of the Egyptian Feminist Union in 1923 (Ahmed 1992; Badran 1995). The quest for women's equality was always intrinsically connected to the broader political question of national emancipation, be it from colonialism in the first half of the twentieth century or from the shackles of different modalities of authoritarianism at the beginning of the twenty-first century (Al-Ali 2000; see chapter 2). Collective action around gender issues has been characterized by multiple identities, issues, framings, institutional forms, strategies of engagement, and relationships with the authorities, civil society, regional and international actors.

Collective action for gender equality has gone through different phases, at times corresponding to change of leadership from one president to another. In some instances the different phases overlap with two leaderships but correspond to changes in political economy policies or radical change in political culture (ruptures). For example, although Egypt experienced a change of leadership in 1981, this period is described as one phase on account of the continuation of the Sadat regime policies during Mubarak's first twenty years in office.

The first phase of collective action for gender equality (1920s–1940s) included the establishment and growth of a feminist movement against the backdrop of colonialism, characterized by the accentuation of a nationalist struggle for independence. It was also a phase that witnessed burgeoning political and civil society characterized by high levels of cultural and political pluralism. During this phase a counterfeminist movement emerged that drew its inspiration from the growing popularity of reviving Islamic social and political order.

The 1950s and 1960s—the period in which Nasser ruled Egypt—is represented as one phase on account of the central role that the Nasserite government played in shaping the trajectory of all forms of activism. It was characterized by the co-option and repression of all autonomous civil society initiatives, including nonstate women's collective action, and by the birth of state feminism under a highly centralized system that laid out the foundations of a nationalist, welfare society.

The coming to power of Sadat marked a new phase because of the gradual but significant departure from Nasser's policies, which had a dramatic impact on the organization of women. The most influential change brought about by the shift in leadership was ideological (vis-à-vis the leftists and Islamists). Yet this phase is also associated with a shift in political economy (from state welfare to welfare pluralism and from one party system to a limited degree of political liberalization).

This phase (1970s–1990s) included the NGOization of women's collective action through the formation of charitable and developmental women's organizations. This phase occurred against the backdrop of the welfare state's erosion and the embracement of an open-market economy and controlled political liberalization. Many factors contributed to the NGOization of the women's movement in Egypt. The politically repressive context in which activists operated meant that working through a nongovernmental organization (NGO) became the only survival strategy for public work that the government tolerated. In addition, the replacement of Nasser's state welfare policies with welfare pluralism, in particular after Egypt embarked on a structural adjustment program in 1991, elevated the role of civil society in the new neoliberal paradigm embraced by the authorities.

Several nonstate actors became involved in establishing NGOs in Egypt. Some development NGOs assumed a depoliticized approach, focusing on the integration of women in the market economy and addressing socially mediated forms of gender discrimination (such as female genital mutilation [FGM] and early marriage). However, among women activists, political orientation influenced the emergence of cliques in the NGO terrain. Women activists belonged to three key political affiliations: leftist, Nasserite, and liberal (right of center). The ability to forge a unified movement out of diverse NGOs was undermined by competition over donor resources, ideological disputes, and absence of legitimate leadership. In fact, these obstacles often played an inhibitive role in elevating collective action beyond the level of networks in Egypt, as will be shown in chapter 4.

The fourth phase (2000–2010) is associated with the quangoization of the women's agenda through the formation of national women's machineries over which the first lady presided. The two women's machineries were the National Council for Childhood and Motherhood (NCCM) and the National Council for Women (NCW). *Quango* is a term coined by Alan Fowler and is short for quasi-nongovernmental organization, or an organization that relies on state funding but is not formally subsumed under government. In Egypt national women's machineries relied on a combination of state funds and Western donor support. Although the national machineries were not formally subsumed under the government, they did not enjoy political autonomy from the ruling regime because they were headed by the first lady (see chapter 2).

The emergence of the NCW did not so much represent a shift in ideological terms or political economy policies as it raised some fundamental questions of who speaks for Egyptian women. It touched on issues of ownership, representation, and accountability. Women's nonstate activism was significantly weakened with the emergence of the national women's machinery in 2000, as funding, technical support, and political endorsement was diverted from civil society to these quangos. However, the failure of forging a united feminist movement may have allowed the NCW to go unchallenged on some occasions.

The 2000s was also a period characterized by the emergence of foreign-funded and foreign-led coalitions. There were several attempts to form coalitions in Egypt throughout the 2000s, both before and after the Egyptian revolution of January 2011. Some were quite successful for a while, such as the Convention on the Elimination of All Forms of Discrimination against Women (CEDAW), whereas others degenerated into networks or a set of grantees bound together with donor funding. This is a phenomenon that I refer to as *collective action lite* (see below and chapter 5). Magda Adley argues that in view of the deeply entrenched differences between NGOs in Egypt in the 2000s, it was easier for activists to come together to work through campaigns rather than through coalitions (interview by author, July 2009).

The most recent phase of collective action for gender equality (2011–13) represents another new phase in women's activisms marked by the Egyptian revolution that ousted Mubarak. This period witnessed one of the most intense backlashes against women's rights but also spawned new forms of organizing around gender justice agendas that are groundbreaking in many respects. There were several changes of leadership during this time, from Mubarak to the Supreme Council of Armed Forces to the Muslim Brotherhood to an interim civilian government backed by the military. The fate of present-day Egypt remains opaque, though indicators up to the end of 2015 suggest a severe encroachment on civil liberties and on spaces for contestation by civil and political society to freely express itself. Ironically, there are signs of renewed, albeit selective, governmental engagement with women's rights such as on matters pertaining to sexual harassment.

My primary question in this book is what enables or frustrates the emergence of collective action to advance gender equality in Egypt? What makes collective action a one-off event like the protests of December 2011, and what accounts for sustained activism around gender equality?

This book is a case study of collective action around gender of relevance beyond the Egyptian context. It shows ways in which citizens defy, comply with, circumvent, resist, and sometimes internalize red lines that are constantly changing. Shifts in red lines are sometimes subtle and sometimes seismic, but they rarely remain the same. The story of women and men collectively mobilizing behind shifting red lines is of relevance to scholars of gender studies, sociology, politics, and development studies. In this book I aspire to combine an inductive approach to theorization with a practical discussion of policy and development practice.

The rationale behind *Resistance, Revolt, and Gender Justice in Egypt* is to interrogate how collective action around gender justice issues influences and is influenced by different regime orders, ruptures, processes, and outcomes. Although this book tries to capture the dynamic interfaces between the agential and structural and between the internal and external factors that produce different configurations of power, ultimately, the focus is on collective forms of mobilization associated with women's rights. This is not a study of the changing reality of women and men and the relations between them in contemporary Egypt, although these lived realities are referred to when relevant to the discussion of collective action.

International scholarship on collective action around gender has benefited from research comparing similar women's movements within a single region and analyzing the impact of women's movements on state policy and vice versa. However, Beckwith (2013) argues that there are two strategies of analysis that are less common. The first comparative strategy is to pursue a "cross-time comparison of the same women's movement in a single country" (422). The benefits of this longitudinal study are that it allows for an examination of a women's movement's internal transformation of its issue framing, its understanding of gender issues, paths of political learning, mobilization/demobilization cycles, and the extent to which opportunities are capitalized on or missed. The second comparative strategy that offers opportunities for enriching the framework of analysis is "the cross-sectional comparison of different women's movements in a single country" (422). The advantage of this strategy is that it allows an examination of variations in state response to different women's movements. It examines how the state bestows or denies its favors upon different groups and the evolution and nature of relations between different forms of organized women's activisms (422–23).

In this book I aim to address the gaps in literature on mobilization around gender matters in the two ways identified by Beckwith. I perform a *cross-time comparison* of feminist collective actors by examining the transformations in discourses and modalities of engagement from Mubarak's era to the aftermath of the 2011 revolution, when there was a seismic shift in the nature of political opportunities for engaging in public space. I also provide a *cross-sectional comparison* of different forms of collective action that have a bearing on the gender agenda. I examine the manner in which they relate to each other and the state, including feminist voices, women in revolutionary groups, women in civil and political society forces, Islamist groups, and informal youth-led movements working on gender-based violence.

This book is underpinned by two normative assumptions. The first is that this work is guided by a belief that collective action matters for eliciting positive social change irrespective of the nature of the regime in place. The modalities of organizing under different regime types may vary according to political opportunity and a variety of other factors. However, my analysis in this book shows that the strength of working collectively matters even when the opportunities for internal influence are very limited. The strength of collective action is manifest in the ability to mobilize a constituency, create common platforms for making demands, and forge alliances that strengthen the political or social weight of the collective actor and action. Through a study of cases of successful and more stunted attempts at collective action around gender equality under different regime types and political leaderships, I argue that that there are many recurring internal determinants that enable effectiveness of movement building and influence. These include but are not restricted to some minimum level of unity in diversity, legitimate and inclusive leadership, ability to establish alliances and coalitions with sympathetic actors, the presence of a constituency that can translate into greater leverage in political bargaining processes, and a sense of local ownership.

By examining the first revolutionary rupture (2011; see chapter 1), I show that the strength of collective action during Mubarak's era influenced the ability of women's rights advocates to make their claims after his administration's demise. The various coalitions, groups, NGOs, networks, and initiatives during Mubarak's era would have been better positioned to seize the limited political opportunities for influencing Egypt's new political settlement under SCAF if they were able to sustain a united front. The strength of collective action or the ability to forge a united front in leadership, in demands, and in mobilizing a constituency are critically important in times of ruptures, when the ability to leverage political weight to influence processes of change becomes particularly important. However, there were clear instances between 2011 and 2013 in which the ability to organize collectively played a powerful role in challenging government's stance on gender equality. The threats to women's rights experienced after Mubarak were some of the impetus for unified action, though other political factors also came into play.

The second normative element thread throughout the chapters of this book is that not all kinds of collective action and conceptions of reforming gender orders or women-led mobilizations are necessarily supportive of gender equality. Case studies described herein problematize the notion that there is a common denominator in all forms of women mobilizing as women. As I demonstrate in chapter 2, the common denominator argument is premised on the idea that women's exercise of agency in a collective mode represents a challenge to patriarchal gender hierarchies. An examination of different ideological and political modalities of women's collective organization suggests that some forms of women's organizing are anathema to expanding the conditions under which women's freedoms can be enhanced. These are the antifeminist movements. In essence, these movements contribute to masculinist restorative projects even when they use the language of rights and freedom (Kandiyoti 2013). In this book I describe how the Muslim Sisters and the women of the Salafis, though powerful as political expressions of voice in and of themselves, promote agendas that ultimately circumscribe women's formal and informal political agency at large.

The ideological position on gender, rather than the identity of women as women, becomes a powerful predictor of how people mobilize collectively and coalesce into political blocs. This book confirms the postulation presented in scholarship that, irrespective of the ideological and political orientation of various forces (Islamists, liberals, leftists, revolutionaries), they prescribe to viewpoints and political actions that often reflect deeply patriarchal values. This is evident in my discussion of the patriarchal overtones of youth revolutionaries who excluded women from leadership and the non-Islamist political forces who often paid lip service to women's equality (chapter 5). Where ideological orientation matters is in instances in which policy proposals are being put forward that would challenge the gender power hierarchy in fundamental ways. Ideology is not a predictor of whether non-Islamists will participate in coalitions for or against gender equality, nor is it a predictor of whether they will act as a bloc in support of or in opposition to patriarchal gender hierarchies. A number of complex political calculations come into play. For example, some youth revolutionary movements and some liberal political parties were opposed to the institution of a quota for women in Egypt's first post-Mubarak electoral law in 2011. In other instances, such as the writing of the constitution in 2012 and 2013, many (not all) of these actors endorsed the introduction of more rights for women.

Conversely, ideology was a predictor of the organized Islamist political forces with respect to the agenda they pursued on gender equality matters. As I describe in chapter 8, across the spectrum of organized Islamist actors and in spite of their political and ideological differences, blocs would form around the gender agenda to oppose measures that could potentially challenge the patriarchal gender hierarchy. This was manifest in their position against the Commission on the Status of Women's action on gender-based violence in 2012 and their position on women's rights in the constitution of 2012 and 2013.

Mobilization around agenda rather than gender identity is a critical determinant of whether collective action enables positive social change or not, as per the empirical evidence from Egypt. Islamist feminist women's movements that challenge unequal power hierarchies (even those that are violations of Islamic law) did not emerge in Egypt. However, there are gender justice movements comprising women and men who mobilized under a justice and human dignity platform and affirmed women's rights to express their voices in public spaces without violation of their bodily integrity (see chapter 1).

### Mapping the Conceptual Terrain

*Labeling Ideology in Relation to Women's Agency*

In view of the salience of politicized religion in the Arab world, including Egypt, ideology must feature in any analysis of collective action identity. However, it cannot be analyzed in a nuanced manner independent of its historical unfolding and in relation to factors of political economy. The literature on women activists in the Middle East that has emerged in the past decade tends to distinguish between secular activists who advocate a human rights–based approach to gender equality (e.g., CEDAW) and those who advocate for the advancement of gender rights within religious parameters (i.e., endorsed through the Shari'a). In the early 1990s, Dr. Azza Karam provided a more nuanced perspective, suggesting that women can be defined as secular feminists, Muslim feminists, and Islamist feminists. Islamist feminists reject gender equality but do recognize women's oppression as part of a wider sociopolitical injustice. Muslim feminists aim to show that "the discourses of total equality between men and women are Islamically valid" (Karam 1997, 22). They believe that "a feminism that does not justify itself within Islam is bound to be resisted by the rest of society and is therefore, self-defeating" (22). Karam contrasted Muslim and Islamist feminists with secular feminists who "firmly believe in grounding their discourse outside the realm of any religion and place it instead within the international human rights discourses. . . . Religion is respected as a private matter but is totally rejected as a basis from which to formulate any agendas on women's emancipation" (24).

The above dichotomy between the secular and religious platforms for advancing gender equality in Egypt may have represented the different standpoints in an earlier phase, but by the late 1990s these views had changed (Al-Ali [2000] arrives at the same conclusion in her study of women's activisms in the 1990s). Virtually all activists who espoused a gender rights agenda, whether as individuals or through collective platforms, framed their case by emphasizing the compatibility of their platforms with Islam. This fundamental shift in strategy of engagement was a direct reaction to the increasing Islamization of space, politics, and social norms. It is also significant that the Egyptian government itself, when seeking to advocate gender reforms, has been keen to frame its calls as deriving from Islam and emanating from Muslim scholars' endorsement (see chapter 5). The extent to which this fundamental shift in engagement represents an ideological shift in personal belief systems is impossible to decipher. What is clear is that the use of the religious framework by movements is subject to change according to the power configurations in society and state.

In this book, *Islamist* refers to women and men who advocate for governance that is compatible with, and derives its vision from, Shari'a. This term is distinct from *Muslim*, which refers to people whose religious affiliation is to Islam the religion but who do not necessarily endorse an Islamist political project. It is also to be distinguished from *Islamic*, which refers to matters associated with the values and practices of Islam. The variations among women in Islamist movements are very important. These variations emerge as a consequence of being in different organizational structures with different leaderships and at times different ideological nuances and political goals. Women who belong to the Muslim Brotherhood as a movement have some similarities with but also major differences from women in the Salafi movement (see chapter 6).

The term *secular* is problematized on account of its interchangeable deployment to suggest those who do not espouse an Islamist political project. Islamist political forces have used the term *secular* in a derogatory manner to tarnish the image of their opponents. In view of the polarization that emerged in Egyptian society between supporters and opponents of Islamist political parties, it is perhaps best to use the terms *Islamist* and *non-Islamist* while recognizing that there are major political and ideological variations within both camps. The term *non-Islamist* is used to refer to women activists whose political project is not guided by the installation of an Islamist state, though their position on the extent to which governance should conform to the Shari'a may vary dramatically. Within the non-Islamist political stream, there are women activists whose internal demarcations are as deep as the demarcations that distinguish them from women in the Islamist movement. These demarcations are along ideological lines (leftist, Nasserite, liberal [right of center], conservative) as well as between different groups/cliques and sometimes content of agenda (affirmative action, reproductive health, etc.).

*Collective Action Lite*

Collective action lite is about donor-driven modalities of collective action that are run like development projects. They are not so much a reflection of the weaknesses of locally driven forms of collective action as much as of the tensions between the creation of an enduring and legitimate front for local activism and its ownership by external actors. What I argue in the upcoming chapters is that Western funding has, over the course of twenty-five years (since the 1994 International Conference on Population and Development in particular), played an extremely important role in supporting gender activism. Western funding is critical for supporting women's equality in a context in which nonstate funding sources tend to direct donations to charity. Western donors endorsed the formation and strengthening of women's NGO activity in the 1990s and through 2000. Such support, in the form of funding and technical assistance, peaked around key international events such as the International Conference on Population and Development (ICPD) in Cairo in 1994 and the International Women's Conference held in Beijing in 1995.

At the end of the twentieth century and the beginning of the twenty-first, donor policies increasingly shifted toward a discourse of building scale, supporting joint work between partner organizations, and networking. There have also been incidents in which enabling donor practices have supported the emergence and consolidation of successful coalitions for gender equality (i.e., the FGM Taskforce and the CEDAW Coalition in its early phase; see chapter 5). However, when a donor's relationship to collective agency around gender equality becomes one of owning/leading the initiative or running the collective actor as one would a development project, the outcome is a pseudoform of collective action. By pseudocollective action, I mean that it has the semblance of being a collective actor on account of its self-label as a coalition or movement with an organizational framework intended to stir the initiative. Yet it has a credibility deficit on account of its lack of local ownership credentials. The participation of a select number of activists in its structure and its implementation of activities may give it the pseudoappearance of being a collective platform, but because it operates as a donor, disbursing subgrants to grantees (local actors), it lacks the kind of local leadership, cohesion, and grounding needed to make it locally driven. I have defined this phenomenon as collective action lite because of its resemblance of some locally driven forms of collective agency in its structure and activities. Others might argue that it is more akin to failed collective action rather than collective action lite.

It is not this type of organization's reception of foreign funding that gives it a collective action lite quality. Rather, it is its leadership coupled with its *projectivization*; in other words, its treatment as if it were a gender and development program activity or project (see chapter 5). Collective action lite suggests not a failed kind of agency but a negative kind of agency. Its negativity lies in giving a false external front of being a thriving collective actor to the outside world when it is in fact hollow. At critical times such as ruptures, actors that meet the definition of collective action lite have had no mobilization power whatsoever. Those who wished to work collectively chose other organic modalities instead.

The nature of the initiative's ownership is especially important for collective action to be sustainable and legitimate. Pseudomodalities of organizing that give semblance to being organically owned movements (collective action lite) are particularly counterproductive for building cohesive, effective collective movements. Modality of organizing can betray a front that has no legitimate leadership, constituency, or mobilization power, and this phenomenon is intrinsically associated with the role of Western donor practices. Just as in one historical phase there was an awareness of how the NGOization of a movement may lead to its depoliticization, so too can an external donor posing as a local movement be counterproductive to genuine solidarity building efforts on the ground.

### Gender Justice Movements

Unfortunately, the courageous cry of women in Tahrir Square in 2011, "Come and strip us all!" became a self-fulfilling prophecy. The incidents of what were believed to be politically motivated sexual assault against women in protest spaces (in particular Tahrir Square) increased dramatically in 2012–13. It is difficult to uncover the identity of the perpetrators in all of the incidents of sexual assault. The Egyptian security apparatus under Mubarak has a long history of using sexual violence against women dissidents (Amar 2011). In post-Mubarak Egypt, there were several incidents in which the Muslim Brotherhood and the Salafis were directly implicated in acts of sexual assault (Shash 2013; see chapter 8). These acts of politically motivated sexual assault as well as more generic forms of socially motivated sexual assault are indicative of the denigration of women's status in revolutionary Egypt. However, they are also manifestations of a country where rule of law collapsed, criminal groups thrived, and where the entire population suffered from the absence of personal and communal safety.

The phenomenon also spawned informal youth-based forms of activism that resorted to some highly innovative approaches to engagement. Initiatives arose that sought in part to fill this security vacuum (police seemed to have abandoned the role of maintaining law and order in public) and in part to defend women's rights to participate in political life through activism. Men and women formed vigilante groups, campaigns, and online platforms. These groups hold promise of becoming a nascent movement that, although lacking a feminist identity, are able to deliver on gender justice in some distinct ways (see chapter 8).

### Revolutions as Ruptures

Defining the events that have shook Egypt and the region has been the subject of much contention: uprising, intifada, revolution, coup, or counterrevolution? These labels carry deep normative and ideological underpinnings according to whose view is presented. Both the regime changes that occurred in 2011 and 2013 were revolutions if we conceive of revolutions as ruptures. The term *rupture* describes an event in which people's uprising leads to the breakdown of a ruling regime, challenging the status quo in a dramatic way. Although not all Egyptians endorsed the uprisings in 2011 and 2013, the majority of those who chose to express their opinions publicly were in favor of the demise of both presidents.

Describing the popular uprisings in January 2011 and June 2013 as ruptures also allows for a differentiation between the events themselves and their outcomes, that is, whether they fulfilled the objectives of the protesters (bread, freedom, and dignity). The 2011 rupture was followed by a military takeover and the initiation of elections. The Islamists' six political parties won a clear majority of seats (71 percent) in Egypt's free democratic parliamentary elections in December 2011/January 2012. The Freedom and Justice Party acquired 46 percent and the Al-Nour Party acquired 25 percent of the seats (see Rabie 2012b for detailed election results). Six months later, however, when the presidential elections were held, the Islamists' electoral performance had dropped. Muslim Brotherhood candidate Mohamed Morsi beat his opponent, Ahmed Shafik, a remnant of the Mubarak regime, by a margin of approximately 2 percent (51.73 percent Morsi, 48.5 percent Shafik). Morsi's year in office was also characterized by intense violent clashes with youth revolutionaries and frequent protests that included women. The expectations for Morsi's government to bring economic prosperity, political inclusion, and citizen security (safety) were high. Within a year unmet aspirations of power sharing, economic betterment, and social and political inclusion culminated in massive protests that were far bigger than those of 2011. Irrespective of the democratic outcomes of the ruptures, the mobilization of the people in both instances led to the overthrow of two different kinds of authoritarian regimes, one dictatorial and one theocratic.

Although scholars of democratization and the Middle East celebrated the emancipatory power of the 2011 uprisings, they have struggled to speak similarly of the overthrow of the Muslim Brotherhood–led regime in June

2013. President Morsi's overthrow via a popular uprising has been labeled as a coup because it removed a democratic order (Gerges 2013). I contest this label in two interrelated ways: (1) the extent to which the political trajectory of Egypt could be described as democratic under the Muslim Brotherhood, and (2) the reductionist juxtaposition of civilian rule with military rule. In addition, theocratic rule is also anathema to the civility of the state in many ways. If scholars challenge the essentialist association of democracy with electoral practice and the reductionist association of militarism as being the only threat to civility, it is possible to conceive of the January 2011 and June 2013 uprisings as driven by emancipatory politics. The first revolution overthrew an authoritarian ruler; the second uprooted a theocratic regime. These definitions have important implications for feminist scholarship on ruptures and regimes. They confirm leading feminist theorists' conception of democratization as a process that entails more than holding elections, and they beg for a critical probe by feminist scholars into how modern theocratic regimes, not only the military, represent threats to engendering transitions.

Indeed, Egypt did gravitate between rule by a military dictatorship and an authoritarian theocracy in the months between the overthrow of Mubarak in February 2011 and the overthrow of Morsi in July 2013. When describing Egypt's political trajectory during these eighteen months, most Western political analysts tended to refer to the country as being "in transition" (often used synonymously with democratic transition or democratization). This definition was disconnected from the mainstream domestic narrative of a regression into authoritarianism and the struggle under the banner of an ongoing revolution.

The Egyptian case study exposed many of the theoretical inadequacies of the transition literature in interpreting change. It also highlighted the challenge of defining revolutions in terms of their ability to achieve their goals and democratic outcomes. The rupture that brought down the Mubarak regime through eighteen days of sustained collective action on the part of millions in January 2011 ended with the military assuming control of the country. Yet it was a revolution insofar as it involved a mass revolt that challenged the power configurations in a fundamental way. Similarly, the June 2013 revolts ruptured the status quo in a deeply structural way, even though its democratic outcomes are highly questionable thus far. Although I do not make claims of Middle East exceptionalism in this book (nor claim that Egypt is exceptional from other countries), I do sound a cautionary note on the power of transition theory to predict the *outcomes* of rupture processes (see chapters 6–8). I critique transition theory on theoretical grounds and in terms of its influence on international policy discourses about post-Mubarak Egypt.

One of the reoccurring themes in this book is that international policymakers' engagement with a transitional Egypt has suffered from an overemphasis on elections as the litmus test or benchmark for democracy. Although elections are important, the ballot box is not the only way of capturing the will of the citizenry. In the aftermath of the January 2011 revolution, there was a sustained level of political dissatisfaction with the reproduction of authoritarian modes of rule, absence of security, and economic suffering. Yet transition experts ignored the daily instances of dissatisfaction and focused on the centrality of elections as the channels through which citizens should seek change.

The transitologists and consolidologists determined that as long as Egypt had elections that were characterized by multiparty competition, it was on the path to democratization (Tadros 2013b). But as Miller et al. (2012, 295) rightly point out, when comparing the processes of regime change in Arab countries with that of sub-Saharan African and some Latin American countries, the level of population mobilization witnessed in the former is a crucial difference: "Popular expectations and continued pressure will be more important to the outcomes of the Arab Spring than in some previous transitions." The people's involvement in unruly politics (see Tadros 2012c) suggests a different kind of political action that does not indicate regional exceptionalism but rather a distinct form of political engagement that goes beyond the conventional mechanisms of liberal democracy (i.e., elections).

Another failure of the transition literature is its narrow focus on civilian, nonmilitary rule and its ignorance of the threats that theocratic rule pose to the civility of the state and existing governance system. Miller et al. (2012) highlight the importance of ejecting the military from civil government in Egypt, a necessary political move that is strongly associated with breaking free from the ancient regime and is a critical factor for democratization. Although they concur that in the case of Turkey and Chile the military was gradually removed from power over several years, they argue that such a scenario is not one that can be emulated in Egypt because of how deeply entrenched the military is in the old Mubarak politics. With the military reassuming governance of Egypt after the ousting of President Morsi on June 30, 2013, Miller et al.'s (2012) thesis is likely being proven true. There is no telling the long-term outcome of the second revolts, and fear of the military spearheading a counterrevolution to empower the remnants of Mubarak's regime is not unfounded. What Miller et al. (2012) do not discuss, however, is that the threat to civilian rule could also come from the establishment of a theocracy.

Much of the Western democratization literature analyzing the prospects for Egypt's transition did not consider adequately whether a democracy with an Islamist focus, such as that created by the Muslim Brotherhood, would pose governance problems. In the case of Miller et al. (2012), the fact that they drew their analysis from the experiences of Eastern European, sub-Saharan African, and Latin American countries may explain why they overlooked the threat of theocracy to civilian rule. Their mapping did not have cases of Islamists assuming power through competitive elections. One of the key areas of struggle between the Islamists (comprised of the Muslim Brotherhood, the Salafis, the Gama'at Islamiyya, and offshoot parties of the Muslim Brotherhood) and non-Islamists during President Morsi's time in office was the constitution, which is discussed at length in chapter 8. The articles that the Islamist camp introduced to the Egyptian constitution did bring it closer to constitutional theocracy by empowering the clergy to assume oversight of the legislative and judicial branches of the state (Article 4); deepening and expanding the religious basis of governance (Article 219); and adding qualifiers to citizens' rights, including those of women and religious minorities, which could potentially dilute them on religious grounds (see chapter 8 for in-depth analysis).

A combination of gender-specific and generic articles such as Article 219 would affect women in potentially all aspects of their lives. The threat to Egypt's identity and civilian rule were sufficient to convince many political forces to openly withdraw from the constituent assembly. Yet many Western analysts privileged procedure over substance, considering the arrival of a new constitution a successful milestone without due regard for its implications for inclusionary politics (see chapter 5).

Transition literature is also flawed because of its teleological approach to political change, which is premised on the idea of transition phases leading to democratic consolidation and/or the use of the term *transition* instead of democratization. The transitologists' denouncement of the prospects of a future democratic outcome in the aftermath of the June 30th revolution emanated from the fact that Egypt's political pathway did not follow standard blueprints. Transition literature produced before the late 1990s often focused on such blueprints: fundamental procedures inherent in any democratization effort; that is, a set of models that determined the path (Rustow 1970). But a shift in thinking about transitions eventually emerged and teleological assumptions began to be contested. In a pivotal critique of transitions titled "The End of the Transition Paradigm," Thomas Carothers (2002) analyzed twenty-five years of regime changes in seven regions of the world and contested a number of assumptions: (1) regime change necessarily shifts toward democracy; (2) there are phases through which democracy evolves (from breakthrough to transition to consolidation); (3) the determinative importance of elections; (4) the necessity of elite agreements to arrive at a new governance strategy; and (5) democracy and state building are mutually reinforcing endeavors. Carothers instead suggested that countries often assume political pathways and outcomes that are more akin to being in "gray zones" and that involve all kinds of power configurations that do not fit into preconceived, democracy-promoting models.

Although Carothers's conceptual breakthrough moved scholars away from a checklist approach to countries that have experienced regime changes, there is still an element of teleological assumptions informing contemporary approaches to examining regime changes in the Arab world. For example, Miller et al. (2012, 1619) "use the term transition not to imply that countries undergoing political change tend to follow a set, linear pattern but, rather, to indicate our concern for the process of democratisation, in particular, the ways it can be influenced and the possibilities for how it can unfold." In other words, the process is still assumed to be leading in a particular direction, namely the establishment of democracy, even if the sequence-of-phases approach is rejected.

The outcome of the application of a Western-centric framing of democracy produced new disconnects in understanding the rupture that occurred on June 30, 2013. During the year of Morsi's reign, youth revolutionary forces, political parties, and important members of civil society argued that the situation on the ground represented an ongoing revolution. The discourse focused on the need to reconfigure the top-level power dynamics because they reproduced the old pattern of governance witnessed during Mubarak's reign. A contending discourse propagated by President Morsi and the Muslim Brotherhood leadership was that Egypt was transitioning to democracy after the democratic election of its president and was now moving toward complete democratic transformation (see *Al Jazeera* 2012). The Western discourse, in particular that of the United States and the European Union and its member states, disregarded the narrative of the nonstate actors in Egypt and assumed that Egypt was transitioning to democracy—a process that needed deepening.

At the heart of these contending narratives of ruptures and change lie conflicts of interest but also divergent views of what democracy is and should be. Contrasting opinions on the nature of regime change (revolution versus coup) had clear gendered implications. Whereas the Western media celebrated the image of the Egyptian woman in protest during the January 25, 2011, revolution, and there was much interest in it from feminist scholars, the reverse occurred after the June 30, 2013, revolt. In the latter, there was a disregard for and muting of women's agency in the three-day revolt, despite the fact that the number of women and their diversity were dramatically greater than that experienced two years earlier.

Many feminist scholars, democracy theorists, and policymakers committed to engendering processes of regime change and strengthening the voice and role of citizens in these processes have critiqued the assumption that elections are the yardstick for democratization (Waylen 1994b, 2007) and the top-down understanding of democratic practice (an exclusive focus on reform of government institutions). Some of the opportunities and pitfalls emanating from comparative feminist scholarship on processes and outcomes for gender justice during democratization are highly relevant for Egypt and are discussed in chapter 6.

## Positionality and Methodology

I identify myself as an Egyptian feminist whose research is informed by my position as both an insider and an outsider. I have been deeply engaged in feminist circles in Egypt for more than fifteen years and more recently with some of the new, informal youth-based initiatives that emerged after the revolution. On the other hand, I am an outsider insofar as I have always worked on the fringes and have been peripheral to the central decision-making core within Egyptian feminist groups.

The research in this book is based on many years of personal and professional engagement with gender issues in Egypt and internationally. Such engagement stretches back to the late 1990s, when I joined *Al-Ahram* weekly as a journalist and began to cover gender issues, following in the trails of the pioneering journalist Dina Ezzat, whose reporting on women's equality was unparalleled in its accuracy, astuteness, and passion.

I was a member of the FGM Taskforce until its dissolution in 1999, and I learned a great deal about the opportunities and challenges of working collectively from that experience (see chapter 3 for coverage of the FGM Taskforce). Marie Assaad, the taskforce coordinator, opened the doors of her home to all of us and held many meetings there. People of all ages and backgrounds met in such invited spaces, where people could articulate and discuss ideas, challenge each other, reflect on their personal experiences, and debate how to navigate pathways laden with landmines. I learned a great deal from watching Marie Assaad's extreme sensitivity to every word, grimace, and silence in the group as she worked to ensure that no one's voice was left out and no one felt sidelined or negated. She had a highly developed radar to capture people's temperament, and if she identified any verbal or body language suggestive of unease, she would immediately follow up the next morning with a personal phone call. It was a style of inclusive leadership that was key to cohesion. Her long history of active engagement with gender issues and her integrity gave her a moral authority that granted her much legitimacy in the eyes of the taskforce members.

As a journalist I attended countless meetings, workshops, conferences, roundtables, and performances on gender issues in Egypt. Sometimes I got bored. It was the same kinds of events, held in the same four- or five-star hotels, with the same crowd preaching to the same converted audience. The same rhetoric and jargon was being used over and over again, and it did not seem to go anywhere.

From the mid-1990s up to the early 2000s, I spent weekends working as a volunteer development practitioner in the villages and in poor urban squatter settlements. I was struck by the disjunction between what was happening in the five-star hotels and the language, framings, and content of what women spoke about in the villages and settlements. I was also struck by how it was not only the feminists but also the gender and development groups that were disconnected from reality. If the injustices of poor women were only given lip service, it was even worse for poor Coptic women. There was a complete negation of how belonging to a minority religion (Christians amount to approximately 10 percent of the Egyptian population) subjected them to exceptional practices of discrimination.

However, many factors prevented me from taking a cynical view of feminists and gender and development activists. The invisible workings of power are subtle and operate in pervasive ways to encroach on committed activists' and practitioners' choices and agency. For example, to outsiders, cooperating with the state security investigations (SSI) apparatus (the secret political police) may seem anathema to autonomous feminist activism, but the reality of living under Mubarak's reign necessitated sharing information on planned workshop activities and participants with SSI officers. Failing to do so sometimes meant a denial of the right to have the events in the first place. The invisible power at work was not only the internalization of modes of compliance with authoritarian governance structures, but also an appreciation of the role they can play in facilitating activism. For example, when activists hold a regional conference and a Palestinian participant is held at the airport, they might call the SSI officer to intervene with the passport authorities as a favor. Sometimes activists are embedded and entangled in a web of relations that are not always reflective of their preferences and exercise of choice because they have to adapt to living under authoritarianism.

I use a multidisciplinary approach in this book, drawing on political science, sociology, feminist studies, and development studies. I studied a diversity of sources, including media outputs, autobiographies, and literature, in addition to performing conventional social science research. This book is the cumulative output of research I undertook over several years using qualitative and ethnographic methods. Chapter 1 is based on dozens of interviews with women activists, literature review, press content analysis, discourse analysis of state-sponsored feminism, and participant observation of feminist events and encounters. Chapter 2 relies on interviews in 2006 and 2010 with leaders and partners associated with the FGM Taskforce, as well as interviews with policy analysts and a review of secondary literature (see appendix for a list and description of interviewees). I also draw on ethnographic data from 1998 that I gathered by participating in an FGM Taskforce initiative intended to elicit change in community views of and behaviors surrounding female genital mutilation in a poor rural community. This research also relied on field visits to NGOs working in Beni Suef and Asiut (two upper Egypt governorates), which were made possible through the kind assistance of Magdy Helmy.

Chapters 3 and 4 are based on research on six women's coalitions (three in Egypt and three in Jordan) that I did for the Developmental Leadership Programme (DLP). I conducted semistructured and open-ended interviews with no less than thirty leaders of the coalitions as well as founding and other active members. Interviews commenced in April 2010 when the initial test interviews were conducted.

For the CEDAW Coalition, Network of Women's Rights Organizations (NWRO), and Karama–Egypt case studies, I am extremely grateful for the incisive research assistance of Hind Mahmoud. Hind and I interviewed many people as part of the research that appears in chapters 4 and 5 (see appendix).

Chapters 6, 7, and 8 benefited from the capable research assistance of and interviews by Mohamed Hussein el Naggar, human rights activist and researcher, and Robeir el Fares, journalist and writer (see appendix for a list and description of interviewees). This work was complemented by my interviews with key informants, in particular with members of the

Muslim Brotherhood whose names have been withheld in accordance with their wishes to remain anonymous.

In chapter 8 I draw on interviews with individuals of all political orientations, including those representing political parties (the Muslim Brotherhood's Freedom and Justice Party, the Salafi's Al-Nour Party, the Wafd liberal right-wing party, and the left-of-center Egyptian Democratic Party) and representatives of youth movements, the Coptic Church, and other organizations. Robeir el Fares did several interviews in 2012 with members of the constituent assembly who were delegated with writing the constitution (see appendix).

I developed chapter 9 from my documentation of actors, networks, agendas, and processes associated with gender-based activism in Egypt that I collected from 2012 through 2014. The findings emanate from a database of actors developed in conjunction with the Social Research Center under the leadership of Professor Hania Sholkamy, as well as from a workshop with various stakeholders and in-depth interviews and life histories with women and men involved in youth-based and gender-based violence initiatives. Shaza Abd el Latif, who has an encyclopaedic knowledge of youth-based activisms on gender and social justice issues, ensured the thoroughness of our scanning of informal youth-based actors engaged in the struggle against gender-based violence. We extended a workshop invitation to all possible actors so as to corroborate our evidence. Finally, the very gifted anthropologist Rasha Habib completed twelve intense life histories with men in three gender-based movements.

In chapter 10 I rely on several interviews with members of the constituent assembly who drew up the 2013/2014 constitution, an analysis of the constitution itself, and an extensive press and literature review.

**Organization of the Book**

This book is organized chronologically from 1994 to the aftermath of the January 25, 2011, Egyptian revolution and up until December 2014, six months after the ousting of Morsi's government. The choice to organize chronologically rather than thematically was a purposeful one that privileged the analysis of social and political phenomena as embedded in historical and political context.

Chapter 1 engages with the theoretical debates around the significance, role, and nature of collective action in relation to gender identities, interests, strategies of engagement, and outcomes. It examines the empirical evidence highlighting the importance of collective action for global gender equality and how this theme has been approached in feminist praxis and academic literature. It puts forward several arguments and draws on three case studies from Egypt to challenge the positive correlative association between the female profile/identity of participants in collective action and the advancement of gender equality in academic scholarship.

The first case for disentangling identity from cause in collective action around gender equality originates from men's central role in defending women's claims against gender-based violence in post-Mubarak Egypt. The existing conceptual definitions of women in movement, women's movements, and feminist movements are bound by a common variable: the identity is assumed to be female, even if the cause varies. However, movements whose identity is not premised on a common female cohort have played a central role in people's mobilization against sexual harassment in post-Mubarak Egypt. Drawing on Goetz's work (2007, 2008), I define these anti–sexual harassment movements as gender justice movements and show how their different compositions have implications for their framing of issues, representation of identity, and engagement with advancing equality.

The second case for rethinking mobilization with women as the common denominator behind promoting gender equality are those movements that directly intend to circumscribe women's choices. I argue in chapter 1 that the antifeminist movements may be emancipatory for women who participate in them on a personal, experiential level and in terms of group solidarity; however, their ideological underpinnings serve to undermine the conditions under which women can freely exercise choice. The second part of the chapter discusses definitions and classifications for understanding the different modalities of collective action (networks, coalitions, and movements). I argue that although diversity in modalities of action to support women's empowerment is indeed a necessity for survival under different regimes, at critical junctures a movement needs to have the sum of all its parts united around a common agenda under consensual, collective leadership to enable it to leverage the power of a cohesive front.

The challenges of building a feminist movement in a context of authoritarianism and a civil society that is by and large hostile to women's rights are discussed in chapter 2, which analyzes the key political factors influencing women's collective action in Egypt during Mubarak's reign (in particular during his administration's final twenty years). It focuses on the nature and role of collective actors who explicitly advocate a women's equality agenda and on the relationships between each actor and with the wider political forces. I discuss three trends in chapter 2: securitization, Islamization, and quangoization. The securitization of women's agency exposes the increasing role of the SSI apparatus in controlling and regulating women's collective agency. The Islamization of women's activism shows the increasing salience of religion as a normative framework for engaging with gender matters in Egypt and its implications for discourses and strategies of engaging different political forces and forging a constituency. I argue that these three dynamics—securitization, Islamization, and quangoization—have influenced the political opportunities for the emergence of cohesive collective actors that endorse gender equality issues in Egypt, though, as demonstrated in chapters 3 and 4, they have not entirely blocked them.

Chapter 3 examines the rise and demise of the FGM Taskforce, a coalition that was formed by feminists, activists, and development practitioners united by their commitment to ending the practice of female genital mutilation through a multipronged approach that worked on various policy levels as well as on the grassroots level. The FGM Taskforce was the offspring of the ICPD political moment, the critical juncture at which Cairo hosted the International Conference on Population and Development and which saw intense global-local feminist mobilization to advocate for women's reproductive health rights.

The FGM Taskforce challenged the political agendas of different actors: the Egyptian government, the official Islamist establishment, the Islamist movements, the medical profession, radical Western liberal feminists, donors, and the families who defended circumcision as a social custom. The taskforce framed multiple discourses for different audiences and was very responsive to the political moment. On the other hand, the taskforce's strategy of eliciting social change may have underestimated the full implications of the practice's medicalization on a grassroots level. Moreover, the FGM Taskforce's decision to dissolve itself raises important questions about whether it is possible to sustain organized activity in the absence of a legal entity in a highly authoritarian context, such as that of Egypt in the 1990s and early 2000s.

In the fourth chapter, I highlight a successful example of forming a collective entity, with its moments of heightened mobilization and phases of dormancy, in the case of CEDAW. CEDAW is one of the longest surviving coalitions to have emerged in the Middle East. Initially established by a group of activists and practitioners who wanted to use the coalition as an instrument of holding the Egyptian government accountable, it struggled hard to survive internally as a collective entity and to weather challenges to cohesion and leadership. In chapter 4 I examine how the coalition sought to withstand co-option, fragmentation, and political dilution of its cause during Mubarak's reign. I explore how the coalition withstood the volatility of the political context and its deployment of the CEDAW shadow report as an instrument to influence the gender agenda. I also describe how the coalition mobilized to hold the Egyptian government accountable in international spaces when opportunities for engaging domestically were blocked.

Challenges to building strong cohesive movements are not only associated with working in a highly inhibitive political environment. In chapter 5 I argue that the political economy of aid led to the emergence of a pseudoform of collective action on gender equality, which I call *collective action lite*. The chapter includes two case studies that shed light on this phenomenon. The first is Karama, an initiative that claimed to be a movement against gender-based violence in Egypt but which was in reality a development project funded by a donor that was financing the implementation of small-scale activities by grantees. The second is the Network of Women's Rights Organizations, funded by the German International Development Agency, GIZ (*Deutsche Gesellschaft für Internationale Zusammenarbeit*), which initially sought to become a coalition but ended up becoming a local network with limited mobilizational capacity.

Although both initiatives are distinct, the ownership deficit and the pro-jectivization of collective action are common factors.

Chapters 2–5 shed light on what it means to work behind red lines in Mubarak's time and to discover where the amoebic openings occur and where they become severely circumscribed. It also engages with the agential responses of various actors (as individual associations but also as movements) to these changing political spaces. I argue that the state of constituency building and mobilization during Mubarak's era had an impact on the quality and nature of capacity to influence unfolding configurations, at least in the immediate phase after his administration's demise (in particular the first year).

In contrast to the demobilizational impact of donor-led efforts to forge collective entities that promote equality in a highly hostile political context at the end of Mubarak's reign, the Egyptian revolution of 2011 catalyzed the mobilization of thousands of women and men to engage in collective action. Chapter 6 examines women's participation in social and political movements after the end of Mubarak's reign, how feminist voices reorganized into new collective actors, and how women belonging to Islamist movements also sought to influence the emerging political order. The chapter presents a scope of the different collective forces and movements that characterize the postrupture political scene in Egypt. It discusses why the participation of women in the January revolution did not translate into recognition of a women's rights agenda. The chapter exposes how the new political culture of the revolution revealed how politically inept feminists are engaging citizens in the streets, and it shows the disjuncture between the gender rhetoric and the public. It also shows how gender blind the youth revolutionary movements were toward internal power differentials and their implication for equal representation and recognition for women leaders and activists. Moreover, it discusses how new openings affected the Muslim Sisters and how they sought to influence the political scene. In chapter 6 I examine why a collective front around gender equality did not immediately form and I probe the factors that inhibited the formation of intergroup and intragroup alliances, both in terms of the reconciliation of competitive visions of democratic pathways of change as well as the forging of inclusive, legitimate leadership and internal cohesion.

This discussion is followed in chapter 7 by an in-depth examination of the opportunities and challenges of incorporating gender equality issues in the new political order under SCAF rule and with the political ascendency of the Islamists to power, formally and informally. It discusses both the causes and implications of the disjunction between the international and national discourse of Egypt's democratic transition and the revolutionaries' stance that the revolution is ongoing and its aims have yet to be achieved. The chapter compares and contrasts Egypt's experience of engendering the transition processes with that of other countries in which authoritarian regimes were overthrown. It examines feminist attempts to influence institutional politics on several fronts, such as the restructuring of the national women's machinery to make it more representative, pressing for the introduction of affirmative action in electoral law, and engaging the new power holders in parliament on their agenda setting. I argue that although the political configuration of power was extremely antithetical to recognizing any demands for gender justice, activists' ability to forge a collective front influenced their ability to seize power and elicit the kind of change they wanted. What accounts for collective mobilization or inertia is discussed at length.

Chapter 8 is set against the backdrop of Morsi becoming president in July 2012 in an extremely volatile political and economic environment and with high public expectations for a new social contract between the people and the ruler/state. One of the first challenges facing Morsi and the Muslim Brotherhood, which came to power in 2012 for the first time since their inception eighty years prior, was to arrive at a new constitution for the country. The first part of chapter 8 engages with the politics behind negotiating gender in the constitution-drawing process by analyzing the actors, agendas, and relations that informed the inclusion and exclusion of contested articles. I also examine the outcome of the constitution, not only in terms of gains and losses for women's rights but also its legitimacy in the eyes of sidelined parties and its implications for generating a countercoalition against the regime in power. The second part of the chapter addresses the new government's engagement with gender matters on national and international policy levels, how they have sought to navigate the institutional politics of advancing their own agenda, and strategies for circumventing sources of opposition and resistance.

Shifting from top-level politics to politics on the grassroots level, chapter 9 presents a case of one of the most powerful new modalities of collective action to have emerged in post-Mubarak Egypt and to have reached its peak resistance under Morsi. The new gender-based violence initiatives gained momentum because a trigger and a political opportunity paved the way for the coalescing of actors into collective activism. The trigger was the increased sexual violence against women that occurred with laxity in maintaining law and order on the streets. The political opportunity was both structural and agential. Structurally, there were new open political spaces for youth activism and engagement in street politics. Agentially, the revolutionary fervor that had gripped Egypt created a fertile ground for mobilizing youth for political engagement. Their framing, strategies of engagement, and strong volunteer base distinguished them from the prerevolutionary forms of collective action around gender issues.

The prospects of building a nascent gender justice movement from these new, informal, youth-led forms of mobilization as well as the challenges that may undermine their influence are discussed at length in chapter 9. I also raise the question of whether youth-led initiatives that effectively operated as vigilante groups in protest spaces could substitute for a police force in protecting citizens from sexual assault. No amount of preparation or coordination efforts could prepare these groups for the intensity of sexual violence witnessed from June 28, 2013, to July 3, 2013, when millions of Egyptians took to the street to pressure Morsi to step down from the presidency.

Chapter 10 commences with documentation of the mass revolts that erupted alongside the unification of the non-Islamist political and social forces against Morsi. Yet the outcome of the revolts, namely the ousting of Morsi via military intervention, led to extreme fragmentation and deepened fissures over the new status quo within political society and among feminist and gender justice actors. The chapter discusses women's participation in the June 30th revolution, contested narratives over the nature of the rupture (revolution or coup), and the tensions between gendered processes and outcomes that the new power configuration has elicited. The second part of the chapter discusses whether we have reverted back to the same old political scene under Mubarak's tenure: are we back to mobilizing behind red lines?

In the final chapter of the book, I reflect on the main findings from the previous chapters, presenting a nuanced discussion of the effects of the imposition of new red lines and the reproduction of old ones on the various political actors contending to influence the country's gender agenda. I discuss the ways in which the Egyptian political trajectory influences the existing literature on regime ruptures and affects understanding of the interface between structural and agential factors in changing gender outcomes for various stakeholders: the ruling government, political and civil society, and transnational feminist activism.

# 1

## COLLECTIVE ACTION FOR GENDER EQUALITY

*Revisiting the Theoretical Terrain*

The scholarship on the significance, role, and nature of collective action in relation to gender identities, interests, and strategies of engagement is rich and varied. But in light of the emerging new modalities of organizing and the complexity of new identities that engage with gender matters, scholars need to revisit the existing categories of analysis. Here I propose a typology that builds on pioneering feminist scholarship. Though it stems from inductive theorization from a case study of Egypt, I am hopeful that it is relevant for other contexts as well.

In this chapter I postulate that scholarly literature has been primarily informed by the gender *profile* of the movement, that is, the unit of analysis has always been associated with women as participants or leaders in movements. The emergence of gender justice movements led by and comprised of women and men challenges the association of gender interests with gender identity. These movements do not fit comfortably in any of the existing definitions of women in movement, women's movements, or feminist movements. In practical terms, their emergence means that the framing of gender equality, the mode of expression, and the nature of engagement are fundamentally changed as a consequence of this differential composition in the collective actor.

This chapter also challenges the notion that women's collective mobilization is by default an act of empowerment on account of their exposure to collective oppression. I argue that the antifeminist movements may present opportunities for personal journeys of emancipation for the women who participate in them; however, their impact for the advancement of women's rights as a collective is anathema because these movements do not create the conditions in which women can freely exercise choice. The opportunities for solidarity building around gender rights agendas may be greater among movements that have minimal women in leadership and are not particularly gender friendly or are gender blind than among women-led collectives that represent antifeminist movements. Although diversity in modalities or strategies of action to support women's empowerment (e.g., campaigns, networks, groups, and coalitions) is welcomed, at acute junctures a movement needs to have the sum of all its parts united around a common agenda and leadership (even if it is a collective leadership) to leverage the power of the collective.

The nature of the ownership of the initiative is a significant element in the sustainability and legitimacy of collective action. Pseudomodalities of organizing that give semblance to being organically owned movements— what I term *collective action lite*—are particularly counterproductive for building cohesive, effective collective movements. The modality of organizing can betray a front that has no legitimate leadership, constituency, or mobilizational power, and collective action lite is a phenomenon that is intrinsically associated with Western donor practices. Just as in one historical phase there was an awareness of how the NGOization of a movement may lead to its depoliticization, so too an external donor posing as a local movement can be counterproductive to genuine solidarity building efforts on the ground.

The legitimacy, ownership, unity, and mobilizational power of collective action around gender equality become particularly important at critical junctures. Events such as regime overthrows represent historical phases that contain dramatic reconfigurations of power. They can offer opportunities to engender the new status quo and/or threaten to circumscribe or revoke existing rights. One such critical juncture in Egypt was the popular ousting of President Hosni Mubarak. Political opportunity structure has often been used as the analytical prism through which to examine the interface between collective action in relation to gender action and ruptures in political orders. Through the Egyptian case study, I argue in this chapter that the unity of a movement and its ability to mobilize its resources to garner the political weight necessary to effect change are essential factors in its own success.

## Why Collective Action for Gender Equality Matters

Weldon and Htun's (2013) comparative case studies of pathways to policy change in seventy countries between 1975 and 2005 established that the single most important and consistent factor driving positive policy change in relation to gender-based violence is feminist activism. They wrote that feminist activism plays "a more important role than left-wing parties, numbers of women legislators, or even national wealth. In addition, our work shows that strong, vibrant domestic feminist movements use international and regional conventions and agreements as levers to influence policy-making. Strong local movements bring home the value of global norms on women's rights" (231). They also describe how autonomous feminist movements succeeded in championing the social perspectives of marginalized groups, transformed social practice, and changed public opinion. By and large, where successful policy change was secured, it was because these movements prompted various stakeholders, including voters, civic leaders, and activists, to pressure policymakers to respond to their demands. In addition, the movements often found empathetic allies within such policymaking circles (247).

The Pathways of Women's Empowerment Consortium also performed comparative country case study research, this time across fifteen countries in five continents. Their findings indicated the centrality of collective organizing as a pathway of women's empowerment:

> Organising is a major route to change and a key pathway of empowerment. Women's organisations and movements are vital in building constituencies for gender justice. For women in low-paid, under-valued jobs, organising provides opportunities to gain rights and recognition and is vital in their struggles for empowerment. Women's organising has an important role to play in governance, holding states to account for their commitments, and monitoring implementation of laws and policies affecting women; as in the example of Pathways Brazil's work monitoring the new domestic violence legislation. Pathways research

shows that gains that have been achieved in relation to women's sexual and reproductive rights are substantially due to women's organising at the local, national and transnational level. (Pathways of Women's Empowerment 2012, 9)

One of the consortium's key findings is that supporting women's organizing can transform pathways of empowerment into pathways to justice and equality (Pathways of Women's Empowerment 2012). The cross-country research discusses the multiple benefits of collective mobilization (e.g., bestowing women with their own sense of self-worth), the intersections of oppression that women are subjected to, and the practical, concrete gains made in conditions for women (e.g., in the informal employment sector). The consortium's report concludes, "it is much harder to achieve lasting change through legal or policy reform without active engagement by those for whom the changes are intended" (Pathways of Women's Empowerment 2012, 26).

Collective action certainly is not the only pathway for positive social change. Governments have sometimes used top-down interventions, including legal and policy reform and other institutionalized mechanisms, to respond to women's needs, and they have invested in nationwide programs and projects to integrate women's issues in development plans. However, when such actions occur in an environment that lacks space for collectivized forms of action for advancing the gender agenda, it becomes more difficult to hold the state accountable. The sustainability of top-down initiatives that have no ownership within the broader polity is also questionable. In cases in which the promotion of a particular version of women's equality is associated with a certain government or leadership that then fails, there is a risk that the gender agenda, in whatever form, becomes vulnerable to a fierce backlash. Hence, delivery of gender equality is important, but so too is the process, the constituency behind it, and the extent to which it can draw its legitimacy from socially embedded constituencies.

## Collective Action, Gender, and Framing

In the introduction, I suggested that this book is informed by two normative assumptions: first, that collection action counts, and second, that not all forms of mobilization around gender equality are conducive to expanding choices for women. To unpack these assumptions, an engagement with a political, sociological take on what constitutes collective action is critical, as is looking to feminist scholarship on mobilizing around gender equality. Finally, both assumptions need to intersect with development studies insofar as development actors played a key role in funding women's equality in Egypt as in many other countries.

Collective action is "coordinating efforts on behalf of shared interests or programs" (Tilly and Tarrow 2007, 5). By collective actors, I mean individuals and/or organizations that have chosen to coalesce around a common cause, which forms the basis of their common mobilization. The analytical framework guiding the analysis of gendered collective action is informed by an understanding of collective action around gender issues as being a subset of social movement.

There is a large body of feminist literature (Batliwala 2007; Beckwith 2007; Kretschmer and Meyer 2013; Kuumba 2001; Nazneen and Sultan 2014; Viterna and Fallon 2008) that has pointed to the usefulness of engaging with women's movements as a subset of social movements. Social movements are "collective challenges to existing arrangements of power and distribution by people with common purposes and solidarity, in sustained interaction with elites, opponents and authorities" (Meyer and Tarrow 1998, 4). In that sense, the literature on the attributes of social movements, their strategies of engagement, and their power relations with other actors can be useful in shedding light on the dynamics of women's mobilization. Beckwith (2007, 313) argues whether "mounting collective challenges to powerful actors, whether opponents in civil society, state authorities or economic elites; women's movements, as social movements, have engaged in sustained challenges to powerful actors both within and outside the State." The work of political sociologists such as McAdam, McCarthy, and Zald (1996), Meyer (2004), and Tilly and Tarrow (2007) has been highly influential in providing the analytical lens through which to examine how social movements seize political opportunities, respond to the political moment, frame the message, build a constituency, manage relations with the state, and build internal cohesion (see, e.g., Nazneen and Sultan 2014). Social movement theories originally did not engage with gendered forms of collective action, which were largely ignored at the time. It was feminist theorists that engendered social movement theory by drawing on empirical case studies to contribute to this body of knowledge.

The concepts developed in social movement theory and contentious politics are also relevant to a wide array of collective actors who do not necessarily fit the label of social movements. Collective actors could, for example, include campaigns, coalitions, and alliances. Concepts of political opportunity, repertoires of collective action, and strategies of engagement have been particularly useful for analyzing the interface among collective actors, social and political society, and the state in Egypt.

## Typology of Collective Action

Feminist scholarship has contributed to many identity demarcations, which are fluid but helpful for analytical purposes. However, the notion of a typology that classifies or categorizes has also raised concerns over its potential reification effect. For example, labels may essentialize complex phenomena that cannot be contained in a particular category and they can create artificial binaries. Molyneux (2006, 235) notes, for example, that the idea of strategic and practical interests was intended to be used in a relational manner, yet became appropriated in such a manner as "to form of a too rigid binary, with practical interests set against strategic in a static, hierarchized opposition. If this occurred, it is far from what was intended and contradicts the original formulation."

Inserting complex phenomena into categories may misrepresent a dynamic reality as if it were static. Binaries can be deceptive in essentializing collective actors who are far more complex. One example of this misrepresentation is how secularists use religion as an entry point for influence or use religious framings in relation to certain audiences while still being spoken of as secularists versus Muslim feminists (see chapter 2).

Categorization can also be used for the exercise of power over relations. Moncrieffe and Eyben (2007) note how labels can be used to entrench biases, and Moncrieffe (2006, 43) writes that "as expert researchers, policymakers, programme managers and evaluators, we all harbour biases that are not displayed publicly but that may be the subject of our private conversations. . . . Our own socially acquired meanings (stated and unstated) that we then assign to labels . . . influence how we perceive issues and shape the encounters that we willingly and less willingly engage in." This assertion is highly relevant for the appropriation of the "secularist" and "Islamist" labels used to describe those aligned with different political projects as it led to a binary understanding of identity that proved to be deeply polarizing.

Nonetheless, the fact that there are possibilities for misappropriation of categories of analysis does not make a convincing case for abandoning initiatives to understand, define, and differentiate between different social and political phenomena. As Molyneux (2006, 231) writes, "all theories and concepts run the risk of being mis-applied, but this is not usually reason enough to abandon them . . . what is needed, however, is some greater refinement in its treatment and caution in its deployment."

I argue that the categorization of women's collective agency would benefit from such greater refinement. Its three conventional classifications are women's movements, women in movement, and feminist movements. I would add two additional classifications to this list: antifeminist movements and gender justice movements.

## Women's Movements

What distinguishes women's movements from other social movements, from the perspective of many feminist scholars, is their membership and distinct women's identity. Molyneux (1998) suggests that a women's movement is comprised of majority women even if it does not exclude others. Beckwith (2007, 314) argues that women's movements are those that make "gendered identity claims as the basis for the movement, where they explicitly organize as women, or as mothers, or as daughters, asserting a female gendered identity distinguished from other possible overlapping or competing identities."

Movements can sometimes be described as "feminine," that is, they appeal to women's roles as mothers, daughters, and wives. Examples include the mobilization of women in Nicaragua, Argentina, and other Latin American countries as mothers seeking redress and justice for their children, the victims of political murders. Bayard de Volo (2003) studied the Mothers of Matagalpa in Nicaragua, who joined together to fight for redress for their martyred children. She writes that the mothers "initially understood and portrayed their activism as within 'proper' gender roles (in this case, this often meant being a good mother) and became increasingly critical of 'old' expectations about women" (100), though they did not necessarily become an explicitly feminist organization or solicit feminist objectives. Such examples demonstrate that although initiatives may initially emerge without contesting patriarchal gender hierarchies, one of the unintended outcomes of mobilization is that through organizing and engaging, members become aware of how their positioning as women is reflective of unjust power relations. As a consequence of this awareness, their relationship with gender inequality in their activism changes.

Case studies from Latin America and elsewhere also challenge the rigid binary of feminist versus nonfeminist categories in that many forms of women's organizing serve feminist causes or have positive outcomes for feminist agendas even if they deliberately choose not to use feminist banners or identify themselves as such. Such decisions are often guided by strategic as well as pragmatic concerns and in relation to what they consider to be the most effective framings of their cause in a particular social or political context. The blue bra vignette in the introduction of this book represents a case of women's collective organizing as women. Although the women in Tahrir Square that day cannot be described as a movement per se because there was no sustained collective action except that one protest (see definition of movement below), they were there to protest the way women were being treated as women. What bound them together was their gender identity, even if their political identities varied.

*Women in Movement*

Sheila Rowbotham (1992) differentiates between those who mobilize around various interests (women in movement) and those who mobilize explicitly around feminist interests (i.e., some women's movements). The protest surrounding the blue bra woman that is described in the introduction would not be categorized as women in movement because the citizens who congregated in Tahrir Square were mobilizing explicitly on the basis of their identity as women.

The analytical significance of women in movement is that it broadens the scope of coverage of women's political agency in ways that an exclusive focus on gendered identities and interests denies, and it recognizes the diversity of issues around which women mobilize. Women in movement are also distinguishable from women's movements in that they do not necessarily have a women's leadership/membership or the explicit goal of women's emancipation like that of a feminist movement.

Undoubtedly these demarcations are both fluid and dynamic. Women may take part in broader social movements but then, on the basis of their experience, decide to collectively organize around gender-specific interests. Haj (1992), Ray and Korteweg (1999, 51), Safa (1990), and Schirmer (1989) all give examples of ways in which transformed agendas and causes ended up having feminist outcomes though they did not necessarily start that way. Another example of how demarcations between women's movements and women in movement may be blurred is the analysis of women in religious movements. Even if they have a separate organizational platform, they may not necessarily represent themselves as separate women's movements. For example, the Muslim Sisters have their own organizational structure yet the majority of the members that I interviewed identified themselves as part of the Muslim Brotherhood (and represented themselves in the public sphere as such). This presents a dilemma: Do we categorize the Muslim Sisters as women in movement (i.e., women participating in a broader religious-political movement), or do we identify them as a women's movement in recognition of their distinct organizational structure and practice of organizing *as women*? Such a categorization is not merely a question of which slot to fill; it essentially touches on themes of autonomy and political identity, both of which are quite fluid and dynamic.

Many of the women who participated in the youth revolutionary movements in 2011 could be defined as women in movement. They were members of emancipatory movements working to overthrow oppressive regimes. These women raised the banner together with the men of the "bread, freedom, and social justice/dignity" movement, but their conceptions of these demands were not particularly gendered. They were not antifeminist, either, insofar as they did not endeavor to circumscribe women's freedoms. They simply pressed for the benefits of bread, freedom, and justice to be for all.

## Feminist Movements

Feminist movements are bound by more than a woman's identity—they explicitly address gender interests. Batliwala (2012) suggests that some of the key distinguishing characteristics of a feminist movement are that women form the critical mass of the movement, they adopt a gendered analysis of the problem or situation, they espouse feminist values and ideology, and they adhere to the following criteria: "They have systematically built and centered women's leadership in the movement. The movement's political goals are gendered. They seek not only a change in the problem, but a change that privileges women's interests and seeks to transform *both* gender and social power relations; they use gendered strategies and methods. Strategies that build on women's own mobilizing and negotiating capacities, and involve women at every stage of the process; and they create more feminist organizations" (6, emphasis in the original). Along similar lines, Baldez (2002, 14) defines feminist movements as those that "explicitly challenge conventional gender roles." Hassim (2004) identifies them as those that "seek to challenge [women's reproductive and domestic labor] roles and articulate a democratic vision of a society in which gender is not the basis for a hierarchy of power."

There are common themes among these definitions: the critical mass of women in membership and leadership, the challenging of gender roles in explicit and systematic ways, and the emphasis on transformation on a structural level. The role of feminist organizing for eliciting positive social change has long been recognized, though challenges such as the generational gap and the absence at times of intersectionality have also been identified as having influenced the social bases of these movements.

## Antifeminist Movements

Not all forms of women's movements directly or indirectly enhance women's voices, and there is a need for cautious differentiation between feminine and antifeminist movements. Kretschmer and Meyer (2013, 393) define antifeminist movements as "those meant to counter the claims and gains of feminist movements, protecting or restoring traditional gender norms. They are, understandably, generally conservative in nature, defending traditional gender roles for both men and women."

Kretschmer and Meyer (2013, 404) suggest that in some cases the emergence of antifeminist movements was inspired by the desire to counter the success of feminist movements. This is particularly meaningful in the Egyptian historical context with respect to the political trajectory of one of the most famous (if not *the* most famous) Islamist woman, Zeinab el Ghazali. El Ghazali was a revered member of the older generation of the Muslim Sisterhood and a close confidante of the founder of the Muslim Brotherhood, Hassan el Banna. El Ghazali's autobiography describes how she established the Muslim Women's Society in 1936 after she participated in the first feminist organization in Egypt, the Egyptian Feminist Union. She formed her organization specifically to counter the union's vision of women's empowerment, which she found as incongruent with her conception of gender roles derived from Islamic values and culture (Abd el Hady 2011; Badran 1995; Cooke 2001). In other instances, women join or belong to movements that were not established as counterfeminist movements (i.e., they were not formed along specifically gender lines); however, these movements' broader political projects encompass antifeminist objectives. In this book I describe women who belong to the ultraconservative Islamist movements in Egypt (e.g., the Salafi movements) as representing such an antifeminist stance.

Salafi women follow a line of Islamic thinking that is characterized by rejection of any revisionism and revival of the tradition of living in the time of the Prophet Mohamed and his companions. For these women, faithfulness to the way of life and organization of society as prescribed and lived in that first century is critical, as is the struggle against any thinking and way of life that deviates from the time of the Prophet and his companions. It is from this standpoint that Salafi women have actively fought against any reconfiguration of women's positioning in relation to men.

Although these women do express their voices in deeply political ways, they do not fight for political inclusion of women. Herein lies the paradox: They use their (informal) political power strategically to press for the political exclusion of women, including themselves, from formal political decision-making platforms such as legislatures. In December 2011/January 2012 Egypt held its first parliamentary elections since the overthrow of Mubarak (see chapter 6 for details). Parties were required to put women on their lists (though they were free to place them wherever they wished on the list). The Salafi Al-Nour Party objected vehemently and women members mobilized against women's representation in parliament using the pretext that it is religiously prohibited for women to assume leadership over men.[1] According to the Salafis, women should be hidden from the public gaze, their voices not heard, and they should certainly not, under any circumstance, assume leadership positions in the public sphere, especially if the positions are over men. To accommodate the electoral law (although they ignored it in many instances and did not have any women for some of the electoral districts), the Salafis presented a number of "ghost" women on the list. These women were relegated to the bottom of the electoral list, thereby making it almost impossible for them to win parliamentary seats. In campaign flyers showing the list of candidates for the Al-Nour Party, their husbands' names, not theirs, would be inscribed, and instead of their faces, there would be a blank space or a rose. In some rare instances, their names would appear, but nothing else. Interviewing these women was very difficult and only possible via the telephone.

For this research, Robeir el Fares interviewed one Salafi woman in December 2011 who was placed at the end of the Al-Nour Party's list for a seat representing a heavily populated area of greater Cairo, the electoral district of Giza (a combination of suburbs and shanty towns such as Imbaba, Dokki, Agouza, Kit Kat, Mansheyet el Kanate, and El Wahat). Her placement at the bottom of the list made it unlikely that she would win a seat. When asked what constrained her chances of winning, she answered, "Who said I lost? My party won therefore I won." She recognized that people have accused the party of placing women candidates at the end of the list and therefore defended her party, arguing that they

---

1. This section on Salafi women's participation in elections draws heavily on a book chapter that I wrote on women in Egypt's first parliamentary elections after the outset of Mubarak (Tadros 2014).

offered to put her in third place and she refused (incidentally the four top names on the party list made it to parliament). Whether the party offered her a place at the top of the list is questionable given its stance on women's political leadership positions and its failure to place any woman candidate at the top half of any of its electoral lists. Regardless, the reasons she gave for refusing to head the list are interesting:

> Now, I have Eman [woman] and Ahmed [man] whom should I vote for? God said the strong is the faithful. The woman is by her nature weak. I felt I could get weak but of course the man is stronger than the woman and because of this I refused to be placed as number 2 or 3 [on the party proportional list] because I would prefer to be at the tail of what is true than to be at the head of what is false. (interview by Robeir el Fares, December 2011)

This Salafi woman leader and many others like her are deeply engaged in society, providing emotional, spiritual, and welfare assistance to thousands of families. The fact that she sees herself as weaker than men is indicative of her belief in (or at least her public espousal of) the notion of gender identities and roles being driven by nature, in which women are biologically weaker than men. It also shows a strong conviction in the gender hierarchy of the Salafi movement and its logic. This belief in women and men's behavior being shaped by their nature informs the leader's perception of herself. She spoke of Al-Nour's favorable position on women's employment in social services, teaching, and health. Yet when she was asked whether Al-Nour approves of women becoming judges, she said that she can only speak for herself and not for the party: "If they make me judge I will immediately declare the accused innocent if he cries because our nature [as women] is different from the nature of the man who rule by their mind." This representation of her own weakness is at odds with the formidable role she pursues in public. She has a bachelor's degree, identifies herself as a journalist who writes for an Islamist publication, *Al Mokhtar Al Islami*, and is the director of an Islamist welfare NGO. She is also a preacher or *da'eya*, which is defined as someone who is involved in the *da'wa* or proselytization of the Muslim faith and who calls people to piety.

Although Salafi women should not, like all other women with different political orientations, be judged according to some universalist normative criteria of what constitutes feminist or nonfeminist, my argument here is that this Salafi woman leader is actively mobilizing against the inclusion of women in politics (even though she herself is politically engaged in the informal arena). Such mobilization aims to narrow the space for women's expression of political agency in a way that is conspicuously counterfeminist, even by Egyptian social standards.

*Gender Justice Movements*

In the aftermath of the Egyptian revolution of 2011, women experienced increased exposure to sexual assault in public spaces because of a complex configuration of factors. This increase was notable in scope, frequency, and intensity (see chapter 8). To address the situation, men and women citizens began to form initiatives that acted as substitutes for the police (vigilante groups), exposed the scale of sexual assault (via online media, conventional media, and other sources), and acted as change agents in society, seeking to raise awareness through street action. It is difficult to classify these initiatives under one of the three categories: women's movement, women in movement, or feminist movement. They could not be identified as women's movements because these initiatives comprised women and men, and this composition was reflected in their leadership and membership. They could not be identified as women in movement because they did not comprise women who had joined a movement with a non-gender-based cause. Combating violence against women in public space and standing up for women's dignity was an explicitly gendered cause. These initiatives' interventions were aimed at addressing unjust social practices that discriminate against women or challenge hegemonic conceptions of masculinity and femininity. Moreover, the term *women in movement* recognizes that although women may channel their political agency in non-gender-specific movements, they may not necessarily assume leadership of these movements. In these gender-based initiatives, leadership ultimately comprised women and men, and its membership almost always featured both.

As with women's movements, the postrevolution initiatives are different from feminist movements in that their composition is not predominantly women. However, they differ from feminist movements in that their point of departure is not to challenge patriarchy per se but to promote social justice and dignity for all. The framing of the issues is not feminist, although it ultimately serves feminist causes. What my research proposes in terms of rethinking the relationship between identity and organizing around interests is that movements may focus on challenging gender hierarchies in very direct ways without having a feminist identity.

The absence of a critical mass of women in leadership or membership does not necessarily make an initiative less feminist in its advancement of feminist goals. Many interviewed members of the initiatives that emerged in Egypt to counter gender-based violence rejected the term *feminism* even when it was described as challenging gender relations. They argued that the impetus for their work was to establish a democratic society in which women's rights, as women, were not infringed upon. However, even when rights language was being used, it was intrinsically associated with a broader vision of a new social order in Egypt. It is noteworthy that the initiatives that did not reference women/feminist in their names were the ones that were most likely to have a high percentage of men in leadership and composition. They were also likely to have a broad-based constituency (Tadros 2012a).

The commitment of many of these men and women to the cause of defending women's rights to bodily integrity meant that they were willing to put their lives at risk, and their exposure to psychological and physical harm did not deter them from sustaining their political activism. Their "gender credentials" should not be appraised on the basis of their feminist identity or deployment of feminist language, but rather on the substance of their cause and the outcome of their actions. Members of these initiatives confided privately that some feminist organizations think of them as less sophisticated because they do not have feminist credentials (language, understanding of the deep structural causes of inequality, and experience in policy engagements). Others, they argued, sought to bring them into the fold on the basis that they were too young and inexperienced to work without the necessary support. These movements challenge conventional categorizations of collective movement analysis in that they do not conform to the nexus of gender identity interests.

*Gender justice* is a term that has emerged in feminist and development scholarship and can have multiple meanings. Gender justice is defined here along Goetz's (2007, 31) conception:

> The ending of—and if necessary the provision of redress for—inequalities between women and men that result in women's subordination to men. These inequalities may be in the distribution of resources and opportunities that enable individuals to build human, social, economic, and political capital. Or, they may be in the conceptions of human dignity, personal autonomy and rights that deny women physical integrity and the capacity to make choices about how to live their lives. As an outcome, gender justice implies access to and control over resources, combined with agency. In this sense it does not differ from many definitions of 'women's empowerment.' But gender justice as a process brings an additional essential element: accountability.

Although Goetz's above definition focuses on gender justice in terms of the desired outcomes, what is equally important is the conception of gender justice as a practical project in which

> organized constituencies of *women and men* would express outrage about unjust social practices that *discriminate against women or circumscribe men's roles*. They might join or form political parties and compete for representative seats in political institutions in order to put gender justice on the legislative agenda, or they might lobby politicians and political assemblies for changed laws. They would demand that public actors answer for the effect of their policies on equity in gender relations—in other words, they would insist upon *a gender-sensitive form of public accountability*. (Goetz 2007, 31, emphasis added)

There are limitations to the appropriation of the term *gender justice* to describe the new type of collective actor who mobilizes around gender-based violence in the context of post-Mubarak Egypt. The movements themselves have not used this term in self-description, and the term is not translatable into Arabic in a way that makes sense because the word "gender" is not commonly found in the Arabic language. Ultimately, the classification of these movements as *gender justice movements* is used for analytical purposes to show how their composition and the critical juncture at which they emerged generated a new kind of collective struggle that was deeply gendered but not in the ways that has been conventionally defined through women's movements, feminist movements, and women in movement. The implications are conceptual but the intention is not to suggest a hierarchy within the typology. As will be shown in subsequent chapters, there are junctures at which feminists played a central role in the struggle for gender equality (in particular during the 1990s). At other times, women in movement were essential for pressing for justice (e.g., women in workers' movements), whereas under Morsi's tenure gender justice movements played a critical role, and generally in between ruptures all of these movements had sometimes different but important roles.

Goetz's (2007) notion of public accountability as comprising state and nonstate actors is an important one. Many of the gender justice initiatives sought to hold both the government and society accountable for violations of women's rights to bodily integrity. However, the modality through which they pursued these goals significantly affected their influence.

**Modalities of Collective Action**

Not all modalities of collective action bear the same mobilizational power. Social movement and feminist theorists (such as Charles Tilly and Maxine Molyneux, respectively) concur that there is a need to differentiate between movements and other collective entities. Tilly (2004) argued that social movements are those that have WUNC (worthies and unity of cause, numbers and commitment). Molyneux (1998) notes that the term *movement* should best be reserved for those forms of collective action that are of substantial number and scale, thereby amounting to a phenomenon of some significance. "A woman's movement does not have to have a single organizational expression and may be characterized by a diversity of interests, forms of expression, and spatial location. Logically, it comprises a substantial majority of women, where it is not exclusively made up of women" (Molyneux 1998).

It is possible to identify different levels of collaboration that require a lower level of collective mobilization than that which amounts to a movement. A *network*'s collaborative work requires the least level of collectivism. A higher level of collaborative work can be witnessed in a *campaign*, which usually is bound by time and space, whereas *coalitions* require more of a sustained form of collective action.

Wasserman and Faust (1994) define a social network as consisting of a set of actors (nodes) and the relations (ties or edges) between the actors. The nodes may be individuals, groups, organizations, or societies. The ties may fall within a level of analysis (e.g., individual-to-individual ties) or may cross levels of analysis (e.g., individual-to-group ties). Katz et al. (2004) suggest that in any social network, there are often multiple kinds of ties operating simultaneously, such as: (1) communication ties (who talks to whom, or who gives information or advice to whom); (2) formal ties (who reports to whom); (3) affective ties (who likes whom, or who trusts whom); (4) material or workflow ties (who gives money or other resources to whom); (5) proximity ties (who is spatially or electronically close to whom); and (6) cognitive ties (who knows whom). They note that networks typically involve multiple types of ties or actors who share more than one type of tie (307).

In networks, the lowest common denominator can be a shared interest in information sharing or invitations to participate in mutual activities. Networks can potentially create a higher level of organization and mobilization, but one that requires a higher level of "glue," ideologically and organizationally, and a political and legal environment that allows them to thrive. For example, in Zimbabwe, Women in Law and Development in Africa (WiLDAF) formed in 1990 and comprised faith-based groups (mainly the women's wings of churches), trade unions (under the ambit of the Zimbabwe Congress of Trade Unions), women's rights and legal rights organizations, and community development organizations. Although the network included some explicitly feminist organizations, the general theme of common engagement was the use of law as an entry point for gender and development. Diluted gender and development language concealed deep ideological differences and was less threatening for organizations that did not wish to pursue a confrontational strategy with the state. In 1994, WiLDAF took on the more contentious topic of women's deaths due to backstreet abortion. As Win (2004, 23) notes, "the march was very badly attended by members of the network itself. It was clear that the issue was so divisive for the network that it was not going to progress far. Advocacy on this issue has not been revived since."

Another dimension of the "glue" that is lacking in networks, which hinders their ability to serve as platforms of mobilization, is the presence of a legitimate form of leadership that can act authoritatively in steering the movement ahead and making decisions at critical junctures. As Gladwell (2010) espouses, "because networks don't have a centralised leadership structure and clear lines of authority, they have real difficulty reaching consensus and setting goals. They can't think strategically; they are chronically prone to conflict and error. How do you make difficult choices about tactics or strategy or philosophical direction when everyone has an equal say?" But networks need not be run in a democratic or consensual manner; they may be vertically organized, involving patron-client relations of varying degrees of power.

Campaigns tend to be bound by issue, space, and time, therefore allowing the coalescing of activists in a way that requires less collective work than coalitions. Tilly and Tarrow (2007, 119) define a campaign as "a sustained, organised public effort making collective claims on targeted authorities . . . [extending] beyond any single event." Campaigns "always [link] at least three parties: a group of self-designated claimants, some object(s) of claims, and a public of some kind" (119). In Egypt, there was a proliferation of campaigns occurring throughout the 1990s and 2000s in which various NGOs coalesced and joined forces. The word *hamla* (campaign) became quite widely used. Examples include the campaign to allow women to become judges, the campaign against lenient sentences in rape, and the campaign to grant Egyptian women married to foreigners the right to pass on their nationality to their children (see chapter 2).

Coalitions may use networks and campaigns as methods of communication and intervention, respectively; however, they require a greater repertoire of collective action. Hogg and Leftwich (2007, 4) suggest "a coalition is best thought of as an association of groups and organisations working to resolve specific problems or to achieve specific goals that are beyond the capacity of any individual member of the coalition to resolve or achieve on their own." In campaigns, collective action is around a particular issue, but in coalitions actors work around a broader goal, usually requiring more sustained action. Bobo et al. (1991, 70) define a coalition as "an organisation of organisations working together for a goal," and they caution that "coalitions are not built because it is good, moral, or nice to get everyone working together. The only reason to spend the time and energy building a coalition is to amass the power necessary to do something you cannot do through one organisation." Perhaps one way to distinguish between campaign and coalition is that the former involves a strategy of intervention, whereas the latter involves an institutional setup that thrives even after it has completed its campaign because the cause requires continued action.

It is possible to analyze the configuration of power in coalitions along two axes: vertical and horizontal. Vertical coalitions are collective entities in which decision making is concentrated in the hands of one or a few powerful leaders but in which there is a broader membership base. Sometimes there is an open way of selecting the few who will manage the coalition on behalf of others; in other cases, the underlying power relations consist of patron–client relationships between the power holders and the members, which are symbiotically useful to both parties. Leading power holders can boast of having a coalition comprised of many members (thereby giving the coalition political weight), and members on the periphery can be connected to powerful individuals or organizations that can provide forums for participation, visibility, and funding. Horizontal coalitions, by contrast, are characterized by the sharing of decision-making powers among many leaders who have an equal stake in running the collective entity. It is a structure in which power is more evenly distributed among participating leaders/organizations.

Analysts such as Beckwith (2007, 319) use the term *coalition* to describe a strategy rather than an institutional actor: "Feminist movements also employ a coalitional strategy, making alliances with nonfeminist groups." In feminist literature, coalitions and campaigns can be used interchangeably, but in Win's (2004) discussion of the role of coalitions in Zimbabwe, she cautions that coalitions are more than merely a strategic intervention or activity; they are political actors in their own right. She suggests that "rather than seeing coalitions as mere functional organisational formations, they should be seen as political institutions, with political issues to deal with, both internally and externally" (26).

There are many important qualifiers for conceptual analysis of modalities of collective action. Although this typology is premised on distinguishing criteria regarding type of leadership and level of cohesion, in reality, demarcations can be opaque and blurred. In addition, collective actors involve dynamic processes: they may begin with the goal of becoming a movement and instead become a network, or they may begin with the goal of organizing a short campaign and in the process become a coalition. Coalitions may be active and then go through a period of hibernation. Hence, they are fluid processes that should be analyzed as such rather than as static entities with clearly defined lines or identities.

### Collective Action and Ruptures

Scholars have argued that transitions from authoritarian rule represent political opportunities for organized activism to influence political outcomes. This body of literature has been inductively drawn from the experiences of transitions in Latin America, where organized feminist activisms identified the overthrow of dictatorial regimes as political opportunities to press for more gender-equitable democratic orders (Jaquette and Wolchik 1998; Razavi 2000; Waylen 1994b). The pioneering comparative work on transitions by Waylen (2007) showed that transitions can allow for a reconfiguration of power favorable to women's rights if there is a pre-existing organized feminist movement that is able to seize new political opportunities to influence the political will. Sternbach et al. (1992, 397), in reference to the Latin American experiences, argue that during periods of flux generated by transitions to democracy, all classes of women may find the "political opportunities" to push for change.

There are many important qualifiers with respect to transitions as moments full of political opportunity for progressive social change. Political opportunities are gendered because the actors bear particular gender-normative values and beliefs and because the environment that they operate in is deeply gendered. In other words, advocates of democracy may not necessarily believe that gender equality should be prioritized as part of the reform process, nor are institutions necessarily open to becoming gender responsive (see chapter 6).

It is not only the existence of a political opening that is important, but also the cognitive dimension of political opportunities (Kuumba 2001). Do people perceive of the changing reconfiguration of power as a political opportunity? Do they engage with it as such? I would like to emphasize the cognitive dimensions of understanding the political situation as perceived by key actors *then* and *there*. The interpretations of reality and consequently people's choices of engagements and understanding of political opportunity are determined by temporal and spatial factors: what political cues were given at the time that informed people's assessment of their choices? Where were people situated, what spaces were they engaged in (circles of influence and power), and what were their perceptions of both? An understanding of the temporal and spatial dimensions can be captured through people's narratives, that is, stories that reveal their perceptions of power hierarchies and relations.

In the case of post-Mubarak Egypt, proponents and opponents of women's empowerment recognized the demise of his administration as a political opportunity to influence the new order. Many women's rights activists responded to the unfolding political events with a determination to be in the formal and informal spaces where negotiations were being held (see chapter 6), though sometimes they were completely excluded. However, so did antifeminist movements, who seized the anti-Mubarak sentiment to mobilize against the legislation and policies that had been issued during his tenure, under the pretext that these were imposed by the first lady and were alien to Egyptian culture (see chapters 6 and 7).

Research findings agree with existing feminist scholarship that the strength of collective action in favor of gender equality matters a great deal in times of reconfiguration of political power. When collective action around gender equality (expressed via a silent demonstration in Tahrir Square) was weak in March 2011, the impact was negative in that it incurred a high individual cost for the participants and it was not able to elicit positive social change on the ground.

The typology I present in this chapter is useful in delineating how having a plurality of modalities of collective action around gender equality can fulfill various purposes. However, at critical junctures such as ruptures, there needs to be a minimal level of (1) local legitimacy (as opposed to collective action lite), (2) cohesion (as opposed to casual networking), and (3) external show of unity (coalition or movement). Each level is briefly highlighted below and elaborated on in chapters 5–9.

### Local Ownership and Legitimacy

Although collective action lite forms of organizing such as those described in chapter 5 can thrive in contexts of political inertia, in moments of rupture, when there are struggles over the delineation of a nation's new identity, nationalist sentiments may be heightened and the pressure to prove one's indigenous credentials may be higher. In such a context, it is essential for collective actors to establish credibility and legitimacy by showing that they are firmly embedded in the social fabric of the country and that they are locally owned and led. It is therefore not surprising that when Mubarak's regime was overthrown the networks sponsored by the German International Development Agency (GIZ) and the Karama Coalition became marginal platforms for women's mobilization (see chapter 4). Many of the women activists who continued to press for women's rights post-Mubarak chose to work together, but this work was primarily undertaken through new coalitions that they forged, rather than pre-existing ones. My point here is that collective action lite is unsuitable for organic mobilization because it is too closely aligned or associated with a particular form of organizing that is tied to an external donor.

### Level of Cohesion

In my earlier discussion on networks in this chapter, I suggested that they may be useful for sharing information and for building repertoires of relations, but that ultimately they required a minimal level of cohesion insofar as commitment to a cause and a collective response (though they may develop in that direction). I also suggested that campaigns can be very effective in responding to a strategic opening or threat, conjuring the political forces around an issue, and mobilizing around it, after which demobilization occurs. This is perhaps why Magda Adley (see introduction) spoke of activists in Egypt finding it easier to work through campaigns rather than coalitions. However, in times of rupture, a certain level of cohesion of a coalitional or movement type is needed because these turbulent phases of political change require sustained collective engagement in which the sum of all parts is able to present a (relatively) coherent narrative about the desired change and political outcome. Without such internal cohesion, the political weight that can emerge from a combined constituency is not manifest.

*Unity*

Whereas cohesion has to do with internal organization, unity has to do with the ability of an organization to conjure a unified collective front to leverage its political weight to build alliances, be in a stronger negotiation position, and withstand opponents' efforts to divide and rule. At critical junctures after the overthrow of Mubarak, the government resorted to divide and rule tactics to undermine the emergence of a united voice concerning the national women's machinery. It purposely spoke to leaders active in the women's rights domain about pursuing different scenarios with respect to the National Council for Women. The outcome was a political reconfiguration of power that was unsatisfactory to everyone. Conversely, when faced with the increasing threats of encroachments on women's rights in 2012–13, alliances among youth coalitions, political parties, and women's rights led to organized collective street action that was strong and defiant in its defense of women's rights (see chapters 5–7).

It is always a constellation of factors that influence any political process and outcome. These determinants of the kind of collective action conducive to influencing the gender agenda at a time of rupture are neither a recipe for successful influence nor a set of boxes to tick.

## Conclusion

This chapter reviewed some of the worldwide scholarship that demonstrates how collective action matters for policy influence, women's empowerment, and engendering new orders after the downfall of authoritarian regimes. In this chapter I question the common theoretical underpinning of all forms of women's organizing: that it has a positive impact on women's agency. Some of the determinants of collective action's success have also been proposed (ownership, internal cohesion, and unity), and these determinants will feature throughout the upcoming chapters. Such elements are lacking in collective action lite, which is not just a weak form of organizing (like networks) but a highly disruptive and illusionary one.

By broadening the existing typology of the identity (female/male profile) of collective actors working on gender equality, the empirical data challenge us to rethink the many ways in which the identity of collective actors influence the gender equality agenda. In the first part of this chapter I argue that antifeminist forms of collective action do not by virtue of their women's constituency lead to the inclusion of women in politics, even when they themselves are politically engaged. I use the example of the Salafi women, who endorsed the sabotage of women candidates on the party electoral list so as to exclude women from becoming parliamentarians, even when other Islamist political parties accepted women's role in government. This chapter also examines the use of the term *antifeminist* as part of a broader theoretical engagement with thinking on collective action and identity. I showed how antifeminist movements significantly circumscribed women's freedoms, even by local normative standards governing political life. The association between women's collective agency and gender equality is challenged through another case study: that of the initiatives that emerged in post-Mubarak Egypt to counter the growing problem of sexual violence. These initiatives do not have a shared gender identity because they comprise both women and men and the mobilization of their constituency is not premised on a common experience as women. They cannot be defined as women's movements, feminist movements, or women in movement.

My intention is not to privilege one identity-based type of collective action (i.e., gender justice or feminist) as being necessarily more conducive to promoting gender equality, though the adverse impact of antifeminist movements on gender equality should be taken into consideration. As I will argue in the chapters to come, different types of collective actors are instrumental in challenging the red lines of gender equality in different spaces and at different junctures.

# 2

## SECURITIZED, ISLAMIZED, AND QUANGOIZED

*Women's Activisms under Mubarak*

Egypt under Mubarak had feminist voices without a movement and several women's movements without feminists. During the Mubarak years, there was strong women's leadership and participation en masse by women workers who organized around everyday issues and women belonging to the Islamist movements. Feminist voices played an important role in challenging discourses inimical to women's rights, but rivalry, fragmentation, and the absence of a constituency on the ground undermined their ability to work collectively. Rather than focus on the internal organizational dynamics of various actors, the focus of this chapter is the relations between feminist activists and various competing voices around identity, framings, and national women's agendas.

The Mubarak era is one of deep contestation between different actors over who has the authority and legitimacy to speak on behalf of Egyptian women. Under Mubarak, women's activisms in Egypt thrived in a context in which, politically, an authoritarian regime controlled citizen space; ideologically, religion became the normative framework for public engagement; and organizationally, the national women's machineries claimed representation of Egyptian women's voices and interests. The rise and salience of these forces emanated from a complex power struggle encompassing global, national, and local actors.

In this chapter I examine two sets of struggles that are to a large extent intertwined. The first is the struggle between various forces, not always neatly demarcated between the secular and the religious, over Muslim identity in relation to women's issues. The second is the struggle over voice, representation, and agenda setting between feminist voices in civil society and the national women's machineries. The last twenty years witnessed an increased pervasiveness of religious values and frameworks used for engaging policymakers and an intensification of the political struggle between Islamist opposition groups and the Egyptian government over who represents Islam and are the most faithful custodians of its precepts. For women's activists in Egypt to openly contest an increasingly conservative and religionized gender regime would have incurred high costs to their legitimacy, maneuvering space, and ability to engage a grassroots Muslim constituency. The costs of articulating an openly feminist voice— one that uses a human rights standpoint to advocate for women's rights— are particularly high. Accordingly, many secular feminist voices became increasingly framed in religious terms to accommodate the Islamization of society, challenging the conventional secular versus Muslim/Islamist dichotomy. The space for engaging policy and practice for women's activisms, in particular secular feminist voices, is also shrinking due to the establishment of national women's machineries and their claim to represent women's interests in Egypt. I argue that since 2000 women's activism has increasingly been affected by the process of quangoization of women's issues, namely, the establishment of institutions that organizationally seem as if they are independent of the government but in essence are controlled by the ruling regime and its entourage.

## Feminist Activisms in Mubarak's Egypt

Feminist voice refers to women's rights advocates who believe in CEDAW as a yardstick for the measurement of women's rights while being open to the use of multiple framings and entry points for engagement in women's rights. The significance of this feminist voice is how it challenges the red lines set by the government and Islamists over what is culturally and religiously acceptable in terms of a set of demands. The importance of feminist voices lies in their public articulation of a gender equality agenda in a political and social climate that is extremely hostile to such articulation.

This chapter focuses on feminist voices from 1994 until the ousting of Mubarak. Throughout the chapter I draw heavily from the comprehensive and detailed exploration of the origins and political trajectories of feminist activists in the seminal work by Nadje Al-Ali (2000), *Secularism, Gender and the State in the Middle East: The Egyptian Women's Movement*. A brief overview of the period prior to the 1990s is found in this book's introduction.

A small group of women activists expressed feminist voices in Mubarak's Egypt. These women tended to come from professional backgrounds, work through NGOs, coalitions, and campaigns, and often were engaged in multiple struggles (against the inheritance of the presidency, academic censorship, police brutality, etc.). Toward the end of the 1990s, feminists were particularly active in engaging on a policy level; they stepped up advocacy campaigns to challenge gender-discriminatory codes and laws (the most infamous of which is the Personal Status Law) and campaigns against practices such as sexual harassment and domestic violence. Although they did not have a significant constituency to champion their causes, they often were successful in ensuring that their voices were conveyed in the media, and they sometimes succeeded in making women's issues highly debated in public. There were ideological and class ruptures behind the divisions between the minority feminist voices and women's activists who championed other agendas. Ideological rifts emerged between secular feminists who refused to adopt an exclusively religious framework and women activists working through NGOs who increasingly embraced a more conciliatory approach toward integrating "progressive" religious discourses.

The nature of the interests that were being advocated and on whose behalf claims were being made limited mobilization through feminist activism. Feminist voice during Mubarak's reign was generally focused on campaigning for strategic gender interests, specifically those "involving claims to transform social relations in order to enhance women's position and to secure a more lasting repositioning of women within the gender order and within society at large' (Molyneux 1998, 232). Examples include feminist critiques of gender stereotypes in education and the media. However, in practice, women workers and civil servants organized around practical gender interests, or "those based on the satisfaction of needs arising from women's placement within the sexual division of labour" (232). Rowbotham (1992, 306) argues that engaging with women's autonomy and gender relations cannot be abstracted from material circumstances. This reflects the dilemma facing feminists who voiced a feminist agenda in Egypt: intellectually, they were engaged with gender in relation to practical issues, but in practice the necessary links with a constituency that played a leading role in advocacy campaigns were absent. The disconnect between feminist activists and the wider female constituency was in part due to limitations on freedom of association, inexperience in engaging grass-roots communities, and the elitist background of some of the activists.

## Visible and Hidden Regulation of Feminist Activism

The political situation in Egypt at the beginning of the twenty-first century became particularly volatile as it was squeezed by both internal and external factors of influence. The authoritarian regime came under pressure to democratize at various times (in particular from 2004 to 2006 under the Bush administration's democracy promotion initiative in the Middle East). Subsequently the regime allowed controlled democratic spaces to emerge but in a highly contained manner. Women activists of all political and ideological orientations were susceptible to becoming the targets of a state security apparatus. One feminist-cum-development NGO leader confided that members of her organization were perplexed when the state security apparatus unexpectedly sought to prevent their organizing of a workshop to discuss the Personal Status Law for Christians. Interviewed activists said that they thought it was completely random which issues would be seen as within the red lines and which ones would be seen as having towed them.

Yet in spite of this highly repressive and unpredictable political environment, women were openly contesting government policies. They organized, mobilized, and led marches and demonstrations. From the mid-2000s onward, as part of the Mubarak government's strategy to appear tolerant of political opposition, some protests and demonstrations were allowed within a highly securitized and controlled space. The key question became, who capitalized on this controlled space to organize and mobilize people into open political forms of activism? Some women participated in the emerging opposition groups, such as Kefaya! (Enough!), and they protested Mubarak's never-ending presidency and the possibility of succession to his son, Gamal Mubarak. However, their representation in leadership positions remained negligible. These women did deploy a variety of strategies to engage with activisms. For example, they appealed to a thriving independent press that has emerged in Egypt in the past five or six years and has had to exercise a certain level of self-censorship.

Hand in hand with the tolerance of controlled democratic spaces was the continued use of repression by security forces and plainclothes police. The establishment of associations was highly controlled and was one of the most effective ways of containing activism. Women's NGOs, like other forms of nongovernmental organizations registered with the government, complied with a highly restrictive NGO Law. Per the law, the Ministry of Social Solidarity (MOSA; formerly the Ministry of Social Affairs) was the key interlocutor for the NGOs. In practice, though, the secret police pulled the strings.

The NGO Law established strict restrictions for networks and any form of partnership or collective action. For example, any registered NGO is prohibited from joining an international network without first seeking MOSA's permission. It must also notify MOSA of any local networks that it joins. Local networks or coalitions must seek permission for formation from MOSA if they are to assume a legal character. Should an NGO become involved in an informal network/coalition, it may make itself vulnerable to questioning by MOSA employees. In addition to these formal powers, the Ministry of Interior exercised its real informal power through its state security investigations apparatus, commonly referred to as the SSI or domestic intelligence agency. The SSI surveillance spans any organization, irrespective of its ideological orientation or mission.

In some cases, the SSI openly blocked the activity of organizations, including feminist ones such as the New Woman Foundation, which has been active since the 1980s. Previously known as the New Woman Center and registered as a nonprofit civil company to evade the NGO Law and MOSA's heavy-handed bureaucracy, it was eventually forced to apply for registration in conformity with the new Law 84. Law 84 prohibited nonprofit organizations from registering under any other umbrella. When the New Woman Foundation submitted its registration papers to MOSA, the SSI rejected its application on security grounds. It was closed for many months before the court ruled in its favor, but during this time its status was in limbo and many initiatives were temporarily halted.

The SSI also used tactics of intimidation against individual women activists. One activist was incarcerated in the 1990s because she had exposed the way in which the SSI detained women and used threats (and acts) of sexual abuse to put pressure on suspected Islamists to turn themselves in. Because the Emergency Law[1] allowed the SSI to detain citizens without charge, mothers, daughters, sisters, and wives would be suddenly seized and kept for unknown periods of time. This activist exposed multiple human rights abuses to the international media, thus putting the Ministry of Interior in a compromising position.

Irrespective of the political affiliation of women activists, they have had an ambiguous relationship with the state apparatus, and they had to engage the SSI in strategic ways. The situation varied greatly from one activist, one organization, and one political moment to another. The level of compromise on the part of women's organizations and activists when dealing with the SSI was partly influenced by their own negotiating power (derived from their social and political positioning and clout). The question of where to draw the line when engaging with the SSI was a difficult moral quandary for activists. Some notified the SSI counterparts of their forthcoming workshops and meetings but refused to share the names of participants. Others provided a summary of the workshop activities and findings but refused to give details. Some refused both actions but did respond to the SSI when called upon to answer questions. Few would have been able to survive if they refused to engage the SSI at all. This reality is applicable to all political and civil actors in Egypt at the time, not only feminist activists (Tadros 2011a).

### Feminisms and the Constituency Question

Many feminist organizations assumed an elitist character from an organizational and agenda-setting point of view, which undermined their ability

---

1. Emergency Law was put in place in 1981 to counter terrorism after the assassination of President Sadat. In effect, it granted the security forces sweeping powers to haphazardly arrest and detain suspects for extended periods of time and try them in special courts.

to build a constituency on the ground. The NGOization of the Egyptian women's movement occurred in response to the donors' increased interest in promoting civil society. This in turn stemmed from Western economic liberalization policies that were pursued in tandem with the promotion of welfare pluralism. NGOization led to a proliferation of organizations representing different political perspectives but also the creation of a large set of "boutiques"[2] working on gender issues. Competition for foreign funding became more acute in the mid-1990s as donor funding for women's NGOs increased, making it more difficult for organizations to work together through coalitions, let alone movements.

The continued growth of the "boutique" phenomenon encouraged women activists to keep up with the latest development fads rather than be responsive to the pulse of a constituency on the ground. This further deepened the divide between the grassroots and the elites who ran the organizations. The elitism in feminist agenda setting also emerged out of a neglect of issues of economic inequality and distribution. Alliance building with the women workers who mobilized to make demands collectively would have provided feminist activists with an important opportunity for constituency building. By far the largest group to have engaged in organized collective activism were the women workers mobilizing around livelihood issues such as poor wages, delays in or cancellation of bonuses, and the use of fringe benefits as a substitute for raising salaries. Large numbers of female workers, civil servants, and low-income employees took to the street, usually in partnership with men, to protest their meager wages, lack of rights, and soaring prices. These protests occurred in a context in which a sustained economic liberalization program had taken its toll on the poor. The state increasingly privatized its welfare services (by expanding the scope and burden of cost-recovery measures) and state-owned enterprises while social inequalities widened, inflation rose, and deprivation increased (El Naggar 2010; Soliman 2006).

2. I am grateful to Akram Habib for coining the word "boutiques" in reference to individuals who have established organizations primarily for self-profit but under the guise of NGOs.

Given the state's control over them, women workers did not organize within formal trade unions. Instead, they mobilized around specific local contexts; for example, a particular factory at risk of shedding labor as a consequence of privatization, or a public-owned enterprise failing to give workers their wages for months on end. In response to the increasing deprivation and fall in the standard of living, women were at the core of groups who organized protests, sit-ins, and appeals for their rights. They did not organize in their capacity as women, but as fellow workers and employees. They assumed leadership positions, earned through the support of both men and women, and they were chosen to speak out against the injustices and negotiate with the ruling powers over terms of compromise. In doing so, they broke social taboos regarding the appropriate spaces for women to occupy, and they ignored socially prescribed curfews for women (they slept in tents on the streets and in factories during sit-ins).

In many cases, these women and their families succeeded in arriving at deals that secured their rights. In December 2007, hundreds of property tax workers, a significant proportion of them women, staged a peaceful sit-in that lasted more than eleven days. Finding it increasingly difficult to cope with the rising cost of living, they demanded fair pay commensurate with that of other workers on the Ministry of Finance's payroll. Women brought their children and their belongings and set up tents in the streets of central downtown Cairo. The image of these white-collar women, some with their entire families, sitting in tents on some of the city's most vibrant streets, incurred sympathy from the public and represented a major embarrassment to the Egyptian government. The negotiations that followed culminated in a 330 percent increase in their pay. The success of this incident prompted many other groups to consider sit-ins and strikes as a means to making remuneration demands (Rashed 2009).

Women activists participating in these contentious forms of politics organized others in the thousands and had a powerful influence on the outcome of the struggle to secure minimal economic and social rights from the government or the private sector. The activism, however, was not sustained after deals were reached. These were issue-based campaigns that were dismantled once the government responded to their demands (payment of overdue salaries, bonuses, and improved working conditions).

Citizens found their campaigns more successful in eliciting public support and government interest when they were centered on a very specific set of concrete demands (rather than structural demands such as freedom of association or expression). These activists also were at a stage in which livelihood concerns predominated, and they did not want to embark on larger, broader agendas at that juncture. If they had sought to sustain their activism, the SSI would have seen them as transgressing the red lines and would have cracked down on them with greater intensity.

Yet there was still space for building bridges between feminist organizations and women workers' struggles around common issues of economic inequality, including unpaid care,[3] welfare rights, and paid employment. To a large extent feminists excluded these issues from their policy agendas.

**Feminists Negotiating the Sacred**

An important development since the 1980s has been the increased salience of religion in every aspect of life in Egypt. Religion came to represent a normative framework for engaging with all kinds of public and private issues. This change was a result of the rise of political opposition movements like the Muslim Brotherhood but was also due to the state's active encouragement of religion's infiltration in media and society and its competition with the Islamist movements over who was more observant and deferential toward Islam. The increasing prevalence of the Islamist framework influenced how women activists engaged with a sociocultural environment in which religion assumed such a critical role. In addition, women belonging to Islamist movements, in particular the Muslim Brotherhood, increasingly claimed public space to advocate for an Islamist platform. Although their numbers were not as large as the women workers, they did use diverse spaces (e.g., universities, mosques, and the street) to articulate their demands for the application of their movement's agenda and vision.

---

3. Unpaid care includes work such as household tasks (i.e., cleaning and cooking) and care for the children, elderly, and vulnerable members of households and communities. It is often neither recognized in economic policy as work nor is its value calculated in economic terms.

The literature on women activists in the Middle East who emerged in the 1990s and 2000s tends to distinguish between secular activists who advocated a human rights–based approach to gender equality and those who advocated for the advancement of gender rights within the parameters of a religious framework. In the early 1990s, Azza Karam classified women activists as secular feminists, Muslim feminists, and Islamist feminists. Islamist feminists reject gender equality but do recognize women's oppression as part of the wider order of sociopolitical injustice. Muslim feminists aim to show that "the discourses of total equality between men and women are Islamically valid" (Karam 1997, 22). They believe that "a feminism that does not justify itself within Islam is bound to be resisted by the rest of society and is therefore self-defeating" (22). Karam contrasted Muslim and Islamist feminists with secular feminists, who "firmly believe in grounding their discourse outside the realm of any religion and place it instead within the international human rights discourses. . . . Religion is respected as a private matter but is totally rejected as a basis from which to formulate any agendas on women's emancipation" (24).

By the late 2000s, the above dichotomy between the secular and religious platforms for advancing gender equality in Egypt no longer reflected the situation on the ground. Virtually all organizations that worked with a grassroots constituency, the media, and the government (or any other non-Western, nonacademic party) had to show and profess the conformity of their demands with the precepts of Islam. This fundamental shift in strategy of engagement was a direct consequence of the increasing Islamization of space, politics, and social norms. It is also significant that the Egyptian government itself, when seeking to advocate gender reforms, was keen to frame its calls as deriving from Islam and supported by Muslim scholars.[4] Interviews with activists in August 2010 indicated that individual leaders thought that without framing ideas and agendas as

---

4. For example, after introducing *khul'* (a woman's right to arbitrarily divorce her husband via the judiciary system on condition she forgoes some of her financial rights) in 2000, the government was keen to emphasize that it was advancing this law as part of its commitment to the implementation of the Shari'a (rather than advancing gender equality). See Al-Sharmani 2009 for more information.

stemming from Islam, they did not stand a chance of winning campaigns or constituency support.

The extent to which this fundamental shift in engagement represented an ideological shift in personal belief systems or religious values of feminist activists was impossible to decipher. However, what is noteworthy is that religious frameworks became the "natural" pathway for advocating for social change on gender matters. Feminist activists developed a discourse of showing the compatibility of enlightened readings of the Shari'a with international human rights treaties. Enlightened readings of the Shari'a were premised on the more progressive interpretations of religious texts, such as that provided by the late Nasser Abou Zeid, a renowned progressive Muslim jurist. Promotion of these readings was designed to advocate for women's rights through the prism of an alternative interpretation of Islam.

However, as feminists sought to adapt to the increasingly religionized environment, disputes emerged about framings and ideological underpinnings. In one particular instance, feminist activists began to discuss how they would frame their case for more gender equality in family law. The German International Development Agency (GIZ) began this initiative, which was intended to bring together organizations from feminist and development backgrounds (see chapter 4) but was soon faced with a crisis that led to the withdrawal of one of its core NGOs over the question of referencing. The crisis highlighted that the lines of demarcation were not between secular feminists and Islamist leading women activists or even between Muslim and secular feminists. Ironically, the dispute erupted between leaders with a long history of feminist activism who have, in their trajectories, consistently referred to CEDAW as their point of reference.

The first party to the dispute, who later pulled out, was the Arab Women Solidarity Association (AWSA). At the time AWSA was headed by a former United Nations Children's Fund (UNICEF) director who had more than thirty years of experience working with women in development and was from a liberal feminist tradition. Dr. Hoda Badran firmly believed that the document to be shared with the public and used for advocacy purposes vis-à-vis the government, the media, and *Al-Azhar* newspaper should not make any reference to CEDAW. Instead, the document should specifically reference the "enlightened Shari'a." Dr. Badran explained that although she firmly believed in CEDAW, she thought that AWSA must be responsive to the political climate in Egypt, where religion is so salient and so influential (interview by author, July 2010). Furthermore, in light of the fact that the Personal Status Law was already premised on Shari'a law, she conceded the need to be particularly sensitive when showing how the championed policy changes have not deviated from those parameters. In essence Dr. Badran and AWSA sought to maximize opportunities for winning allies and countering the opposition, who were likely to attack any policy reforms proposed in the area of Personal Status Law as a Western imperialist project intended to undermine Islam. Dr. Badran also argued that the insertion of CEDAW in the document signified a bowing down to the donors' agenda because this was the framework through which they operated.

The second party to the dispute involved most of the other feminist activist associations, though some were in the gray zone and remained on the fence. One leader who took a different stance was a founder of the Forum for Women in Development (an NGO) and a renowned leftist writer and activist (of the Tagammu leftist party). She believed that the premise of the associations' work should be CEDAW and the international human rights conventions. She explained that those who adopt an old reading of the Shari'a do not believe in the international conventions, and hence the conventions specifically must be stipulated as part of the feminist standpoint: "In our work, in our workshops, lectures and seminars we have defended the idea that the international conventions are part of our culture too and that we [Egyptians] have contributed to their writing and to the introduction of their articles . . . so the international conventions are not alien to us, they are not imported" (interview by Hind Mahmoud, July 2010).

This leader conceded that insisting on the international conventions sets the normative values that safeguard against the possibility of different readings of the Shari'a that are adversarial to women's rights and that see women as second-class citizens, without recognizing their full dignity and humanity. However, she was overruled by the majority opinion of the initiative's members (see chapter 4), who insisted that their demands for Personal Status Law reform should be framed as deriving from both CEDAW and the enlightened Shari'a. When commenting on this stance, one member of the initiative (who preferred to remain anonymous) said that those who championed mentioning the enlightened Shari'a as a reference were not all on the same wavelength ideologically. For some it was a case of pure political pragmatism: a focus on the compatibility of CEDAW with the Shari'a meant that they could hold middle ground, maintaining their framework of reference while winning maneuverable space in society. For others, their insistence on articulating a stance on enlightened Shari'a derived from their fundamental faith in the superiority of sacred texts over CEDAW and in the possibility of accommodating all women's rights in the Shari'a. It is a position that may not have been adopted universally in the 1990s but one that has certainly grown with the rise of Islamism in society throughout the first decade of the twenty-first century.

The dispute over frameworks and framings was not simply an ideological squabble between feminists of different shades. It had a deep impact on the identity of the group, to the extent that one organization, AWSA, chose to withdraw altogether from that initiative. This rupture was to affect not only the core group in the GIZ-led initiative but also the working relationships between AWSA and some of the associations more broadly, manifesting itself in other spaces and policy forums. The outcome was the increased fragmentation of efforts, which undermined prospects of building cohesive movements that could mobilize the sum of all parts to launch unified struggles against threats to women's agendas or to win battles when political opportunities were ripe.

In addition to their internal struggle over the dialectic relationship between religion and gender issues, feminist circles struggled externally with the organized women's constituency of the Islamist movements in Egypt. By far the most populist of these movements was the Muslim Brotherhood, which was officially outlawed by the Egyptian government but in practice tolerated (albeit they were susceptible to sporadic waves of violent repression and mass incarceration). Women members of the

Muslim Brotherhood consistently expressed the party line in defense of the Islamist political project and its activists (see chapter 7).[5]

An obvious ideological struggle exists between Islamists who view women's equality as only achievable in the context of a just Islamist state and feminist activists who are critical of the Islamist view. On the street, this struggle was won by the Islamists.[6] Politically, there was consensus around the Muslim Brotherhood's ideological positions on some issues, such as the necessity of veiling. Central to the Muslim Brotherhood women activists' strategic use of voice to mobilize was their nationwide access to mosques. It is through these spaces that they recruited and mobilized adherents. The mosque space was (and continues to be) closed to many feminists as long as they do not conform to ideas about religiously prescribed appropriate female behavior, discourse, and attire (and this varies from one mosque to another). This excludes them from one of the most important spaces for dialogue, mobilization, and collective action with women who regularly visit the mosque. The voice of these women activists is highly complex in relation to feminist voice and to the government and wider society. Feminist voices were so marginal on the streets most of the time that the Islamist political forces did not bother to attack them (see chapter 4).

It is only when feminists, for example, sought to build a relationship with clerics at Al-Azhar University (the Sunni establishment's most important place of learning) that members of the Islamist opposition began to openly oppose them because they feared that they would seek to influence policy. By the twenty-first century, however, most Islamists did not bother attacking feminists when they launched campaigns or pressed

5. For example, thousands of Muslim Brotherhood women activists participated in the protests against the Israeli strikes on Gaza. Such protests were driven by a political and ideological commitment on the part of the Muslim Brotherhood to liberate the Muslim *ummah* from occupation in Palestine.

6. For an excellent summary of the increasing Islamization of public space and Egyptians, as well as the rise of the more fundamentalist Salafi movement in the early 2000s, see D. Rashwan 2009.

for policy change because they recognized that they had little to fear in terms of their influence.

The competition between the Muslim Brotherhood and the Egyptian government (as well as the ruling National Democratic Party [NDP]) to show who was more committed to Islam added another layer of complexity to interpreting the increasing Islamization of public life in Egypt in the last three decades of Mubarak's rule. This complexity was brought to the fore through two incidents, one involving the minister of culture openly criticizing the veil, and the second involving the minister of education prohibiting the wearing of the *niqab* during examinations. In the first incident in 2006, the Muslim Brotherhood and the government took the same position in response to an off-guard statement made by the minister of culture about the veil. Both political forces, normally in opposition, were united with the Islamist opposition in their call for the minister's resignation. In the second incident in 2009, the minister of education's position on prohibiting the donning of *niqab* during examinations was met with open protest by the Muslim Brotherhood and with more subtle critiques by different elements of the Egyptian government. Although both incidents are controversial, their significance lies in the reactions and what those reactions suggest in regard to the pervading political culture and the space allowed for deviant voices.

The first incident involved an unofficial conversation between Farouk Hosni, the minister of culture, and a female journalist in which Hosni spoke out against veiling and attributed its popularity in Egypt to the Wahabi Islamist influence. He also lamented that Egypt was going backwards compared to Bahrain and Qatar, where "women are starting to remove the face veil, niqab, while in Egypt people are taking it up" (Al-Dakhakhni 2006). Hosni later insisted that the statements were an expression of his personal opinion and were not made in his official capacity. However, the resultant campaign against him was sustained for weeks, with many female Muslim Brotherhood members participating in public protests. In parliament the Muslim Brotherhood led the campaign, with ruling NDP members chiming in and calling for Hosni's resignation. This was presented as the only appropriate action to be taken in response to his inappropriate comments, which were interpreted as an attack on Islam itself (Mussalam and Yasin 2006). In a context in which the overwhelming majority of Muslim women don the veil, the minister's statements struck a chord with public opinion.

The impact of the Muslim Brotherhood and government reactions was far-reaching for secular feminist activists and others who do not hold the same ideological position on women's veiling. It is noteworthy that Hosni's statement was not made from the perspective of women's right to choose (not to wear the veil), but from the negative implications of a pervasive, imported form of Islam. The normative framework in which discussions about this incident were taking place ostracized voices that expressed alternative standpoints. Part of this normative framework was to pit veiled, righteous women against nonveiled women with questionable morals. Another important element was the presentation of religious dogma in absolutist terms, thus obstructing the possibility of engaging with multiple interpretations and perspectives on the position of Islam on veiling. Conforming to mainstream conceptions of religion had become the norm, and any deviation from this norm was increasingly met with opposition and hostility.

The second incident occurred in October 2009 in response to a policy adopted by Sheikh Mohamed Sayyid Tantawy, the grand sheikh of Al-Azhar University, which banned students from wearing the *niqab* in all-women classes tutored by presecondary Al-Azhar schools. Tantawy explained that the *niqab* is a habit (*'ada*, i.e., he inferred that it is not a religious obligation, or *'ebada*). A conversation between Tantawy and a preparatory school female student who was wearing the *niqab*, in which he obliged her to remove the face veil and insisted that Islam did not require it, was criticized as disrespectful. It is worth noting that there is complete gender segregation among students at all levels of Al-Azhar education in Egypt. Although the content of the conversation remained controversial in terms of interpretation,[7] the minister of higher education subsequently

---

7. Please note that these debates must not be read in the same light as those taking place in France, which are clearly racist and Islamophobic (in my point of view). In Egypt,

issued a policy banning women who wore the *niqab* from university student accommodation. The stance against the *niqab* catalyzed a series of protests and demonstrations by Muslim Brotherhood women activists on account of its violation of the right to freedom of attire. Feminist activists were divided. Some lauded the voice of moderate Islam expressed by Sheikh Mohamed Tantawy, whereas others asserted the right of choice.

Irrespective of how the incident is interpreted, the debates that followed showed the extent to which the prevailing social climate was constrained. In a telephone interview on an Egyptian program, Sheikh Hegazy extolled the *niqab*-wearer and contrasted her with women of immodest attire and prostitutes who do not wear the *niqab*; a woman "who goes out *moutabareja* [without wearing *niqab*] exposes her adornment onto others is a prostitute and hides the devil inside of her" (Nabil 2009). Socially, there is very little tolerance of views considered antithetical to prevailing interpretations of Islam. This is significant for feminist voices who choose to work outside of this normative framework and who find their positions being delegitimized. Even so, they insist on making their voices heard. Azza Soliman, a researcher (not the human rights activist of the same name), waged a lawsuit against Sheikh Hegazy for insulting Egyptian women and insisted he make a public apology (Nabil 2009).

### Feminist Struggle with the Ladies of the Quangos

The national women's machineries actively marginalized the role of feminist groups in civil society and pursued state feminism at the service of the ruling regime and made possible through the support of foreign donors. In Mubarak's Egypt, the national women's machineries were the NCW, a parastate entity established in 2000 that was answerable to the prime minister and presided over by the first lady, and the NCCM, established in 1988 and also led by the first lady. These organizations were hybrids of quangos (quasi-NGOs) and gongos (government-organized NGOs) (Fowler 1997).

---

the government has been implicitly endorsing the Islamization of public space for at least four decades, including the active promotion of veiling. Hence, the historical–cultural–political context is very different.

Institutionally, they typify Fowler's definition of a quango, namely, a para-state body set up by government as an NGO, often to enable better conditions of service or create political distance. They enjoyed the status of autonomous organizations and were considered to be neither part of the government's executive arm nor accountable to any government ministry. They had their own budgets, boards, and internal governance structures. However, in terms of function, national women's machineries served as gongos; they were used to capture or redirect nonprofit funds allocated by the official aid system.

Both the NCCM and NCW received extensive funding from foreign donors. In some cases, foreign donors withdrew funding from civil society initiatives to fund these organizations. For example, as shown in chapter 4, UNICEF diverted its funds from supporting the NGOs' CEDAW work preparing the shadow report for the Commission on the Status of Women (CSW) to fund NCW's efforts to prepare the official government report.

Donors could have pressed for a division of labor, earmarking funding so that the national machineries and civil society would have complementary roles. This would have minimized rivalry. However, there were instances of duplication of work by women's NGOs and national machineries (e.g., work on gender-based violence). Many donors chose to channel funds via the national machineries because of their ability to implement programs at a national level. The implications were that donors strengthened the national machineries' visibility and claims of representation for the gender agenda in Egypt.

If the Islamists' sphere of influence on gender issues was populist, the overriding influence on gender issues in the policy arena was that of women within or close to the regime's political entourage. Women affiliated with the national women's machineries tended to exert direct influence on the policy-making process more than Muslim Brotherhood women activists and feminist voices, whose influence was at best indirect. The national machineries' legitimacy was derived from the political will of the ruling regime, which in turn allowed them political proximity.

The increasing visibility of the national machineries (based on their claims to represent Egyptian women's needs) and the expansion of their role in policy work and development contributed to the more explicit treatment of gender equality issues in the public domain. It has also meant appropriating feminist voices in civil society. Like national women's machineries elsewhere, the NCW and NCCM are not homogenous institutions, and they encompass actors who represent voices of both feminists and depoliticized government bureaucrats. Thus, the exercise of their agency is not singular and the relationships forged are very diverse. For the most part, though, women's machineries' internal governance structures left very little room for inclusion of dissenting feminist voices from within civil society. The nature of the leadership was heavily influenced by the will of the first lady and the secretary general (whom the first lady appoints). In the case of the NCW, the first lady wielded the mandate to appoint one-third of the board of members and to change them every three years, whereas the secretary general had the mandate to appoint all twenty-seven heads of branches. A significant number of those occupying governance positions were also members of the ruling NDP, and the machineries were accountable directly to the prime minister, thereby limiting the potential to influence them given the absence of downward accountability.

National machineries capitalized on their political proximity to the "powers that be" to effect change on gender issues. Yet the focus on influencing the policy-making arena meant that there was little attention paid to the process of creating consensus around policy, nor on the impact of the policy on more marginalized groups. In authoritarian regimes in which the policy-making arena is restricted to a closed circle of elites, political openings for the wider citizenry to influence policy sometimes exist but are few and far between. In effect, most policy reforms in Egypt were achieved without widespread participation from those on whose behalf reforms are being made. For example, in 2001 the ministerial decree that prohibited women from giving their nationality to their children (commonly referred to as the nationality law) was changed, largely through the efforts of a few key organizations and activists who were able to influence public opinion and reach out to policymakers. They used case studies of women whose children's rights were denied as a consequence of the existing law, but these studies were used to support their campaign rather than lead it.

The greater the access feminists had to the circle of highly connected people affiliated with the national machineries, the greater the potential for influence. This posed a dilemma for feminists. On the one hand, if they wanted to strategically influence the government, engaging with senior members within the national machineries could be an effective way of getting political buy-in to the cause being advocated. Some feminists found this productive, especially in terms of the visibility and impact of events done in partnership with national machineries or under the auspices of the first lady. For these feminists, what was most important is to effect change on the ground. If it meant partnering with national women's machineries, so be it. On the other hand, some feminists found that the long-term impact of such a strategy was the appropriation of their demands and struggles in deeply disturbing ways.

Although national machineries did play a highly influential role in eliciting legislative reform, they often claimed sole credit for policy changes. The decades-long contribution of civil society organizations in documenting women's ordeals, raising consciousness on the implications of discriminatory structures, and transforming cases of injustice into public opinion issues did not feature in the official narrative of how change happened. In her assessment of the national machineries of Egypt, Khafagy (2007, 8) noted that "the NWM [national women's machinery] in Egypt succeeded, through lobbying with the parliament, to change the nationality law, the pension law, the tax exemption law, the alimony fund law and introduce the *khul'* law and the family court law." The extensive lobbying by women NGOs and activists to elicit change and their role in publicizing gender issues and getting them debated should be acknowledged. In the case of the Nationality Law, women's NGOs and feminist activists spent years lobbying policymakers, but when parliament discussed the change to the ministerial decree, members made no mention of the role of civil activism in bringing it to the fore. Rather, one member after another stood up to thank the first lady for her benevolence toward Egyptian women.

Authoritarian governments sometimes wish to appear as benevolent patrons who change policy in response to their recognition of the people's needs. This presents a further disincentive for them to recognize the role of civil society organizations. Hence, the attribution of successful policy change becomes highly problematic when different parties are involved in adversarial as well as more backdoor forms of advocacy.[8]

In a similar case to the Nationality Law, the NCCM claimed to be the principle force behind criminalizing female genital mutilation in 2008. FGM was criminalized under the rubric of the Child Law, which ingenuously provided the appropriate framing to minimize opposition (likely to occur with anything framed under women's or human rights). Although the NCCM negotiated and pushed the law forward in parliament, it was really thanks to the earlier work of feminist and women activists that the issue was brought to the fore. Prominent (secular) feminist Nawal el Saadawi was one of the first to speak out against FGM. The FGM Taskforce (see chapter 3) introduced appropriate ways of engaging on the issue to elicit culturally sensitive social change on the ground and to encourage public debate on religious and health perspectives. When Nawal el Saadawi was asked about the promulgation of the new legislation against FGM, she said that the law came as a consequence of the struggles of the Egyptian population.

> I fought a lot against female and male circumcision since sixty years ago, and I lost my job and my reputation and was opposed by religious men and the physicians' syndicate for this cause. And when they issued the law, no one mentioned me and recognition was given to Suzanne Mubarak because she is the President's wife! (Nasr 2009)

The political significance of who gets credit is deeply political; it is about voice, recognition, and agency. As the national machineries became increasingly hegemonic in claiming to represent Egyptian women's interests, feminist activists' contribution to civil society was downplayed and their voices marginalized.

So far in this chapter, I have discussed the role of the national women's machinery in sidelining feminists, monopolizing the right to speak on behalf of Egyptian women, and assuming sole credit for policy reform

---

8. See Gaventa (2008) for a discussion of the problems associated with donor approaches to assessing advocacy campaigns.

on women's equality. The machinery's aggrandizement was made possible through Western support, which was able to accommodate the ideological dispositions of the authoritarian regime in power.[9]

### Western-Sponsored Authoritarian Empowerment

During the first phase of its political empowerment program funded by the United Nations Development Program (UNDP), the NCW provided technical training to female candidates running for elections, specifically the local council and the parliamentary elections. The training of female candidates aimed to provide them with the skills required for campaigning and lobbying. In the 2000 national elections, the NCW claimed that its support was nonpartisan, and the same applied for its support for the 2007 local council elections. After the 2005 parliamentary elections produced the least number of winning female candidates in the history of the country, key female candidate-activists of the opposition had some harsh criticism for the work of the NCW. They indicated that partisan politics prevented the NCW from offering equal opportunities to all parties and their candidates. There were no mechanisms in place for the Egyptian constituency to hold the NCW accountable should it engage in partisan politics, but because this program was foreign funded, the monitoring mechanisms were upwardly rather than downwardly accountable.

The subtleties of the NCW's promotion of political engagement need to be examined against the backdrop of the unfolding political scene in Egypt. In 2007, the president of Egypt launched a referendum on amending the constitution. Opposition parties argued that some of the amendments aimed to restrict political freedom and undermine the prospects of any other party contesting the NDP. Consequently, members of the opposition party in parliament boycotted the parliamentary session in which the vote on the constitutional amendment was cast, and they led a nationwide campaign to urge Egyptian citizens not to go to the voting poll on March 26, 2007, as an act of protest. The NCW mobilized its employees

---

9. Case studies in the following section draw heavily on information from Tadros 2010a.

and members to go vote in the referendum. The very fact that it prompted them to participate in the referendum, even if it did not tell them what to vote, is a partisan political action. The NDP desperately needed to have citizens participate in the referendum to give the impression that the changes passed democratically with the majority of Egyptian voices supporting them, and it is in this context that the NCW's proreferendum initiative must be assessed. Because this activity was being funded by the UNDP's support for the political empowerment project, it is possible that donor money was being spent to legitimize and support the status quo and the regime in power.

Although the theme of the NCW's program was political empowerment of women, the institution's approach was one that diluted the concept of all politics. Political empowerment was reduced operationally to a set of technical inputs involving training and networking. When women engaged in the kind of politics that brought them in conflict with the ruling regime, they could not turn to the NCW. When state security forces incarcerated women for participating in prodemocracy demonstrations, the NCW said that it was not their responsibility to defend these women's rights. The project coordinator of the Women Political Empowerment Program at the NCW argued that it is not in the mandate of the NCW to defend women in demonstrations. This admission showed the extent to which political empowerment became stripped of any potential to challenge the existing power configurations on the ground. When female candidates standing for the parliamentary elections complained to the NCW that their campaigns were being obstructed by the work of hired thugs and by harassment and violation of campaign rules by other contestants who often used gender as a basis for defamation and assault, no actions were taken. It is understandable that the NCW had no authority over the security apparatus; however, it could have used its political clout to lobby the Ministry of Interior to ensure better protection of all candidates running, men and women, especially because its principle constituency (women) were being attacked.

Western policy and funding played a critical role in enabling the NCW to make women's empowerment a project compatible with the ruling authoritarian regime. The approach to political empowerment, as shown above, was the initiation of a set of projects with activities and deliverables. Yet the extent to which these programs show responsiveness to the predicament of women political activists on the ground was not factored in the assessment of the impact or outcomes of these projectivized initiatives. This practice resonates with Marina Ottaway's (2004) observation of American donor assistance to governments for the promotion of women's rights. She noted that this aid "can be translated in practice into many concrete small projects that are not seen as threatening by most Arab regimes and are even welcomed by them as a means to demonstrate their willingness to democratize and modernize."

In addition to the projectivization of women's equality, the NCW allowed donors to selectively filter what types of discrimination to address and which ones to ignore, permitting them to purposely avoid cases in which women face injustice as a consequence of the intersection of their political identity and their gender. For example, the NCW launched a program to address domestic violence funded by the United States Agency for International Development (USAID). The program suffered from a kind of schizophrenia typical of many externally supported programs that fund women's equality under authoritarianism. Under the program, police officers and other stakeholders were trained in how to deal with domestic violence situations. However, when women were subjected to violence on the street rather than at home, such incidents did not fit the project objectives and thus were ignored.

In 2006 significant numbers of women were sexually harassed, and some had their clothes completely torn off while in a crowded public square in front of cinemas in downtown Cairo. The images of youth harassing veiled and nonveiled women who were in the company of their spouses or in groups were captured via mobile phone cameras and later disseminated via bloggers' sites on the Internet. The Ministry of Interior denied the harassment and insisted that no reports were filed at the downtown police station. The NCW did not comment on the incident. Their only reaction was a letter sent by their secretary general to *Al Destour* newspaper. In the letter she reprimanded the paper for criticizing her organization for being silent, insisting that it was not appropriate for the NCW to comment on a matter under investigation by the general prosecution (Tadros 2010a).

By focusing on domestic violence, USAID could avoid the political sensitivities associated with women's embeddedness in relationships of oppression, some of which linked directly to the nature of the authoritarian rule in place.

## Conclusion

In this chapter I examined the predicament of feminist voices that articulated a women's rights agenda within the sociopolitical context and historical trajectory of Mubarak's rule in contemporary Egypt. In terms of collective strength, women members of the Islamist movements far outnumber the organizations and women who express feminist voices. Up until the revolution, women workers and civil servants represented the largest collective mobilization of women that Egypt had witnessed in half a century. Feminists' activisms were politically marginal and were not propped up by a strong constituency, though there were some successful cases (as I discuss in chapters 3 and 4). However, the fragmentation of feminist activists had implications when the regime was overthrown in 2011. When faced with the threat of complete marginalization by the new political actors, they could not conjure a united front that would give them the political weight to influence the unfolding agendas. Ridden with years of fighting over funding, ideological differences, and belonging to different cliques, the feminist activists were too divided in the first few months after the overthrow of Mubarak to collectively press for a gender-sensitive transition.

The absence of a strong constituency also meant that in the aftermath of the January 25th revolution feminist activists became easily displaced by initiatives that could do street work, build a following, and champion gender issues that directly touched people's everyday lives. When control by the state security investigations apparatus was temporarily removed, there were no more excuses that could be made for the prevention of public political action. Yet by and large many failed the litmus test of showing that they could build a large constituency from ordinary women and men. As for the national women's machineries, the "blessing" that they had capitalized on—political patronage of the first lady—became their greatest curse after the ousting of Mubarak.

Although the women's agenda was primarily challenged on ideological grounds in the aftermath of the January 2011 revolution, nevertheless, the political association between the first lady's national machineries and the women's agendas provided the ammunition to Islamists as well as other right-wing forces to attack women's equality as the corrupting project of the former regime. A clear policy message is how imperative it is for national machineries to enjoy full economic and political autonomy and broad-based ownership from nonstate actors. It was not only the national machineries' reputation that was tainted after the revolution, but also the Western donors who supported them.

# 3

## THE FGM TASKFORCE

### A Coalition Possessing a Soul without a Body

One of the earliest attempts at coalitional work across nongovernmental organizations during Mubarak's tenure was the FGM Taskforce, a platform established to address the pervasive practice of female genital mutilation in Egypt. FGM is the outcome of several forms of genital cutting "that involve partial or total removal of the external female genitalia, or other injury to the female genital organs" (World Health Organization 2014).[1] Historically, there have been several champions who have spoken out against the practice, such as renowned physician and feminist writer Dr. Nawal el Saadawi and writer Amina el Said. The FGM Taskforce represented the first collective front formed by different

---

1. The World Health Organization (2014) identifies four types of FGM:
    1. Clitoridectomy: partial or total removal of the clitoris (a small, sensitive, and erectile part of the female genitals) and, in very rare cases, only the prepuce (the fold of skin surrounding the clitoris).
    2. Excision: partial or total removal of the clitoris and the labia minora, with or without excision of the labia majora (the labia are the "lips" that surround the vagina).
    3. Infibulation: narrowing of the vaginal opening through the creation of a covering seal. The seal is formed by cutting and repositioning the inner, or outer, labia, with or without removal of the clitoris.
    4. Other: all other harmful procedures to the female genitalia for non-medical purposes, e.g., pricking, piercing, incising, scraping, and cauterizing the genital area.

In Egypt, the most common practice is clitoridectomy.

stakeholders from civil society to elicit social, political, and legal change to address this practice.

The taskforce is one of the earliest and most successful cases of a collective actor that emerged during Mubarak's reign and distinctly worked on multiple levels: transnational, national, and grassroots. The FGM Taskforce had to navigate its positionality vis-à-vis the political agendas of different actors: the Egyptian government, the official Islamist establishment, the Islamist movements, the medical profession, radical Western feminists, donors, and the families who choose to circumcise their daughters. Some of the successful strategies pursued by the taskforce to navigate through these political landmines are discussed at length in this chapter, including the framing of multiple discourses for different audiences, the strategic choice of issues for campaigning, and ways of being responsive to the political moment. Regrettably, the taskforce followed the cyclical nature of social movements: after experiencing a phase of consolidation, it dissolved. Its dissolution led to the demobilization of the collective character of the initiative, leaving a conspicuous civil society vacuum. The impact was felt during the discussions of a government-sponsored law to criminalize the practice, which were severely compromised by the absence of a taskforce voice.

In the first part of this chapter I examine ways in which the FGM Taskforce's choice of labeling the practice shed light on ways in which it negotiated its positionality and framed its discourses. In the second part of the chapter I give a more detailed account of how the religious establishment and the government medicalized the practice of FGM and I discuss the nature of strategies adopted by the taskforce. The chapter also includes an analysis of the role of the medical practice in perpetuating FGM's medicalization and a particular focus on the taskforce's approach to catalyzing social change on a community level. The final part of the chapter discusses the effects of the taskforce's dissolution on policy and practice.

## The Idea of an FGM Taskforce

The FGM Taskforce was established in 1994 when the silence shrouding the practice of FGM was replaced by an intense politicization of the issue. Eventually, FGM would represent a pawn in the battles between different ideological and political actors. This first became evident at the ICPD, held in Cairo in 1994, which galvanized civil society to convene, mobilize, and put forward agendas for promoting women's reproductive health rights. A CNN documentary film screened during the conference showed a little girl being circumcised by a local barber as she was pinned down and screaming in pain. The controversial footage and the subsequent debates elicited the attention of many different actors, causing a knee-jerk reaction in several directions. Ali Abd el Fattah, then the Egyptian minister of health, responded to the international outrage by promising to outlaw the practice of FGM.

It is in this politically charged context that a group of NGO practitioners, activists, and feminists, concerned about how to appropriately end the practice, joined forces to form the FGM Taskforce. Marie Assaad, a renowned NGO practitioner/scholar who wrote one of the most influential papers on FGM, was nominated to become the coordinator of the taskforce. The majority of the taskforce members were professionals (e.g., doctors, lawyers, journalists, and human rights activists), and many were development practitioners working in community development, health, women's rights, and education. There were a few members who were from grassroots organizations based outside of Cairo.

The taskforce was particularly conscious of two dimensions of its membership: class and number. Members were aware of the privileged position from which they came as well as of the moral and political issues implicit in speaking on behalf of the poor. In addition, although the taskforce was an open membership forum that invited anyone to join as long as he or she shared the same commitment to ending FGM, it remained a small organization up until its dissolution.

From the outset, Marie Assaad was determined not to create an institution, or what she called "an empire." She wanted a forum where members collectively shared ideas, efforts, and time to create a movement that would address policymakers, scholars, media, local activists, and others. The taskforce existed under the umbrella of the National Commission of Population and Development (NCPD), an institution created to represent NGOs working on reproductive health matters after the ICPD. Although the NCPD did allow the taskforce to operate unlike an institution, it eventually became evident that working under another organization's tutelage undermined the taskforce's freedom and autonomy. In terms of its identity, the FGM Taskforce did not label itself "feminist," but its overall position on gender issues did reflect a feminist standpoint. Moreover, many of its member activists (men and women) were self-proclaimed feminists.[2]

The taskforce had to engage with several influential actors, all of whom had their own set of political landmines. At the grassroots level, the taskforce wanted to develop a better understanding of what works and what does not in eliciting positive social change, what has been tested and failed, and what shows promise in facilitating the process of change. Because many of the members were practitioners, they often went to the field and returned to share their reflections in the taskforce meetings. On the national level, the taskforce took on an advocacy role, seeking to win allies, understand its opponents, and work with the media. Opponents at the time of the taskforce's establishment included the head of Al-Azhar University, one of the world's largest centers of Islamic teaching for Sunni Muslims, several prominent doctors and medical professors, and the Egyptian government.

As an indigenous forum determined to maintain its national identity, the taskforce had to establish its position and negotiate relations with a wide and diverse array of international actors, including local and foreign donors, scholars, international NGOs, and the media. Positionality and framing were critical for the group's political survival. The FGM Taskforce's version of positionality included a reflexive awareness of how the taskforce was perceived by different actors in the context in which it operated. The taskforce was aware that in representing itself as an Egyptian entity, some opponents would seek to characterize it as an external actor advocating an external agenda. Hence, members of the FGM Taskforce were particularly sensitive to the spaces in which they appeared, the actors with which they partnered, and the language they deployed in advocating their cause.

2. Including Aida Seif el Dawla, Amal Abd el Hady, Seham Abd el Salam, Azza Soliman, and Nadia Wassef.

## The Merits of Schizophrenic Engagements:
## Framing and Positioning

Aida Seif el Dawla, leading member of the taskforce, professor of psychiatry, and founder of one of the earliest feminist research centers, the New Woman, once said, "I feel I am schizophrenic sometimes. When I am talking at an international gathering, I insist that they must get over their orientalist obsession with female sexuality in the Middle East, and their *focus* on FGM. When I am talking to the government, I highlight the gravity of dealing with FGM as a minor or irrelevant issue, and we press them to prioritize the issue and stress why it is an issue that seriously affects the wellbeing of Egyptian girls and women. When we are working on a community level, we work with a different language and message" (Seif el Dawla, personal communication, 1999; emphasis added). It is this schizophrenic engagement characterizing the taskforce's work that offers one of the most critical lessons in feminist strategies for negotiating different political audiences.

The word "schizophrenic" may suggest inconsistency and even hypocrisy. However, the taskforce's position and policy were characterized by neither—only by the framing and discourse that it altered according to its positionality (with whom it was engaging). This was evident in its interaction with different actors and the choice of terminology its members used to describe FGM.

When engaging with national and international actors, the FGM Taskforce refused to refer to the practice as *circumcision, tahara* (purification/purity), or *genital surgeries*. This choice of terminology reflected their position on the practice. From the outset, the taskforce had to decide on the terminology that they would use on the policy level and in international debates on the issue. They decided to endorse the term *female genital mutilation* because it emphasizes the results of the practice and its violent nature. Seham Abd el Sallam, one of the leading members of the taskforce, explained that the term *FGM* was selected by members because they found it to be reflective of all forms and grades of the practice in that it symbolizes disfiguration of a body part (Tadros 2000). The term *female circumcision* was rejected in its equation with male circumcision (i.e., the removal of the prepuce of a male organ is not equivalent to the removal of the prepuce of the clitoris). The taskforce also refused to refer to it as *tahara* because of that word's positive connotations. In refusing to use both terms (*circumcision* and *tahara*) in policy circles, there was also an explicit rejection of those who sanctioned the practice in the name of religion.[3]

When working in local communities, taskforce members did not use the term *mutilation*. Amal Abd el Hady, a member of the taskforce and a feminist, physician, and practitioner, commented that during her work in the countryside she could never ask a mother a question like, "why did you mutilate your daughter?" because it implies ill will on the part of parents, circumcisers, and respected leaders. "As numerous interactions we have had in the field demonstrated, the terms we use have direct bearing on the acceptability and success of our advocacy efforts" (Tadros 2000, 13). So instead the taskforce members used *female circumcision*, the term used in the community, and then they slowly helped the community realize the essence of the practice (Abd el Hady 2011, 108).

---

3. The taskforce also refused to use the terms *genital surgeries* or *operation* because of the insinuation of the medicalization of the practice. Obermeyer (1999, 113) coined the term *female genital surgeries* and put it forward as an alternative to *FGM* because its use "emphasises the extent of the operations and maximizes dramatic impact. It also makes an assumption about the malevolent intentions of those who carry out the operations, despite good ethnographic evidence to the contrary." She suggested that the use of *genital surgeries* "has the merit of being descriptive without denouncing the practices a priori" (113). Seham Abd el Salam (1999, 320) argued against the use of any term other than FGM: "Both circumcision and 'genital surgeries' are problematic to me, because they use medical terminology to describe a social tradition. . . . Surgeons today are medical professionals and they carry out surgery to remove damaged, unhealthy tissue. The sad fact that some medical personnel agree to perform FGM does not make it 'surgery.'" She also argued that the term does not solve the problem of cultural sensitivity because "no Arab speaker uses the Arabic equivalent of 'genital surgeries' (girahat tanasuleya) to describe the tradition of what is done to the female genitalia. Moreover, it adds to the negativity of the traditional cultural image of women. Only people who are ill need surgery" (321). There are parallel Arabic terms used by women to describe FGM, such as *al youm al aswad* (the blackest day) (322).

The multiple discourses and terminologies did not alter the taskforce's uncompromising position on the nature of the practice. However, it did mean that they were able to escape the polarization in the debate between those known as "universalists" who use the term *FGM* and those identified as the "cultural relativists" who use *female circumcision*. Although the taskforce chose in policy discourse to use the term *FGM*, they were not universalists in that they were stern advocates of a culturally sensitive approach to the practice. Politically, this positioned them well in the campaign—they were not agents of the West, but neither were they blind defenders of tradition.

Although taskforce members chose to use the term *FGM*, they were not uncritical of the positions emanating from the West. As Aida Seif el Dawla (1999, 134) noted in the context of engaging with some Western feminists who essentialized and condemned the issue as the worst form of atrocity, she found herself sometimes being "provoked by the oversimplified, sensationalist way in which the matter is frequently taken up in some Western circles." In its 1999 position statement the taskforce also criticized the hypocrisy of some Westerners in their adoption of double standards when addressing women's rights issues. Seif el Dawla (1999, 134) emphasized that "it is inconsistent for example, to be troubled by the practice of FGM and ignore broader health policies that deprive poor women—who are the majority of women in Egypt—of the basic right of access to the minimum level of primary health care. An organisation that supports the privatisation of health care services in Egypt is hardly in a strong position to advocate the eradication of FGM on human rights grounds."

However, the taskforce's adherence to the principle of cultural sensitivity and its determination to understand FGM in light of the wider political context did not mean that they were cultural relativists. Members of the taskforce did not accept any condoning of the practice nor did they negotiate ways of maintaining the practice while making it safer. They continued to wage battle against the medicalization of the practice and a variety of actors: those wishing to medicalize FGM to perpetuate it and those from the cultural relativist camp who wished to provide parents an opportunity to have the practice performed with minimal pain for the girl and in a safe environment.

## Medicalizing the Practice: FGM Taskforce versus the Religious Establishment and the Government

The FGM Taskforce emerged when the national politicization of FGM was manifest in its medicalization.[4] In the mid-1990s, following the ICPD, unholy alliances arose among a government reluctant to promote a total abandonment of the practice, a religious establishment (Al-Azhar University) eager to find all means possible to maintain the legitimacy of the practice, and doctors, who for profit, ideology, or both were eager to

4. FGM was medicalized in different ways, by different actors, and for different motives. First, there was increasing identification of the issue as a medical practice or "operation," the necessity of which was to be determined by doctors. The most recent Demographic Health Survey (DHS; El-Zanaty and Way 2004) suggests that 97 percent of ever-married women have undergone FGM in Egypt. The DHS also suggests that there has only been a minor change in the proportion of mothers who reported circumcising their daughters (50 percent in 1995 and 47 percent in 2004). There was also a minor decline in the proportion of women intending to circumcise daughters in the future (from 38 percent in 1995 to 31 percent in the 2000 and 2003 surveys; El-Zanaty and Way 2004, 105). Medical staff play a primary role in performing the practice. According to the government, 49 percent of FGM cases are performed in private medical clinics, 30 percent through midwives, 10 percent through nurses, and 10 percent through barbers. The 2003 DHS revealed that more than half of cases of FGM are performed at the hands of registered doctors. It also indicates that the percentage of cases performed by members of the medical profession has been steadily increasing. For example, only 9 percent of Egyptian women ages forty-five to forty-nine were circumcised by trained medical personnel, but 50 percent of those women had their daughters circumcised by trained medical personnel (El-Zanaty et al. 1996). According to El-Gibaly et al. (2002), the adolescence and social change survey (Population Council 2011) conducted in Egypt in 1997, which provides information on circumcision for more than 1200 randomly selected girls and women, corroborates evidence from the DHS of the medicalization of the practice: "The ASCE survey found that 47.5 percent of adolescent girls were circumcised by a doctor. When doctors are combined with nurses for comparison with DHS, the total reaches 55.1 percent. Indeed, doctors are the most frequently mentioned type of practitioner performing the procedure, followed by a daya (traditional birth attendant; another woman or man specializing in performing the practice in the community), 10.8 percent; nurses, 7.6 percent; male barbers, 5.6 percent; and relatives, 1.1 percent (other response category equals 2.6 percent)" (El-Gibaly et al. 2002, 214; parenthetical information added).

further medicalize the practice. The taskforce made some strategic choices that were more successful with some players than with others. Here I describe the choices they made in relation to the government, religious establishment, and the professional medical sphere, and on the grassroots community level.

Although the history of the position of Al-Azhar on FGM is by no means homogenous, religious leaders tended, irrespective of whether they condemned or condoned the practice, to support their arguments with religious evidence. An interesting phenomenon in the debates that ensued from the mid-1990s onward was that members of the religious establishment began to substantiate their positions by referring the matter to the medical professionals. One of the most influential fatwas (religious opinions) to be issued on the subject was that of Sheikh Gad el Haq, the grand sheikh of Al-Azhar. In 1981 he issued a fatwa from Dar al Ifta (the highest body responsible for issuing religious opinion), the substance of which was reissued in 1994 at the time of the ICPD. The crux of his fatwa was that although FGM is not obligatory as in the case of male circumcision, it is still required by Islam and is a *sunna* (not required but preferred) that should not be neglected by anyone (El Banna 2005, 34). Sheikh Gad el Haq began the second part of the fatwa by arguing that if female circumcision is professed by Islam and its manner is guided by the teachings of the Prophet, then it is not acceptable that an opinion or position on the issue should be sought from any other source, including a doctor, because the nature of medicine is that it is ever changing and the position of doctors on this subject varies.

The above statement suggests that the position of medicine is insignificant, yet the fatwa went on to explain how some doctors have provided medical evidence of the necessity of the practice and how these medical opinions are commensurate with the teachings of the Prophet. Sheikh Gad el Haq argued that procircumcision doctors have shown that circumcision reduces the sexual urges of adolescent girls. He then suggested that circumcision reduces the fatty emissions that cause inflammations in the urinary and reproductive tracts, which then cause malignant diseases. He added that procircumcision doctors have also suggested that girls who are not circumcised grow up to have volatile moods and negative temperaments in their childhoods and adolescence. The fatwa claimed that in light of the gender mixing that characterized daily social interaction (such as in public transport systems), circumcision protects a girl from amorality and deviation (El Banna 2005, 34).

Although other Islamist scholars such as El Awa strongly contested the content of El Haq's fatwa, his ruling was politically very important. His reissue of the fatwa, which was reprinted and distributed nationwide, was a major stumbling block for efforts to contest the religiosity of FGM. Moreover, in his role as the sheikh of Al-Azhar, he was a figure who represented the highest religious ground in the country. He was also not thought to have been co-opted by the government, which further enhanced his credibility and legitimacy in the eyes of the people.

Conversely, there was another important figure from Al-Azhar who yielded significant power but condemned the practice of FGM. Sheikh Mohamed Tantawy, who as grand mufti also issued a fatwa framing the matter in medical terms in the aftermath of the ICPD. The content of the post-ICPD fatwa was different from an earlier one he issued in which he condoned the practice and insisted that the "procedure" should be in conformity with the Prophet's instructions that part of the clitoris be excised not in its entirety so that women's sexuality is not madly aroused but at the same time their ability to experience sexual pleasure is not eliminated. The new fatwa's content, unlike the first one, concluded that FGM is a social tradition that is not required by any religious text and is not practiced by most Islamic countries. However, the concluding paragraph of his new fatwa opened a dangerous loophole:

> The decisive word on the issue of female circumcision is up to the doctors, if they deem that the procedure is harmful we will abandon it because they are Ahl al Zikr (the people who have the knowledge). If they say otherwise, then it is the responsibility of the Ministry of Health in Egypt to take all necessary legal measures to allow the undertaking of this operation for girls in a way that guarantees for them protection, chastity and human dignity and which protects a girl's femininity. (El Banna 2005, 63)

Sheikh Tantawy's position was in perfect conformity with that of the government. The minister of health issued a medical decree in October 1994 allowing FGM to be performed in hospitals and forbidding nonmedical staff from performing it. The minister argued that families would be counseled against the practice and only if they insisted would the practice be performed. He also argued that this new decree would prevent the "operation" from being performed by unskilled individuals in unhygienic conditions (Tadros 2000, 7). As expected, there was no counseling, and instead "patients" got a ticket after paying the necessary fee for the "circumcision operation." Although decrees that were subsequently issued by other ministers of health banned circumcision in hospital, in many cases the new decrees were not widely disseminated and many hospitals continued to offer this "service."

At this time the FGM Taskforce made the strategic decision not to launch a campaign in favor of more stringent legislation against FGM. The political moment was not appropriate and any such campaign would have backfired and delegitimized the efforts of the taskforce. Their subsequent decision to take legal measures was a reaction, rather than a well-studied initiative, to the international scandal that ensued after the screening of the CNN film at ICPD. The Egyptian government had been forced to "make a statement in which they denounced the practice and promised to legislate against it. That promise however, was not to the Egyptian people, since the overriding need at that moment was to appease the opinions of the international community" (Seif el Dawla 1999, 131). Hence, the FGM Taskforce was responding not to the content of the government's proposed legislation (i.e., a ban on FGM) but to the political context in which it was being released. It was conspicuously obvious that in banning FGM the government was bowing to foreign pressure rather than responding to an issue it identified as worthy of national attention and effort. To support this legislation would have been political suicide for the taskforce because opponents would have framed it as a case of the taskforce supporting the West's hegemonic meddling in the cultural and social fabric of other societies. Moreover, the level of social awareness of the nature of FGM was very limited at this time, and the issue was still associated with significant social stigma in some circles. Therefore, while they were careful to insist that the reasons behind the perpetuation of the practice must be understood, the taskforce concurrently chose not to conform to the culture of silence surrounding FGM, which had been propped up by claims of protection of cultural identity and values against the West.

The position of the FGM Taskforce against new legislation may have been politically appropriate in 1994; however, by 1996, such a strategy required revisiting. Seif el Dawla noted at the time that the taskforce said in a statement issued in December 1996 that existing law had sufficient provisions to allow for the criminalization of the practice (interview by author, January 2000). However, the ministerial ban still contained some loopholes that allowed chairs of medical departments to permit the practice in cases in which it was "required." The taskforce had the foresight to not simply celebrate the ban as a step forward; they recognized that it gave doctors authority to claim that they undertook the "operation" because of medical necessity. It was as if doctors were being trained in medical school to perform FGM "operations" according to rules, criteria, and conditions described in their medical textbooks.

### FGM Taskforce (Sort of) Takes On Board the Medical Establishment

Other than the religious establishment and the government, there were three groups in favor of the medicalization of FGM: local doctors who saw it as financially profitable, doctors who were ideologically in favor of the practice on social and religious grounds, and, ironically, Western cultural relativists who saw it as a harm reduction strategy. Although the FGM Taskforce did not have to engage directly with this last group, I argue in this chapter that the manner in which FGM was medicalized by local doctors challenges the assumptions upon which medicalization as a harm reduction strategy have been advanced. The FGM Taskforce was uncompromising in its denunciation of all forms of the medicalization of FGM, but it did little except hold its ground.

Strategically, the taskforce did not do much to hold the medical establishment accountable or to launch campaigns against the establishment's overt role in condoning and perpetuating[5] the practice. Perhaps the medical establishment that has explicitly and (more recently) implicitly supported the medicalization of the practice has been responsible for the silence around the medical syndicate's failure to take a zero-tolerance stance toward doctors who perform this practice. Following the death of a young girl at the hands of a doctor performing a circumcision in 2007, a spokesman from the medical establishment said that it was a case of medical malpractice because the doctor should not have combined the professions of anesthesiology and surgery. He added that there needed to

5. A study conducted by the community medicine department at the University of Alexandria showed that more than half of the 330 students enrolled in fifth-year medical school who participated in the study were in favor of FGM, and almost three-quarters were in support of its medicalization. These findings are significant in that they emanated from one of the country's largest and most prestigious universities, where the student population was predominantly urban (77.2 percent from urban areas; urban slum residents, 11.7 percent; rural dwellers, 11.1 percent). The study reports that despite the fact that more than half of the students (51.3 percent) knew that there were no medical reasons to perform FGM, almost three-quarters of them (73.2 percent) were in favor of its medicalization (Mostafa et al. 2006). Only half of those in favor of its medicalization believed that this was a step toward its prevention. In other words, the other half did not believe that medicalization was aimed at elimination of the practice. Those supporting its medicalization thought it would minimize the pain or reduce risks to girl's health if performed under hygienic conditions (582). What is equally striking is their knowledge of the ethical and legal aspects of FGM. According to the study, less than one-third of the students (27.9 percent) recognized that a medical professional's performance of FGM violates the principle of "do no harm." Only 16.8 percent of the students were aware that Egyptian law prohibits performance of FGM by nonphysicians. The attitudes of these future physicians are strong evidence of the perpetuation of the practice: 31.9 percent of them answered affirmatively to the statement, "I intend (as a future father/mother) to subject my daughters to this practice." To raise awareness among future doctors about the nature of the practice would have required not just the political will (permission from the Ministry of Higher Education, the university president, the medical school dean, etc.), but also support for stopping the practice from the medical leadership. As is evident from the positions of the medical syndicate and some leading gynecologists in the country (of course, many gynecologists and doctors were equally firm in their opposition of the practice), the medical leadership was likely in favor of perpetuating FGM.

be a clear differentiation between the practice of FGM and "plastic surgery operations." This statement once again opened a loophole, this time for the practice to be continued under the premise of "plastic surgery."

One year later, Muslim Brotherhood members, representing the strongest Islamist opposition group in the country, objected to legislation against the practice. They argued that the legislation was unjustified because it would criminalize cases of girls in need of "plastic surgery." This timing may be more than a coincidence given the long historical association between the medical establishment and the Muslim Brotherhood as well as the substantial evidence suggesting a lack of separation of religion and medicine in the medical union. The implication of an implicitly pro-FGM medical syndicate was that the taskforce could not rely on them to hold doctors accountable for promoting the practice. But, then again, neither did the taskforce.

The doctors who were ideologically in favor of maintaining the practice on religious grounds monopolized the public policy arena and received substantial media coverage. These doctors severely hindered the work of the taskforce and any other actor seeking to elicit social change on this issue in local communities. They were very vocal in rejecting any restriction on the practice and often advocated that if the religiously prescribed version of circumcision was performed, then there would be no medical hazards, but rather only medical benefits. The doctors argued that complications occur because FGM is performed at the hands of unspecialized personnel who do not comply with the medical and religious prescriptions regarding the right way to perform it. One of the most famous gynecologists and surgeons to become a reference for the Islamists on the desirability of female genital mutilation is Dr. Hamed Al-Ghawaby. He defended the practice on the grounds that if it is performed according to the Prophet's instructions for reduction of the clitoris and not its obliteration, then no harm would occur. Dr. Al-Ghawaby argued that there were six benefits for women from what he referred to as "female circumcision." These included a decrease in irritability, bad odor, and masturbation (Hendy, n.d., 57–58).

Another gynecologist and surgeon who advocated female genital mutilation and was widely cited by the Islamists is Hatem Saad Ismail, a professor at the second largest university in Cairo, University of Ain Shams. He argued that women risk becoming infertile if they are not circumcised. Islamist lawyer Sheikh Yusuf El-Badry quoted Dr. Ismail in the lawsuit waged against Minister of Health Ismail Sallam after the minister issued a decree against the performance of FGM in 2007 (El-Badry 2007). Dr. Ahmed Shafiq, one of the country's most famous gynecologists in the twentieth century (at one point he held the position of head of surgery at Cairo University), openly announced that the performance of "female circumcision" positively prevents AIDS (El-Badry 2007). Dr. Mohamed Farouk Fikry, a professor of gynecology at University of Ain Shams, espoused the dangers of not performing FGM on women's sexuality. Female circumcision, he and others argued, protects women from being sexually aroused (El-Badry 2007).

These vocal doctors and professors not only advocated for female genital mutilation on medical grounds, but their narratives on controlling/inhibiting women's sexuality went unchallenged. Although some would argue that these figures are long forgotten, it is noteworthy that up until 2015 Salafis were referencing their work to advocate against the restriction or criminalization of FGM. Many such doctors hold highly prestigious positions in Egyptian universities. They espouse medical ramifications of not performing FGM and proclaim its benefits, and they have not shied away from using Islamic references to endorse their "medical" positions. These doctors have consistently served as references for medical evidence against the criminalization of the practice. For example, in 2008 the NCCM put forward a Child Law that included an article prohibiting FGM. El Sayed Askfar, a Muslim Brotherhood member of parliament (MP), openly challenged the proposed criminalization, quoting yet another professor of gynecology, Mounir Fawzy, on the medical necessity of female circumcision for preventing diseases. He then referenced another doctor, Ali Abd el Fattah, the minister of health who prohibited FGM except in hospitals, suggesting that the minister's actions were evidence that the practice is desirable if performed in a medically appropriate and equipped setting (H. Rashwan 2008).

As for the unaccounted number of doctors who are performing FGM "operations" either strictly for profit or for profit and ideological reasons, there is no shortness of demand for their services in urban and rural communities. One doctor who works in a poor upper Egyptian village told me that many of his colleagues do perform FGM and he knows that because he often has parents ask him to circumcise their daughters. He explains to them that it is medically detrimental and that it is a ritual without any benefits, and he says that they usually nod, smile, and go find another doctor. "I know that they have gone to another doctor because they come back to me afterwards for treatment of urinary tract infections and other problems" (interview by author, December 2010). This doctor conceded that in many instances his colleagues do not just respond to a supply for "circumcision operations"; they actively promote the practice to maximize profit. He spoke about one obstetrician who struck a deal with a midwife whereby the latter gets a certain percentage or commission for each FGM case she brings in. To give the ritual medical camouflage, she tells the parents of each girl that they must bring with them the cotton wool, syringes, alcohol, etc., for the anesthesia. After charging each girl a fee, the doctor takes the supplies, does not use any of it, and then returns it to the pharmacy for reimbursement. Most doctors tell parents that it is a simple beautification procedure and often charge no less than fifty Egyptian pounds for it (approximately eight US dollars).

### The Taskforce in the Field

The position of the taskforce in relation to its approaches to social change on a community level was clear. The taskforce advocated adopting what they termed the *sociocultural approach*: asking people why they circumcise their daughters and helping them deconstruct the link between preservation of chastity and the actual procedure. The sociocultural approach was pursued with all members of the community including children, and it did not target only girls and mothers (as was common with previous development approaches addressing FGM).[6] Moreover, the taskforce

6. Emerging field data from successful cases of community abandonment of the practice in Egypt (Abdel Hadi 2006), Senegal, Sudan, Mali (Easton, Monkman, and

was against the strategy of highlighting the medical ramifications of the practice because they argued that doing so was an insufficient trigger for people to change their behavior.

Here it is important to distinguish between two completely different ways in which FGM became medicalized. The first, mentioned above, was that doctors assumed responsibility for the performance of the practice. The second, which is totally unrelated, involved highlighting the negative health effects of the practice in an effort to encourage people to abandon it. Whereas the former method may or may not have aimed at promoting the abandonment of the practice (in the case of Egypt, it did not), the latter certainly did. The FGM Taskforce suggested that the problems with emphasizing the negative medical implications of the practice were twofold. First, the long list of medical complications that may result from the practice are not universally experienced. Some may suffer from frigidity and some may enjoy fulfilling sex lives. Some may suffer from infections, others not. Second, if medical complications occur as a consequence of the practice, could they not be avoided by seeking the "right" medical care? The FGM Taskforce believed that the medicalization of the practice as surgery to be performed by a doctor was a consequence of the focus on its negative medical implications.[7]

---

Miles 2003), and Kenya (Mohamud, Radeny, and Ringheim 2006) all point to two common features: creating community consensus and linking FGM with women's overall empowerment.

7. "In even more dramatic terms, the joint statement of WHO, UNICEF, UNFPA, and UNDP in 1995 labelled the medical basis for anti-FGC policies a 'mistake.' The reasoning of the joint statement suggested that much of the medical discourse—at least as it was applied locally—was exaggerated and consequently counterproductive. The second problem with the medical reasoning was more surprising. Essentially, medicalization had been too effective. By making FGC safer, the international community had undermined the urgency that originally motivated the eradication of the practice. The organizations attempted to recapture some of that urgency in their repackaged message: FGC had negative health consequences, but—more importantly—it was a violation of women's rights" (Boyle 2002, 550).

Increasing evidence suggests that the taskforce's sociocultural strategy reflected an understanding of why and how social change happens; namely, people see FGM as no longer necessary or relevant to their lives. However, whether completely downplaying the medical implications of the practice was equally effective in community attitudinal change is contested. Evidence from the field suggests that the medical dimensions cannot be ignored because they are still important in eliciting social change.[8]

Many taskforce members felt uncomfortable reporting on practicing doctors in the villages because they were worried that they would be seen as resorting to heavy-handed mechanisms to repress members of their own community. However, not holding local doctors accountable was also

8. For example, when the DHS asked women why they would not circumcise their daughters, they gave more than one reason. The majority of women (61 percent) said that they no longer believed in the practice, hence confirming the validity of the sociocultural approach advanced by the taskforce and giving privilege to the question of why girls are circumcised. The second most prevalent response (42 percent of women) was concern about potential health complications. In addition, the data from the Adolescence and Social Change in Egypt (ASCE) survey show that when girls ages 10–19 who reported having undergone circumcision were asked to give their opinion on the practice, 13.6 percent said that they thought it was unnecessary (28.4 percent said they did not know and 58.0 percent said it was necessary, although half of those in favor of the practice could not explain why). Reasons cited by circumcised girls who were against the practice were quite significant: 33.3 percent could not give a reason why they thought it was unnecessary; 24.2 percent cited its harmful health outcomes; 7.7 percent said it was not a religious requirement; and 14.2 percent said it was a meaningless tradition (Population Council 2011, 216). In regard to the one-quarter of circumcised girls who objected to the practice on health grounds, some of them must have had FGM performed by a doctor (in light of the high prevalence rate of doctors performing the practice) and are therefore not confident that going to doctors eliminates health complications. Even if doctors advertise pain-free, 100-percent safe and hygienic operations, in reality, there is an abundance of articles every month on girls who die when going to the doctor for FGM. One such young woman died at the hands of a high-ranking doctor from the Ministry of Health who put her under anesthesia and circumcised her before she bled to death (Khattab, Fouad, and Helmy 2004, 28).

problematic because they were blocking and inhibiting change. Strategically, not taking action against practicing local doctors represented a missed opportunity for the taskforce in its campaign.[9]

9. The medicalization of FGM had a conspicuously negative impact on attempts at eliciting change. Grassroots activists' claims that the practice was undesirable and unnecessary were contested by local doctors. In some communities local religious leaders were also communicating a message that it is up to the doctors to decide whether the practice is desirable. In an internal evaluation of a program aimed to raise awareness among children and youth of a variety of human rights issues relating to their well-being, the children in one village were asked whether their views on FGM had changed. One group said that after listening to the local sheikh talk about how the issue should be left to the doctors for them to decide on the necessity of FGM, they became unconvinced by the message against FGM. Again, it is this medicalization of the practice by the Muslim religious establishment, even on a grassroots level, that undermines prospects of unilateral rejection of the practice.

In places where doctors were performing female circumcision, it became very difficult to convince people that it was not necessary. Even if the social approach was used, grassroots activists spoke about the high status of doctors in villages and how if doctors were in favor of the practice, this affected the legitimacy of their message. When doctors are performing FGM, it is more difficult to convince people of the negativity associated with the practice than when the practice is performed by a midwife. Grassroots practitioners also pointed out that when they told people that FGM is against the law, they took it with a grain of salt. People would retort, "if it is against the law, then why is it that doctors are performing this every day and getting off scot-free?"

If doctors were not performing FGM and were actively discouraging the practice, would the prevalence rates have gone down significantly because there would not have been the "medical" alternative? There is no concrete evidence in support of this scenario. ASCE (Population Council 2011, 218) concluded that "as parents turn away from traditional practitioners of circumcision, they are opting to obtain the operation in presumed 'safe' circumstances under a doctor's supervision. We assume that many of these parents would be reluctant to return to traditional practitioners, and that they share some of their children's reported ambivalence toward the practice. Thus education efforts and more effective enforcement of the existing ban among doctors and nurses might dissuade those families from the practice in the future." The latter suggestion—more effective enforcement of the ban—perhaps could have been used by the taskforce to make the sociocultural approach work on the ground.

### Dissolving the FGM Taskforce: A Cause without a Movement

By 1999, the taskforce had gained momentum. It was considered an authoritative voice on any matter relating to FGM in Egypt. A journalist writing about FGM would almost always refer to the taskforce. The taskforce was also being proactive. Seham Abd el Salam, who was responsible for scanning research and media relations on behalf of the taskforce, was scrupulously monitoring the media; every time FGM was discussed in an inappropriate way, the taskforce responded by writing letters and contacting persons responsible. Western and local researchers were also using the taskforce and the significant resources it had accumulated on the subject as an important source of information. Reflections and discussions about field practice were generating more interest and therefore research on how to inform policy.

One of the main factors behind the success of the taskforce was the inclusive and consensus-building leadership style of Marie Assaad. Assaad's role as coordinator was the glue that connected individuals with very different ideological orientations. She could speak "in different tongues" to individuals from different backgrounds. Marie Assaad's idea of dissolving the taskforce came at a moment when several dynamics were in play. There was a growing friction with the National Commission for

---

The education of practicing doctors requires significant attitudinal change, and this is not always possible when there are other motives behind performing such procedures (i.e., profit). Evidence from Senegal and Mali shows that a greater knowledge of the practice and its medical complications among health workers did not lead to a reduction in the performance of the practice because the health workers themselves must go through a process of attitudinal and behavioral change (Diop and Askew 2009, 139). It is clear that turning the matter over to doctors contests the validity of the harm reduction strategy, which assumes that doctors who perform FGM are necessarily guided by the objective of minimizing pain and toward the abandonment of the practice. Evidence suggests that doctors in favor of performing FGM are not guided by the long-term goal of elimination, but rather perpetuation of the practice. For ideological reasons or profit-making incentives or both, they are in a position of advocating the practice instead of being "forced" to perform it to reduce health hazards. Medicalizing the practice allows them to render further legitimacy to the continuation of the practice rather than reduce its harmful impact.

Population and Development as they began to interfere in conspicuous ways in the work of the taskforce, possibly because they were somewhat insecure about the taskforce's level and scope of publicity and recognition. Working under the NCPD umbrella was no longer feasible and the relationship desisted in 1999.

Marie Assaad was determined not to institutionalize. The taskforce became a loose, decentralized structure where the work on FGM was carried out through the commitment of its members' organizations. Assaad justified this decision on the basis that "the taskforce was always a movement of inspired and committed people. It was never meant to be a perpetual empire. It was designed to evolve in the direction that would best serve the issues facing us at the time and the ultimate commitment to stop this practice which degrades us as women, as a country and as a culture" (Tadros 2000, 21). The taskforce was not quite a social movement, if Charles Tilly's (2004) definition of a social movement was applied (worthiness of cause, unity of members, and numbers and commitment of members; see chapter 1). The worthiness of cause and the commitment of individual members existed, yet unity was very much tied to the existence of the taskforce. Without some sort of informal or formal structure, it did not exist. Moreover, the number of members was an obvious limitation. Because the taskforce was operating in such a hostile environment, the more members it had, the more it would have seemed like a cause with a constituency rather than a small, distinct group of like-minded activists.

Another important factor influencing Marie Assaad at the time was the National Council for Childhood and Motherhood, which approached Assaad about introducing a nationwide outreach strategy on FGM using the taskforce's grassroots approach. The NCCM hired two taskforce members as consultants to the program, one of whom was Magdy Helmy, who became the NCCM's deputy coordinator. He sought to apply in the village models the ideas drawn from the evidence-based work of the taskforce. The NCCM's grassroots work to reduce FGM had attracted significant funds from a large number of donors outside of Egypt. Its foreign funding was a weakness that the Islamists capitalized on in their campaign against criminalizing the practice. The NCCM's strategy was multidimensional and quite successful. It produced an understated yet moving advertisement against FGM that was broadcast on mainstream television (in a country where television reaches 99 percent of the population). It also complemented this advertisement with more sustained work with the media. In terms of its grassroots-level work, the NCCM established links with local councils to secure an enabling environment. It closely followed the taskforce's approach, establishing partnerships with local NGOs who then drew their own strategy of work, guided by the principles set by the taskforce (i.e., the importance of working with men and not just women as well as working with local leaders on different levels and with different backgrounds). After some years of work, signs of change became decipherable in the communities in which the NCCM had partnered with local NGOs.

Marie Assaad once reflected that there was no longer a need for a taskforce when a nationwide strategy was being mainstreamed that was in accordance with the ideas of culturally appropriate approaches to social change. Her logic was that because the cause had been assumed by an agency with the commitment and resources to make it a reality, there was no longer the need for a taskforce. Assaad convinced the other members that the dissolution of the taskforce was a better option than co-option or the formation of an independent NGO. The assumption was that members had formed a repertoire of relations that would sustain the work informally (Tadros 2000). Yet the dissolution of the taskforce meant the withdrawal of the kind of leadership, cohesion, and collective vision without which there was little incentive for people to work together.

In the absence of a coalition or movement, a vacuum emerged. The NCCM, representing the government, sought to fill this vacuum but it had a credibility deficit[10] that severely undermined its impact. One case in point was the march against FGM organized by the NCCM on June 18, 2007, after a child named Bedoor died from an anesthesia overdose on the operating table in a physician's private clinic. According to one newspaper account there were 3,000 mothers and girls participating in the

---

10. A term coined by Marina Ottaway (2004) in reference to the US promotion of democracy in the Middle East.

march, which was held on the day of Bedoor's burial (Rashwan and Thabet 2007) and attended by Moushira Khattab, the secretary general. For the government to orchestrate a march for Bedoor when there were severe restrictions on public action and extensive repression of civil society could only be interpreted as hypocrisy. If the FGM Taskforce had initiated some public event on behalf of Bedoor, it would have been seen as a civil society action responding to a citizen's tragedy.

It was highly problematic for the government to organize action against one form of gender-based violence when only a few months earlier several hundred women were openly harassed in downtown Cairo on the first day of the 'eid (feast), in the absence of any government security presence and despite repeated calls for help. Other forms of gender-based violence had also been tolerated, so why take action against FGM in particular? The NCCM was a champion of a comprehensive campaign to stop FGM, yet its commitment to this cause was not shared by other parts of the government. The march may have contributed to keeping the issue alive, yet the NCCM's profile as a quasi-governmental agency did not allow it to assume the role of civil society activist, one that would have been more appropriately led by the taskforce.

The full implications of the lack of a civil society voice that is neither government nor representative of partisan political interest became evident in the discussions before and during the parliamentary deliberations over criminalizing the practice of FGM. Article 61 of the amended Child Law, which was passed by the People's Assembly on June 7, 2008, pronounced that anyone found guilty of practicing FGM would face a fine of 1,000–5,000 pounds and a prison sentence ranging from three months to two years. This was not the first legal measure introducing a total ban on the practice.

In the aftermath of Bedoor's death, Minister of Health and Population Hatem El-Gabali issued Decree 271 in June 2007, prohibiting the performance of the practice by any health service provider (physicians and nursing staff) or others (paramedics or related personnel). FGM was not allowed in government or private practice. The decree stipulated that professionals who perform FGM are considered in violation of the laws and regulations of the ethical code governing the medical profession. Such individuals will be subjected to penalties and punishment from both the Ministry of Health and the medical syndicate. However, because there were so many ministerial decrees prohibiting, narrowing, and allowing FGM, the general impression left was confusion. Moreover, the medical syndicate could not be counted on to hold doctors accountable.

Had the taskforce continued to exist, would it have been in support of the legal criminalization of FGM? Probably yes, but its positionality would have significantly altered the discourse and deliberations about the law. There are several reasons why the taskforce would have supported the law. The social context in which the law was introduced was very different from ten years ago, and the choice of political moment to introduce the law was opportune. In addition, the proposed law emanated from a political will to address the issue rather than to respond to a foreign agenda. The criminalization of the practice was appropriately introduced under the banner of the Child Law in 2008 (i.e., far less contentious legislation than the Personal Status Law or any other legislation specific to women) and was one of several articles put forward rather than the only article.

In terms of the social context surrounding criminalization, it is well established that using law to force social change backfires. It makes people more determined to cling to their social practices and beliefs, and it can make the practice go underground and/or intensify the animosity and intensity of opposition. Feminists have been suspicious of the historical use of legislation to induce change, especially when it emanates from patriarchal states and institutions. However, in the context in which the law was proposed there already had been ten years of awareness raising initiatives, including a nationwide media campaign (albeit not always a perfect one) to inform the citizenry of the nature of the practice.

At the time of the Child Law in 2008, many communities had already decided to abandon the practice of FGM, and the new generation of young girls was not circumcised. Rahman and Toubia (2000, 62) suggest that any criminal law introduced should be part of a broader governmental strategy to change individual behavior and social norms. In this case, the law was only introduced after the government had in effect implemented a series of measures to affect change in public opinion and on a community level through partner NGOs. As Rahman and Toubia (2000, 62) argue, "a well studied and strategically timed introduction of a criminal law prohibiting FC/FGM is a strong political and legal tool. If social change is well underway, with substantial popular backing and approval from the political establishment, the process of introducing, debating and successfully passing a law could itself serve to accelerate change. On the other hand, poorly timed or hastily introduced laws can backfire by truncating an emerging social dialogue, causing social rifts and driving the practice underground."[11] The law was put forward during a time in which FGM was already being questioned in many circles, yet efforts to reduce the practice were being significantly undermined by the lack of means to hold practicing doctors accountable.

As Rahman and Toubia (2000) have argued, the timing is very important. In the case of Egypt, the political moment is almost as important as

---

11. There have been tragic cases of legal approaches to change causing a backlash and forcing the practice of FGM underground. For example, in Tanzania, the passing of a law in 1998 criminalizing FGM led to continued practice in secrecy by one of the tribes (Legal and Human Rights Centre 2004). The Maasai people living in the Morogoro area began to perform FGM in secret after the law was promulgated. It came to the attention of the Legal and Human Rights Centre that three girls, Neema, Sabina, and Christina, were subjected to the practice by their father in 1999 when they were ages twelve, thirteen, and fourteen, respectively. The girls had not wanted to be subjected to the practice and had run away from their father to the local pastor to seek refuge. Eventually they were returned to their father, who went ahead with the practice. When the Legal and Human Rights Centre investigated the matter three years later in 2002, two of the girls had already gotten married and did not want to testify against their father in court nor pursue the matter any further. Contrary to the will of the girls, the organization went ahead and took the matter to court, where the girls denied their father had subjected them to this practice and vehemently defended him. When the court ordered a forceful examination to see whether they had been circumcised, they adamantly refused to allow the hospital doctor to conduct his examination. The court eventually acquitted the father. Afterward, when the Legal and Human Rights Centre examined the impact of the court case on the Maasai people, it was evident that they were outraged at the prosecution of the father for performing a cultural ritual that was part of their tradition. The incident demonstrates the negative implications of seeking legal action in a context in which there is no awareness nor will to criminalize families, and one in which the agency of young women and their right to privacy is not respected.

the content of the law itself. The criminalization of FGM did not come after any obvious moment of international political pressure. Therefore, it did not appear to be something designed to appease the West (of course, NCCM's work on FGM was entirely foreign funded, so there were accusations that the law was part of a foreign agenda).

The discussions that surrounded the law brought to the fore the need for the taskforce. Members of the Muslim Brotherhood were the most vehement opponents to the passing of the law. Some MPs used the religious argument and some hid religious motives underneath medical arguments. They advocated that the matter should be left to doctors to decide. A former leading member of the Muslim Brotherhood suggested during an interview that criminalizing the practice would prevent doctors from intervening in cases requiring plastic surgery. Hence, it was best to leave it to the doctors to decide which cases need surgical intervention.

Whereas one of the adopted strategies was to try and keep the practice under the power of the doctor rather than the law, the other strategy was to undermine the character of the party proposing the legislation. According to opponents, the government lacked any legitimacy and was adopting contradictory social policies: seeking to criminalize FGM while ignoring the plethora of social ills affecting Egyptian society. Unfortunately, the MPs from the ruling party/government who were defending Article 61 (such as Ahmed Ezz) were unpopular with the public and had a low credibility profile.

The taskforce would have been the strongest civil society voice to comment, critique, and advocate for the law. Its positionality would not have made it vulnerable to accusations of corruption, political repression, and authoritarianism. The presence of the FGM Taskforce would at least have given voice to the development practitioners whose work was being undermined by doctors who performed FGM. The taskforce would have emphasized that the primary targets of Article 61 were the doctors, not the parents. The vacuum created by an absent FGM Taskforce meant that the issue became polarized between the government and the opposition. The dissolution of the taskforce also meant that there was no independent body to monitor the manner in which Article 61 is applied and to act as a watchdog to ensure that a comprehensive development plan is being implemented. The two NCCM consultants that were former members of the taskforce were not in a position to hold the NCCM accountable. No alternative coalition or movement existed that could play the watchdog role that the taskforce had led before it was dissolved. In the absence of a coalition or movement, the dissolution of the taskforce was strategically premature. Although institutionalizing by becoming an NGO would have bore its risks (government intervention through the NGO Law, bureaucratization, loss of spirit, and the question of funding), at the very least it would have filled the vacuum that currently exists. No actor has emerged since the taskforce's dissolution with the same positionality and ability to navigate skillfully among different discourses and audiences.

## Conclusion

The experience of the emergence and dissolution of the FGM Taskforce is significant on many levels. The taskforce's model of collective action as a coalition of diverse actors provided a path for civil society actors who do not normally associate with each other to come together around a common agenda (e.g., faith-based NGOs working in development with left-wing feminist activists). Perhaps the least visible asset and one of the most significant achievements of the taskforce is the repertoire of relations—the cumulative know-how of how to manage different agendas and different actors within and outside the coalition—which informed future attempts at collective action. Another important achievement was the creation of consensus on some highly thorny relationships, policy messages, and actors. Despite the diversity of its members, the taskforce was able to recognize the importance of its positionality and relate to different actors while maintaining its identity. Western donors and feminists were welcome to play a supportive role as long as they were in line with the taskforce's agenda and framing.

The taskforce's relationship with the government involved advocacy against the absence of a genuine political will to address the issue but also cooperation with individuals and institutions within the government who wanted to work in partnership. Its positionality on the role of religion was negotiated at different levels: at the policy-making level, they sought alternative interpretations from key Muslim scholars who affirmed that the practice is not Islamic, whereas on a grassroots level, they always sought the support of the local sheikhs. To achieve such clarity on their positionality, the taskforce had a deep and contemporary understanding of different actors' agendas, politics, and role in the battle. It is this understanding of the less visible layers of politics that is often missed out on in feminist and development work, which leads to positioning in a way that increases vulnerability to compartmentalization and stereotyping.

Furthermore, the taskforce was able to establish appropriate framing of FGM for different audiences. The content changed according to the audience, but the essence—the rejection of FGM in all its forms as performed by anyone, anywhere—remained the same. Framing involved more than simply packaging the message differently; it required an understanding of the power relations characterizing the FGM with the party in question. This became particularly evident in the taskforce's engagement with a wide spectrum of Western audiences: the orientalist/racist and the cultural relativist.

Members of the FGM Taskforce had an exceptional ability to engage on different levels: academic, policy-making, development practice, and national public opinion. They did so by drawing on their repertoire of knowledge, connections, and resources. Different members were able to engage at different levels, which allowed the taskforce to become a reference for different players and therefore increase its outreach while remaining relatively small.

The rise of the taskforce was also a result of its ability to respond quickly and effectively to the political moment. They recognized that the political moment in 1994 was not the right one for pressing for legislation against FGM. It may have cost the taskforce a loss of political credibility in the long run. The political moment in 2008 would have been opportune for the taskforce to intervene; however, they had already dissolved.

The questions raised regarding the taskforce's engagement with the medicalization of the practice are more problematic. Doctors needed to be challenged, but without building the support of important allies such as the medical syndicate, the taskforce put itself in a vulnerable situation.

Finally, and perhaps most crucially: when is a coalition no longer needed as the vehicle for fulfilling a mission? Does the fact that the government adopted the entire agenda advocated by the FGM Taskforce signify that there is no longer a need for the coalition's work? I argue that although Marie Assaad's concerns about institutionalization are well founded, nonetheless, the dissolution of the FGM Taskforce meant that the crucial role they played as an autonomous civil society actor was lost. The vacuum created by their absence was especially evident in policy debates in the ten years after their dissolution.

But perhaps NGOization presents the lesser of two evils if the other option is for the government to assume the role of a civil society actor without having the credibility or legitimacy to do so. With the demise of the Mubarak regime in 2011, the NCCM was dissolved and incorporated into the Ministry of Population; unsurprisingly, one of the first initiatives that was put on hold was the FGM-free village initiative. It was easy to disclaim the intervention on account of its association with the first lady. Perhaps if the taskforce had remained, it would have been far more difficult to challenge the legitimacy of such a well-reputed nonstate actor. In the next chapter I examine another initiative that was the offspring of the galvanization of local activism around gender equality at a crucial transnational moment: the Beijing Conference of 1995.

# 4

## CEDAW COALITION

### *Circumventing Closed Space*

The Convention on the Elimination of All Forms of Discrimination Against Women (CEDAW) Coalition was the longest surviving group of collective actors to emerge under Mubarak's thirty-year authoritarian regime. It is a case study of nonstate actors who were committed to the promotion of women's equality and who negotiated the challenges emanating from the National Council for Women, from the Islamists, and from the divisive impact of international donors on NGOs in Egypt. The CEDAW Coalition went through phases of peak activism and phases of hibernation, yet it succeeded in mobilizing NGOs of very different ideological standpoints and activities to hold the state accountable for its failure to realize its commitments under the CEDAW. It managed to contest in international circles the government's narrative of its progressive advancement of women's status in Egypt. Although it is difficult to discuss the coalition's impact on the ground, the very fact that it could hold the regime accountable without being co-opted, repressed, or inactivated is in itself an accomplishment. The CEDAW Coalition's story is also one of enabling donor practices and disabling funding approaches.

### Building a Collective Front for Holding the Government Accountable Transnationally

The International Women's Conference, commonly known as the Beijing Conference, was held in 1995, one year after the ICPD in Cairo. The Beijing Conference contributed to sustaining the energy and mobilization around gender equality issues, and in the case of Egypt, to ensuring that there was no slump or anticlimax after the ICPD. Through the ICPD and then the Beijing Conference, civil society organizations committed to gender equality became increasingly exposed to new ways of thinking, new modalities of nonstate actors holding governments accountable, and the interface between the local and the transnational in mobilizing for equality. If the ICPD's focus was on reproductive health, one of the key instruments for framing the Beijing Conference was the CEDAW.

Egypt ratified the CEDAW on September 18, 1981. However, upon ratification, the Egyptian government made reservations to Articles 2, 9, 16, and 29. Complying with Article 2 was conditional on its compatibility with the Islamic Shari'a. On grounds of a commitment to equity rather than equality in accordance with Islamic tenets, the Egyptian government has not expressed the intention to lift reservations on Article 16 ("Egypt" 2007[1]). In 2004, Egypt lifted reservations on Article 9 of the CEDAW, which concerns granting women the nationality of their children irrespective of the nationality of their spouses (the rule excepted women married to Palestinian men on alleged security grounds). With respect to Article 29, Egypt has refused to be subject to any international mechanism that calls it to account for compliance or violation of the CEDAW. The government's stance is that "it does not consider itself bound by paragraph 1 of that article concerning the submission to an arbitral body of any dispute which may arise between States concerning the interpretation or application of the Convention. This is in order to avoid being bound by the system of arbitration in this field" ("Egypt" 2007).

The CEDAW is considered a key instrument for promoting women's rights within international feminist circles (Reilly 2009). It has served as a yardstick for assessing progress made by countries in fulfilling their obligations to improve the status of women domestically. One of the mechanisms for holding countries accountable is the CEDAW Expert Committee,

1. This blog post was published by the Coalition Equality without Reservation, a regional coalition established in 2006 in Rabat comprising hundreds of members who pressure Arab governments to remove any reservations on the CEDAW and to sign the optional CEDAW Protocol.

which reviews country progress reports every four years. The committee can take into account perspectives and voices from independent sources, including civil society organizations (CSOs), before drafting recommendations for any government. One way in which these perspectives can be conveyed is through the production of an alternative or "shadow report" to accompany that presented by the government.

According to Brody (2009), civil society organizations play an important role in monitoring their governments' compliance with commitments to gender equality through the publication of shadow reports that also offer specific recommendations for government action. She notes that although the CEDAW Expert Committee cannot oblige governments to respond to the recommendations from the shadow reports, the reports still carry authority and are often highly persuasive. In addition to reviewing shadow reports, the committee engages in dialogue with NGOs that prepare the reports, which provides an important lobbying opportunity. Based on the dialogues, review, and report, the committee is able to establish the "concluding comments" that suggest areas of remedial action to be taken by the reporting state before its next review. In light of the importance of shadow reports, many feminist activists have mobilized since the 1990s to increase the capacity of local NGOs to prepare such reports through training and information sessions (Reilly 2009, 62).

No Egyptian shadow reports were presented to the CEDAW Expert Committee until 2000 because CSOs had not collectively worked toward producing one. The process of preparing a CEDAW shadow report involves collecting and organizing information on the status of women in the country, not according to an issue but according to the specific articles of the CEDAW (and presented in the chronological order of the appearance of articles in the convention). Brody (2009) notes that good shadow reports include strong evidence that reflects the differing ways in which women's rights have been violated and present clear recommendations for action. The shadow report has to be written in a "language" that can be read by the CEDAW Expert Committee, that is, using the same terminology, mode of presentation, etc. The report must be submitted at least two weeks before the official report on a country. For CSOs to prepare a shadow report, they need support to acquire a nuanced and deep understanding of the articles of the CEDAW itself. They also need training to understand the process of data collection, synthesis, and presentation in the style required.

In 1998, Fatma Khafagy, an Egyptian professional with many years of experience working on gender and development issues, was serving as a program officer at the Cairo-based UNICEF office. She invited two renowned international trainers to give a training workshop to approximately twenty Egyptian NGOs on the CEDAW. These NGOs were all part of a network on strengthening women's rights that had been established to follow up on the Beijing Conference. The network was coordinated by Fatma Khafagy and had approximately 105 member organizations. For the twenty participants who attended the training, including many women's activists, this was their first close, in-depth encounter with the CEDAW as an instrument of advocacy on women's rights. "By the end of the workshop, we announced that we are establishing this coalition on the CEDAW," remembered the late Afaf Marei, who headed the EACPE (Tadros 2011c). The workshop served as a trigger for mobilizing the participants into wanting to create a forum of their own that would increase NGO awareness and capacity to work on the CEDAW and produce a shadow report as a means of lobbying policymakers.

Fatma Khafagy responded to participants' excitement about creating their own group by inviting them to meet at the UNICEF offices and move the idea forward. Two factors played key roles in creating the enabling environment for Khafagy to facilitate this initiative. First, the 1990s was a decade in which the Beijing Conference and the ICPD had created a momentum for sustained prioritization and interest in advancing gender rights. Gender matters were high on the agendas of the United Nations bodies as with other multilateral and donor agencies. Hence, the idea of establishing a new initiative on the CEDAW was compatible with the popular development themes of the time (particularly because the members were already part of a network on women's rights that was directly linked to following up on the Beijing Conference).

The other very important factor associated with the political moment of the time was, from Khafagy's view, the exceptional leadership of Bacquer Namazi, head of the UNICEF office in Cairo. "He was one who was very committed to making a difference in Egypt; he was ready to think outside the box and take risks," said Khafagy (interview by author, July 2010). Before committing to the CEDAW Coalition, Khafagy pressured Namazi to agree that the initiative should not be dealt with as a UNICEF project. "I put as a condition from the start that this was not going to be a project but a process. We needed to take our time in building strong relations across the NGOs, and to really invest in the process of building the group rather than stick to a project cycle format."

Khafagy also highlighted how, unlike other projects that involved substantial amounts of money, this initiative stuck to a very small budget for specific activities rather than for all of the undertakings of the coalition (which meant that they avoided the many hazards of the excesses of funding). Hence, for the regular monthly meetings, the only funded item was the train ticket for the leaders coming from organizations outside Cairo. The meetings were held on the UNICEF premises and everything was run on an entirely volunteer basis.

*Building on the Beijing Energy*

In the inception phase, the twenty organizations that showed interest in forming the CEDAW Coalition established criteria for the selection of an NGO that would serve as coordinator to this initiative. They decided on an organization that has a history of working on women's issues, is well reputed, is institutionally solid, and is registered as a nonprofit organization with the Ministry of Social Affairs (now called Social Solidarity). The last item was critically important because UNICEF had to get approval from the Ministry of Social Affairs to create the NGO initiative, and the ministry was not going to agree unless the organization fell under its administrative jurisdiction and could be watched closely.

The twenty organizations voted for Women and Society to serve as coordinator, and member organizations nominated a five-member steering committee to coordinate the work. All parties were keen to emphasize that the funding that UNICEF allocated for supporting this work was very small, and that all of the organizations made voluntary, nonmonetary contributions to building the initiative. According to the rules and regulations drawn by the coalition members, the steering committee must meet once per month or at least once every forty-five days. The steering committee provided direction for the coalition while a general assembly composed of all of the members met four times per year to develop policy and planning, to work collectively on the shadow report, and to approve new applications for membership. The coalition developed clear criteria for eligibility of new members as well as mechanisms for their inclusion, such as an expansion of no more than 25 percent of the membership of the coalition to maintain the cohesion of the group. The coalition also created an ethics charter and developed clear guidelines for the distribution of responsibilities.

All of the former CEDAW Coalition members that I interviewed agreed that in the early years after its inception, the coalition was run in a highly democratic manner. Decisions were made collectively, with the inclusion of organizations from upper Egypt. Maher Boshra, NGO leader from the Better Life Association in Minya, recalls that this was a phase in which there was a high level of commitment from the steering committee, which was composed mainly of the leading feminist activists in the country, to connect and work with associations in upper Egypt. Upper Egypt conventionally has been cut off from Cairo in terms of capabilities, sharing of ideas, etc. (Tadros 2011c). Many organizations said that the inclusion of these organizations often generated greater gendering of their work. However, several participants have suggested that the level of active inclusion of non-Cairo-based organizations in the coalition has waned in the last phase despite the fact that they continue to exist as part of the coalition. In effect, like other women's coalitions in Egypt, the CEDAW leadership remains centralized in the hands of a few Cairo-based organizations.

The initial objective of the first coalition group that was established in 1998 was the development of the first shadow report that would serve as a mechanism for urging the Egyptian government to improve its women's rights record by using the CEDAW as a yardstick against which to measure progress. To involve CSOs in monitoring the situation on the ground, however, other activities had to be undertaken to increase their capacity, such as awareness-raising workshops in upper and lower Egypt, support for research on gender-related issues, etc.

The coalition has gone through several phases of activism and dormancy. The first phase from 1998 to 2003 was when meetings were first held at UNICEF and then at the Women and Society organization where the coalition was homed. Fatma Khafagy recalls that because the twenty organizations that formed the initial group had very different standpoints on gender issues, the first meetings were dedicated to listening to leaders talk about their personal views, ideas, and experiences on gender-related work. These listening sessions were extremely important in creating the safe spaces for members to air their concerns and find common ground among each other.

During this phase, activities centered around building the internal cohesion of the group before working toward preparation of the first shadow report. There was much ideological division over some of the content of the CEDAW articles, and, according to Seham Negm, the coordinator of the CEDAW Coalition, it was agreed that they would focus on the points around which there was consensus and set aside all of the issues that caused division (Tadros 2011c). Each NGO then became responsible for working with a cluster of other NGOs to gather information on the status of women according to its area of specialization, which corresponded to an article in the CEDAW. For example, Azza Soliman from CEWLA would gather information on the legal status of women in the Personal Status Law, documenting cases and synthesizing ones provided by other organizations that were working on legal issues.

Despite UNICEF's partnership with the Egyptian government, the opposition to the work of the CEDAW Coalition was quite strong. The Ministry of Social Solidarity, recalled Seham Negm, would haphazardly send its civil servants to check the NGO's internal paperwork, sometimes as regularly as every two weeks, and threaten them with "let's see what the CEDAW can do for you now" (Tadros 2011c). In the initial phase of the coalition, during the late 1990s, the government was actively repressing the Islamists and therefore their voices were muffled. However, when the government relaxed its tight rein on the Islamists in the early 2000s, they actively attacked the CEDAW as a Western instrument of corrupting Muslim nations and for its advocacy of same-sex rights. They also accused organizations that espoused the CEDAW as being foreign-funded agents of the West. On the ground, there was much resistance to the ideas that were presented to the people and to the NGOs because they clashed with the fundamental patriarchal mores of society. The main argument put forward, which was very much influenced by the Islamist normative discourse that was pervasive in Egyptian society, was "why do we need the CEDAW when Islam has granted women all of their rights?" CEDAW Coalition members were very cautious not to frame the CEDAW as an alternative or competing framework with Islam. They emphasized that because Islam is a religion, it is of a sacrosanct nature, whereas the CEDAW is not and hence there is no basis for making comparisons. They would also emphasize the compatibility of Islam and the CEDAW, and they provided textual evidence of this relationship. This method of framing was effective in diminishing opposition on the ground.

For two years, the organizations worked hard to compile the draft of the first shadow report. The editor of the report (Aida Seif el Dawla) categorically insisted on undertaking the assignment on a volunteer basis. After the report was completed, the coalition organized two major meetings, one in the Delta (lower Egypt governorates) and one in upper Egypt, to share the findings with sixty organizations in each region (120 overall). In 2001, the coalition nominated three delegates to present the shadow report in Geneva. Mervat Tallawy, then the representative from the Egyptian government, was not hostile toward the NGO delegation and accepted its presence. In light of the political hostility shown toward NGOs engaged in international advocacy against the Egyptian government, Tallawy's nonopposition represented a significant step forward. Tallawy's leadership at the CEDAW event was instrumental in reducing the possibility of a government backlash against the Egyptian CEDAW Coalition. One of the early leaders of the CEDAW Coalition said, "I heard after the event that Mervat Tallawy was summoned by the first lady who asked her, 'what is this about there being a shadow report being presented?' Mervat Tallawy assured her that the representative organizations were all registered [with the Ministry of Social Affairs] here in Egypt and were respectable figures. So the first lady said 'khallas' [matter is closed]" (interview by author, July 2010).

During the preparatory phase before the report was released, this coalition leader recalls that they purposely avoided working with the media:

We had very few rapports during those first three years of quiet work. This was deliberate as we worked on building our internal organizational structure. I think this was a very important tactic because when we were working together, we had to work on building unified stances on some highly controversial issues and many of the NGOs had very different stances. Had the conversations been conveyed in the media, it would have been divisive and potentially explosive. After we had the shadow report to which all of the twenty-two organizations had signed to and after our delegation returned from Geneva then we talked to the press. (interview by author, July 2010)

One year after the shadow report was released by the NGOs, the NCW decided in 2002 to work on the CEDAW. This decision had important implications for the Egyptian CEDAW Coalition. Once the government openly takes on an issue, that issue loses its taboo status. It is, as one activist pointed out, like "removing the red line which you could not cross." In addition, the Ministry of Social Solidarity stopped harassing the CEDAW Coalition and its host NGOs after the NCW's decision. Conversely, the NCW approached UNICEF to fund its work on the CEDAW. UNICEF pulled their support of the CEDAW Coalition and provided the funding to the NCW instead. According to Khafagy, this occurred because Bacquer Namazi had left the leadership of UNICEF Egypt and a new director who took a more risk-averse approach had taken over. Nevertheless, the CEDAW Coalition continued to meet, even without funding.

*CEDAW Coalition: Beyond the Donor Incubation Phase*

The second phase commenced in 2003 when, by nomination, the Woman and Development Forum took over the role of hosting the CEDAW Coalition from Woman and Society. Until 2007, the CEDAW Coalition was mostly dormant because the trigger for meeting, mobilizing, and organizing collectively—preparing for the next CEDAW Expert Committee—was still some years away. However, in 2007, work started on a volunteer basis in preparation for the second shadow report. It was completed in 2009 and presented to the CEDAW Expert Committee in 2010.

In 2009, the EACPE, led by the late Afaf Marei, was nominated to become the new host for the CEDAW Coalition. This nomination coincided with the arrival of a generous fund from the European Union. However, the EU fund was different from previous grants in three fundamental ways: it was comparatively much larger; it was in the form of a three-year project; and there was confusion over whether the funding came to the organization to administer the coalition or whether the funding was for the coalition itself, just channeled through the organization.

The arrival of EU funding generated an internal crisis within the coalition. In one of the steering meetings of the CEDAW Coalition, a board member of the EACPE (who was not part of the historical CEDAW Coalition) said to members, "You can only give your opinions on this fund but they are in no way binding, this is the NGO's project." This comment generated anger among the steering committee members who had been involved in the coalition since its inception. One faction was so outraged that it wanted to break away and form a countercoalition, except that members stood up and told her not to do so because this would weaken the existing coalition. They argued that they must fight to reclaim what is theirs collectively. One leading member of the coalition shared the following recollection during our interview (July 2010):

> After this incident, people [members] were very angry and they lashed out at him [the EACPE board member] because they owned this initiative. The condemnation was so intense that this person got a heart attack. He did not expect people to feel that this is theirs so much! We met as the community of elders. We needed to defend the integrity of the coalition....I differed with [the person] who said 'let us create another coalition.' This is out of question. We cannot each take a piece and work on it separately. This does not work....We will work together and we will stick together. We held the coordinator [Afaf Marei] who was from the original group accountable. She told us 'this project was written in the spirit of the CEDAW Coalition and it belongs to the CEDAW Coalition.'

The issue of ownership was resolved and it was agreed that only the steering committee would make the decisions in relation to the coalition and not the board members of the EACPE. This experience prompted the steering committee to put down on paper the relationship between a hosting organization and the CEDAW Coalition.

Meanwhile, as the date for submitting the second shadow report drew near, the efforts that had begun a year earlier on a volunteer basis were stepped up. The process of preparing the shadow report highlighted the importance of leadership as a collective role that required several balancing acts. Leaders needed to allow space and flexibility for the participating organization to make a contribution that spoke to their interests. Conversely, the sum of all parts needed to contribute to a whole that would reflect the collective identity/standpoint and achieve the endorsement of the coalition members.

From the participating organizations' perspectives, this balance was successfully achieved in the CEDAW Coalition, though not without trade-offs. Because individuals have different political and ideological stances on women's rights, in particular on issues that directly have to do with sexuality, the strategy adopted by the steering committee was once again to avoid the controversial, contested issues and to arrive at the lowest common denominator around which consensus could be forged. The trade-off was that in the process, members who thought that an issue had not been adequately represented in the shadow report needed to find an alternative channel for advocacy. Such a trade-off was needed to avoid undermining the internal cohesion of the group. In the last shadow report, CEWLA decided that the research findings they had collected on honor killings were too important to leave out of the shadow report. However, many members of the coalition were uncomfortable at the idea of being perceived as approving of women who deviated from the prevailing sexual mores and values of society. Hence, Azza Soliman from CEWLA produced a separate report on this issue and presented it internationally while also remaining part of the CEDAW Coalition. The coalition accepted that it was the organization's right to campaign on an issue for which it was not feasible to do so under their collective umbrella.

The delegation to the Commission on the Status of Women in 2010 agreed that the CEDAW Coalition's oral statement should be made by three members: Afaf Marei, Seham Negm, and Iman Mandour, and that

Mandour (from CEWLA) should respond to the questions presented by the CEDAW Expert Committee. The meeting was attended by nineteen members of the CEDAW Expert Committee and lasted more than an hour, allowing the CEDAW Coalition more lobbying space. The next day, on Tuesday, January 28, the government's representative and secretary general of the NCW, Farkhonda Hassan, presented the joint sixth and seventh periodic report on the implementation of the CEDAW in Egypt. During the presentation, the Egyptian government claimed that one of the findings presented by the CEDAW Coalition was inaccurate. The CEDAW Coalition was not entitled to respond or participate in the meeting with the official delegates; members only observed the claim. Iman Mandour recollected the following:

> The CEDAW Coalition members phoned Mervat Abou Tieg in Cairo; since her organization was specialized in the domain in which the information was being questioned, she responded immediately, providing the back-up evidence. The CEDAW Coalition back in Geneva translated this information and when one of the CEDAW Expert Committee members went to the bathroom, I followed her to the bathroom and was able to pass on this information to her. When the Expert Committee member returned, she passed on the note to the person in charge, and he was able to raise it with the Egyptian official delegates to confirm its accuracy.

Many tangible successes were directly related to the fulfillment of the CEDAW Coalition's objectives. The shadow report was well received and praised by the CEDAW Expert Committee. Several of the recommendations from the shadow report and deliberations over lunch with the CEDAW Expert Committee members were reflected in the final recommendations that were officially presented to the Egyptian government. Because the CEDAW Coalition left its mark, the official Egyptian delegation realized that it was a political force to contend with. While still in Geneva, Farkhonda Hassan invited the coalition to a meeting upon their return to Cairo to draw up a future strategy for implementing the CEDAW recommendations. Although the NCW certainly does not deal with the CEDAW Coalition as an equal, and the power differentials in this relationship are very conspicuous, the fact that the government put forward an invitation to the CEDAW Coalition to take part in such an event indicates that it recognized the coalition as an important partner and as an actor that can engage in international space.

The collaborative work in Geneva had a very positive impact on coalition morale. Most members said that the organized, effective performance of the group created a positive sense of achievement and impetus to move forward as a *coalition*; in other words, in a collective capacity. When asked why they consider the CEDAW Coalition successful, interviewees often began to tell the anecdote of how they collectively worked together to present a unified force in Geneva and to make a convincing case to hold the Egyptian government accountable before the CSW Expert Committee.

The CEDAW Coalition was the longest running coalition on women's rights in the contemporary history of Egypt (until the 2011 revolution). It achieved its goals of presenting shadow reports to the CEDAW Expert Committee, using them as tools for holding the government accountable, and for advocating for women's rights on an international level. Organizationally, it survived despite two key challenges: the absence of funding for some phases of its existence and attempts at hijacking and turning it into a project by a singular NGO.

The success of the CEDAW Coalition is, like all forms of collective action, attributable to a constellation of factors: some to do with the choices made by the leaders and members, and some beyond their control. One of the enabling factors that worked to the coalition's advantage, which was difficult to replicate for subsequent collective actors, was the international political moment at its inception. The structural or contextual frameworks and policy environment around the world in the 1990s played a significant role in the emergence of many forms of women's collective action. International policy and donor prioritization of gender empowerment all had ripple effects on making gender issues matters of deliberation between national governments and local feminists.

Another important factor that helped increase member commitment to the initiative was a high level of local ownership. The UNICEF leadership responded to the collective desire of workshop participants to form a group and provided an enabling environment for the CEDAW Coalition to emerge. It neither created the coalition nor did it seek to control it. Of all of the people I interviewed about the coalition, there was unanimous consensus that its most successful phase was its inception. The attention and investment in the process of bringing together parties and allowing them the space to develop common agendas was often cited as one of the key elements to building a strong foundation. It also gave members a shared sense of stake in the success of the initiative, which later surfaced after EACPE's board intervention in the internal affairs of the coalition presented a risk of people pulling out and forming a parallel coalition.

**The Looming Threat of a Projectivized, Professionalized Coalition**

The practices of external donors play a pivotal role in the survival of a coalition. On the one hand, the absence of funding may threaten the sustainability of a collective actor or even force it to assume a dormant mode, as happened with the CEDAW Coalition earlier in its existence. On the other hand, large funding has the power to kill the coalition because it dampens people's willingness to contribute to the sustenance of the initiative: if it all can be externally funded, why bother? This attitude in turn creates an image of the initiative as being a funded project, not a local collective actor. It also generates a sense of competition over funding, which only deepens hostilities between competing organizations and fragments collective action.

During the CEDAW Coalition's inception phase in 1998, UNICEF allocated a very small budget to start the initiative from its fund for Beijing follow-up activities. The amount was so small that none of the founders, including Fatma Khafagy herself, remembers how much. It did not cover all of the CEDAW Coalition's activities but helped to cover small workshops in upper Egypt, some meetings and roundtables (others were self-funded by the organizations), and the travel expenses of participants from upper Egypt. The funding from UNICEF, which was channeled to the Woman and Society association, was terminated in 2002.[2]

---

2. Canadian initiatives launched by the Egyptian branch of the Canadian International Development Agency to promote civil society capacity building gave a small fund

The nature of the conceptualization and administration of the funding influenced greatly the collective spirit and internal cohesion of the CEDAW Coalition because it helped make the cause, not the financial incentive, the driver of collective action. It also helped nurture local leadership who would claim responsibility for the initiative. Agentially, Namazi's leadership as director of UNICEF allowed committed local UNICEF leaders to respond to pressure from the Egyptian participants to support—and not manage—the development of their own initiatives. The fact that UNICEF was able to successfully pass the torch of hosting the coalition to a local NGO that was selected by the member organizations is evidence of the importance of local leadership and ownership as a litmus test for the strength of its collective nature.

After the Women and Society organization assumed a hosting role, UNICEF continued to fund very specific activities rather than the whole CEDAW Coalition. Hence, the organization that was receiving the funding was not receiving any substantial overhead for its own internal structure. This meant that there was no conflict of interest between the actual organization and the coalition because there was no funding to fight over. Everyone was proud to note that they and their organizations contributed to the development of the coalition on a volunteer basis. This fact is often mentioned in relation to the near absence of any voluntary work among the major development and women's NGOs, who have become less committed to fighting causes as they become increasingly professionalized[3] and technocratic.

The European Union's treatment of the coalition as a project generated countless threats to the collective nature, internal cohesion, and leadership of the initiative. In 2008, a three-year grant from the European Union

---

to the Women and Development Forum when it was hosting the CEDAW Coalition in 2002. However, the funding was primarily directed at another initiative, which sought to perform media monitoring of women's issues in the press, and the funding available for CEDAW activities was less than that of UNICEF.

3. By professionalized I mean the tendency to increasingly rely on development professionals working on donor-supported projects with limited space for volunteer-led activism.

worth 300,000 Euros was made to the EACPE for supporting the CEDAW Coalition, building dialogue with the NCW, and aiding in the production of the shadow report. UNICEF conceptualized the coalition as a *process*, whereas the European Union engaged with the coalition as a three-year *project*. This difference has impacted the leadership process in various ways. In the early phases, the coalition was not required to abide by a particular timeline of activity implementation and project delivery. Hence, if the process of reaching a consensus on an issue required more time and more internal deliberation, so be it. The activities could be rescheduled and there was no pressure on the steering committee or on the organization that served as the institutional coordinator before UNICEF (Seham Negm, representing the Woman and Society organization). In the EU-run phase of the coalition, the late Afaf Marei had to abide very strictly by the project delivery deadlines set by the European Union, including the dates for output delivery (Tadros 2011c).

Another fundamental problem in the conceptualization of project- versus process-led initiative had to do with the separation of powers and question of accountability. In the UNICEF-supported phase of the coalition, financial accountability rested on the shoulders of the coordinating organization, Woman and Society. However, it was not solely accountable for the CEDAW Coalition, and UNICEF expected decisions on activities and processes to be made collectively via frequent engagements with the steering committee. In the EU-funded phase of the coalition, EACPE had sole responsibility for the financial and technical performance of the coalition before the European Union generated a different dynamic. As far as the donor was concerned, EACPE could unilaterally make decisions on activity and process (as long as those decisions were in the proposal and if not, in consultation with them as the donors) without referring back to the collective leadership represented in the steering committee. Incidences involving EACPE's unilateral decision-making were reported by members of the steering committee but were later resolved internally by confronting the EACPE representative in the coalition and asking her to work through the collective leadership structure in place.

A European Union officer responsible for the EACPE grant at the delegation in Cairo has pointed out that although the European Union in its policy documents recognizes the importance of work through partnerships and networks, in effect the current system of fund management does not distinguish between the different kinds of initiatives and their institutional arrangements. At the end of the day, they are all projects. Hence, the requirements for eligibility, the process of proposal evaluation, and the monitoring of the fund apply to an NGO-led project and a coalition in the same way. In the case of the CEDAW Coalition, the European Union recognizes a legal entity (EACPE) as the only accountable entity. How the EACPE manages its internal relations within the coalitions is entirely up to the organization as long as they abide by what is presented in the original proposal. "There is only so much we can do as donors except ask [the grantee] to stick to the original proposal," the officer said. In the monitoring process, they are only required to follow up with the EACPE on the implementation of the stated activities, not with other members of the CEDAW Coalition. The officer explained that because she is responsible for managing between twenty and twenty-five contracts, a visit to the grantee only once or twice a year "is the best scenario."

These problems are not specific to the European Union but reflect a systemic feature of donor practices: an official discourse of strengthening partnerships, networking, and collective action is at odds with funding practices that conceive of all local actors and actions in terms of projects in which activities and outputs are prioritized. Although donors do support coalitions and there have been some very successful cases (Tadros 2011c), the differences between supporting, monitoring, and evaluating NGO projects and programs versus collective modes of engagement have not been sufficiently enforced in donor practices across the board. The irony is that women's coalitional work needs Western support because there are very few alternative sources of funding, and yet donor practices threaten to destroy collective action in the first place.

## Conclusion

The CEDAW Coalition emerged in a domestically hostile political environment associated with an authoritarian regime that was determined to demobilize any political action that threatened its interests. The Mubarak government had a vested interest in using the gender agenda to boost the first lady's profile as the champion of women's rights (see chapter 2) and to convey to the international community that the Egyptian regime, through its national women's machineries, was sensitive to gender. The CEDAW Coalition posed a threat to this narrative in the international arena, and its ability to hold the regime accountable for its gender agenda is in and of itself a success.

The post-Beijing international moment was one in which women's rights and the mobilization around those rights was still high on donors' agendas. A number of agential factors worked in constellation with that international moment to enable the emergence of the CEDAW Coalition. These factors include leadership and a civil society sector that was not entirely professionalized. The internal leadership within UNICEF was personified in the country director, who unlike his successor was willing to take a politically calculated risk in favor of civil activism, even if the Egyptian government did not like it much. Namazi's successor chose not to risk rocking the boat with the Egyptian government and withdrew support for the initiative. Namazi also was willing to allow staff to experiment with a deprojectivized approach that prioritized process over deliverables and that privileged local ownership over donor control.

On another level, the coalition developed an inclusive, transparent approach to leadership that became institutionalized in their practices. Perhaps it was the process of building leadership and allowing it to brew over time through extensive deliberations that increased people's ownership of the coalition, and when the moment rose that it became threatened, they felt that they had enough stake in it to defend it. However, one of the agential factors that enabled the CEDAW Coalition to work as a minimally funded initiative in which actors contribute to the collective with their own efforts, time, and money, was that NGOs had not yet become fully professionalized. This environment was difficult to replicate in the 2000s.

The close association with "doing" gender work in a particular donor-driven way had a decade later caused structural damage to the spirit of volunteerism, in which people are driven by causes they believe in rather than financial incentives. When the spirit of political activism and citizen mobilization permeated Egypt after the ousting of Mubarak, the energies of the CEDAW Coalition went elsewhere. Like many other collective actors, it became displaced by newly emerging, informal, youth-led initiatives. Many of its individual NGOs continue to be active, but not through the CEDAW Coalition platform.

# 5

## COLLECTIVE ACTION LITE

There is a substantive body of literature (Alvarez 1999; Batliwala 2012; Choudry and Kapoor 2013; Jad 2004) that cautions against the NGOization of women's movements with the help of donor assistance. However, the threat to collective action around gender justice is not only from the NGOization of women's movements but also from their collectivization in a "lite" manner. Collective action lite is not simply an upgrade of NGOization; it is the direct outcome of donors actively seeking to establish and run coalitions and movements in a particular fashion.

Funding the formation and strengthening of networks and coalitions has become quite popular in many Western donor circles, but even this funding has to fit within donors' logical frameworks and project designs. There are signs of this new donor trend in Egypt at the beginning of the twenty-first century. In this chapter I examine the dangers of donors funding the formation of collective entities in which there is neither local ownership nor legitimate local leadership. I do so using evidence from two initiatives examined up until 2010.[1] The first is Karama, which is funded by several donors including the MDG3 Fund that was established by the Dutch government (for more information on the scheme, see Kinoti 2011). The second is the Network of Women's Rights Organizations, funded by the German International Development Agency (GIZ). Both of these case studies suggest a direct correlation between the degree to which an

---

1. These initiatives may have changed in the period thereafter; hence, it is important to emphasize that the scope of the research presented here is from their conception up until 2010.

external actor is involved in "running the show" and the likelihood that sustained collective work is possible. The effects of externally induced interventions are not only giving a deceptive image of mobilization that has no basis in reality, but is also introducing a pseudoform of activism that I call "collective action lite."

NWRO's initial plan was to form a coalition, but then its donor became more modest in their aims and formed a network. In the case of Karama, the founder wished to establish a movement but in practice created a locally based international donor organization that provides funding and networking opportunities for grantees (i.e., locally based organizations apply for and receive funds from Karama for the implementation of their own activities). The trajectories of both initiatives show the dilemmas facing external actors when they attempt to catalyze collective action by treating it like a project. Karama is an extreme example of this situation, but there are important resonances with NWRO as well. In what follows, I discuss these two highly revealing case studies in the dynamics of collective action lite.

### Karama–Egypt

Karama–Egypt's formation was triggered in 2005 when Hibaaq Osman, a Somali-American, asked organizations to join an initiative that was intended to become a movement on domestic violence in Egypt. At that time, Osman was representing herself as a leading member of the US-based organization V-Day, which was designed to support the establishment of an Arab regional initiative on violence. V-Day carries out awareness-raising work on violence against women through innovative communication means.

In its literature, Karama-Egypt presents itself as both a coalition and a movement. Its website in 2010 stated that Karama-Egypt is an initiative fueled by "a coalition of partners as constituencies to build a movement to end violence against women in the Middle East and North Africa" (a parallel organization was also established in Jordan). Its strategy was listed as "a cascading national and regional movement to end violence against women." And in their internal correspondence, communication, and engagements with organizations in Egypt, its representatives describe the organization as a movement. Osman is the chief executive officer of Karama–Egypt as well as the V-Day special representative for the Middle East (V-Day 2005). Karama–Egypt is recognized by the Ministry of Foreign Affairs as an international organization based in Cairo and governed by its own internal board. In 2010, its website stated its objective as "to bring together women, men, governments, activists and artists to examine the impact violence makes on women's health, education and economics, and to come up with campaigns at the national, regional, and international levels to end violence against women, tailored to the cultural realities of the target country." Based on meeting minutes and interviews, the objective of examining the impact that violence has on health, education, and economics seemed to have been one entirely developed by Hibaaq Osman and presented to the participant organizations as an innovative approach to addressing the issue of violence against women.

Karama–Egypt's main grant funding in 2010 came from the Dutch government's former MDG3 Fund to support women's initiatives in the global south. The criteria upon which an organization was assessed for this fund included the origin of the organization (with a preference for organizations based in developing countries), its support base, the quality of its financial and administrative management, and the sustainability of the activity. According to a Dutch senior officer, Karama–Egypt's scores on all of the criteria were relatively high, including that of the origin of the organization since it was considered an Egyptian NGO. Even though the identity of Karama was at the time foreign, the organization's registration with the Ministry of Foreign Affairs in Egypt granted it "Egyptian" status. Moreover, reference was made to the Karama "project." No distinction was made in the MDG3 Fund between funding coalitions and organizations; all were spoken of as agencies implementing projects.

In 2010, Karama–Egypt funded the participation of women NGO leaders in a New York meeting of the Committee on the Status of Women. One of the core activities of Karama–Egypt has been to provide financial support for women based in Egypt and other Arab countries so that they may network regionally and attend major international conferences. The rationale behind this activity is twofold. First, it enables women leaders to establish regional connections and, potentially, region-level initiatives.

Second, it increases Arab women's presence and participation in the international women's fora. Both rationales respond to the lack of opportunity to engage regionally among women activists and the poor visibility of Arab women in international fora. This approach to capacity development was very much appreciated by the leaders of organizations that I interviewed. They argued that attending and participating in these international events allowed them to engage with policy on a very different and necessary level. It is hard to say if their engagement on an international level had any impact on their work on violence against women; however, if the objective was to increase presence and participation of Arab women in the international women's arena, it was certainly achieved.

Karama–Egypt funded and managed two local initiatives in 2010: the violence against women network known as the Karama Network (which was initially intended to be a coalition/movement) and the provision of direct funds and capacity support for individual organizations' initiatives. Karama–Egypt provided seed money to local organizations so they may produce outputs relating to the impact of violence against women in different areas or realms: legal, health, education, culture, media, and economics.[2] These organizations formed into clusters and each cluster examined the impact of violence on one realm. The cluster coordinators were responsible for delegating responsibilities among the member organizations and distributing funding for any activities implemented by partners.

At the time I was conducting research for this book (2010), Karama–Egypt had been on the ground for two years, so the initiative was at a nascent stage and an assessment of the different clusters/realms would have been premature. However, interviewees noted that the interconnectedness between the activities seemed very weak and almost nonexistent at times. Moreover, the sum of all parts (or realms) did not seem to be

---

2. There was supposed to be a seventh realm, the political, but it never materialized because the head of the organization that was supposed to lead it, Nehad Abou el Komsan of the Egyptian Women's Rights Organization, froze her membership in Karama–Egypt and stopped participating. No other organization was invited to lead this cluster of work.

leading toward one collective intervention, an impression that was cor-
roborated by my interviews with partners involved in Karama–Egypt. The
consensus was that a donor does not a coalition make.

The interviewees' reflections seemed to suggest that Karama–Egypt's
capacity to become an Egyptian social movement was undermined from
the very start on account of three factors: leadership lacking in local legitimacy, lack of clarity over the cause (or objective), and the management
of the initiative as if it were a project. These factors all contributed to an
absence of local ownership and the will to work collectively.

The concept of legitimate leadership is critically important for all levels of institution building, but particularly so for movement building. One
of the main elements noted by the interviewees that undermined the prospects of Karama–Egypt having legitimate leadership was the fact that the
founder was an external actor who assumed that women activists would
engage with her as an internal actor because she is a Muslim and an Arabic
speaker. This assumption is in contrast to how Western donors perceived
of her. To Western donors keen on funding collective action, Hibaaq
Osman represents the best of both worlds. She is an established member
of an American organization, V-Day, which is renowned for its feminist
engagements, and, as a Muslim of Somali origin, she can claim solidarity
with Muslim women of the Middle East.

One Karama–Egypt grantee reflected on how the dynamics of leadership affected local ownership in the organization:

> There was a clear lack of balance from the outstart between recognizing
> Hibaaq's centrality to this initiative while also recognizing the contri-
> butions that all the members were bringing to this initiative. When you
> have Hibaaq's business card stating 'Founder of the Karama Movement'
> there is bound to be resistance and an outcry from participants. After
> all, we are talking about NGO leaders with long and established his-
> tories of engagement; they would not simply accept being sidestepped.
> (interview by author, July 2010)

This statement points to another element of legitimate leadership with
which Karama–Egypt struggled from the outset: the absence of a leadership process that allowed for power sharing. Many interviewed members

of Karama–Egypt confided that they thought that the vision of the movement was misguided from the beginning. For them, a movement or a coalition involves an internal process of individuals and organizations coalescing and mobilizing around a cause, deciding on what they want to do and how they want to do it, and then soliciting funding when needed. In the Karama–Egypt initiative, funding was made available (or the promise thereof) from an outsider and members met to secure a portion of that funding (and the possibility of expanding their NGO's activities and visibility).

Although the cause of domestic violence represents a pressing and widespread social problem in Egypt, interviewees shared that some NGO leaders could not help but engage with the issue as another fundable project when it was externally induced from an outsider. Some leaders approached work with the Karama–Egypt initiative as a donor-funded project, never as a cause around which they collectively joined forces to fight for as *activists*. This is largely a problem of agential–structural interface.

Had the CEO introduced Karama–Egypt as an international organization keen to forge partnerships through grant-making and capacity support, the initiative was likely to have been applauded as a case of a successful foreign donor endorsing local women's activisms. Some members of Karama–Egypt expressed disappointment that the regional work was restricted to a few workshops rather than attempting to build a collective initiative. The predetermined objective gave some interviewed members the impression of unmet expectations and suggested an overambitious agenda.[3]

The projectivization of collective action not only undermined local ownership but generated rivalry between different factions of the Egyptian activist circles and competition over funding that is systemic of donor-driven projects. It is interesting to note that in interviews with the donor that funded Karama–Egypt (the Dutch government), references were consistently made to the Karama "project." No distinction was made between

---

3. The regional work of Karama–Egypt was beyond the scope of this study and consequently its regional activities were not explored in depth.

funding coalitions and organizations; all were spoken of as organizations implementing projects. PricewaterhouseCoopers won the bid for monitoring the forty-five initiatives funded by the MDG3 Fund (of which Karama–Egypt was one), with Femconsult, a Dutch organization founded in 1985, offering consultancy services to the gender and development initiatives.

There was a division of work between these two international consultancies that were delegated with the responsibility of monitoring Karama–Egypt and other organizations. An interview with one of the consultancy leaders revealed that there was no differentiation between an international organization that is working with and through partners and a coalition or movement. When asked about whether they monitored Karama–Egypt differently because it was supposed to be an aspiring social movement, the leader answered, "A lot of the *projects* are implemented with partners. I don't know any of the forty-five organizations who do not work with partners" (emphasis added). The idea was that Karama–Egypt had local partners, but that the consultants monitored the work of Karama–Egypt the organization, not that of the partners involved. For these reasons, the monitoring mechanism was not conducive to analysis of the process, contextual nuances, and nature of relationships in Karama–Egypt.

Cracks began to appear in Karama–Egypt's structure. Two groups defected from the Karama network and chose to deal with Karama–Egypt separately as individual organizations (El Nadim Centre and the Arab Solidarity Association). In conversations with leaders from both organizations, they pointed to the same issues: lack of clear, transparent policies and decision-making processes and the extreme competition between organizations over resources, which led to a highly divisive environment. Interviewed members of Karama–Egypt mentioned that collaborative work across the different clusters became minimal and this further enforced the sense of an absence of collective purpose. The only member of Karama–Egypt who thought it was effective as a coalition was reflecting on the fact that the infrequency of meetings (at the time) had given some people the impression that things were going well: "But honestly I think it is better that we are not meeting a lot because now we can focus on implementing our projects rather than gathering to fight among ourselves" (interview by author, August 2010).

**Network of Women's Rights Organizations**

Coincidentally, the timing of the NWRO initiative is similar to that of Karama in 2005. GIZ (the German government's bilateral aid donor) was interested in working with NGOs that supported women's causes as part of its international commitment to promoting gender equality and supporting civil society. However, GIZ only operated in Egypt through working in partnership with the government. In GIZ's conventional practice, they would be given an office on the premises of the governorate and they would work in close partnership with officials there. To work with women's NGOs that are geographically spread across the country, though, their partner in Egypt was the Ministry of Social Solidarity, the government party responsible for overseeing the affairs of nonprofit organizations.

The fact that women activists inside and outside the NWRO initiative referred to it as "the GIZ project" mostly encapsulates why it never assumed the identity of an Egyptian collective actor. For one, actors in the initiative did not coalesce around an issue that required collective action, but instead were selected and brought together by the donor. The initiative was consistently seen as run and managed by a donor, with all of the connotations that such a role brings with it. In addition, it never managed to extricate itself from the framework of a project, and when faced with a highly sensitive issue such as the Personal Status Law, it could not manage depoliticized interventions (as are necessary with some development projects). In this section I examine each of these challenges to building an organic, locally driven collective front.

The trigger to the formation of a group of NGOs was an invitation from the donor, GIZ. The internal staff of GIZ selected the organizations with which to work, rather than permitting the process to be organically led. These NGOs included the New Woman Research Foundation, CEWLA, AWSA, and Women and Memory. All were Cairo-based women's organizations that mostly worked on development and advocacy. Two organizations were later added to show a broader geographical outreach: Better Life in Minya and another organization in Aswan. GIZ selected some of the most established women's organizations to have worked on women's rights issues either through grassroots development and/or advocacy work. However, not all such organizations were invited to join, and in the long run their exclusion may lead to them becoming major opponents of the NWRO.

Once all of the organizations convened, GIZ asked them to choose an issue that they would like to work on collectively. GIZ staff members suggested the issue of informal marriages, namely marriages that are not officially certified but are religiously sanctioned on account of the presence of witnesses. If the marriage fails and there is no certification, it is very difficult for women to establish the paternity of their children if the fathers do not claim them. Moreover, such women's claims for divorce in court are not accepted on account of the absence of official documentation showing marriage in the first place.

Members of the chosen organizations knew that the choice of issue was significant: very few, if any, organizations were able to research an issue with the goals of mobilizing collectively and pressing for interventions. Between 2005 and 2008, the organizations conducted research, organized roundtables, and produced a film on the topic of informal marriages, but the issue was later dropped because some members considered it to be too socially sensitive, and the opportunities for influencing policy were very limited.

An important thread runs through the narrative of the NWRO: GIZ selected the organizations, GIZ convened the meeting, and GIZ established the coalition. One activist from an organization that withdrew from the GIZ initiative recalls the first encounter with a local Egyptian woman hired by GIZ:

> She told us that the GIZ is interested in creating a coalition of organizations and we told her that it does not work that way. People get together because of an issue that makes them want to work together and then see how they are going to work on it, but this way [you are putting the cart before the horse]. (interview by author, July 2010)

The organization whose member is quoted above initially made the decision to be part of the coalition because they were promised funding for an advocacy issue for which they had no resources to support. GIZ told them that it could fit under the general issue that the coalition was going to work on and therefore be possible to fund.

Had GIZ supported emerging collective work among a certain group, it may have had a better chance of serving as an enabling agent rather than a donor engaging in social engineering. Members would have naturally chosen each other and claimed ownership, and therefore there may have been an opportunity for them to continue postfunding if they had worked on establishing a cohesive core. The fact that GIZ chose the organizations in the inception phase undermined the sense of ownership with clear implications for postfunding sustainability.

*Whose Legitimacy, Whose Leadership?*

The NWRO had several layers of institutionalized decision-making processes. In that structure, leadership was in the hands of the steering committee, which consisted of eleven NGO leaders. There was also an executive committee of administrative staff members who belonged to these organizations and who performed the day-to-day work of the network. All administrative convening was led by the GIZ secretariat, which consisted of a project manager (Yousry Mustapha, formerly Fatma Khafagy, one of the founding members of the CEDAW Coalition) and a capacity development expert (Marwa Sharafeddin), who was there from the outset. There was also a division of labor among organizations according to their area of expertise (i.e., working with the media, advocacy, or legal proficiency). One of the activists noted the following about the first phase of the initiative:

> As organizations, we have been accustomed that when a donor is providing funding, they require financial and administrative reports and now and then they would attend meetings to see how things are going, but GIZ acted as if it is a partner so they attend every meeting and attend all events and bring two of their staff like any of us [NGOs] but it was worse [than having any other partner] because they have the money and this became very evident in how relationships played out. (interview by author, July 2010)

Flaws began to emerge in the NWRO as a consequence of ideological and personality clashes as well as rivalry over whose opinion presides and how the funding was being divided. The Women and Memory Foundation left the initiative but did not give a specific reason for doing so. The Arab Solidarity Association pulled out over the framing of a campaign on reforming the Personal Status Law in 2009, but there were some other underlying dynamics at hand. Two associations, Better Life and the organization in Aswan, faced internal organizational issues as the Ministry of Social Solidarity encroached on them, and as a consequence, they too left the NWRO. In effect, by 2009, all of the original six NGO leaders had left with the exception of CEWLA.

The new organizations brought in between 2006 and 2009 were the Association for Women and Development in Alexandria, Association for Women and Society, Badr Community Development Association for Comprehensive Development (BADR), CARE–Egypt, Coptic Evangelical Organization for Social Services, Egyptian Association for Community Participation Enhancement, Egyptian Association for Comprehensive Development, Egyptian Association for Family, Egyptian Association for Family Development, and the Society for Sinai Women's Rights. By 2009, there were eleven organizations in total. The profile of the organizations had changed drastically; there was a significantly higher representation from nonfeminist developmental organizations. Moreover, with the change in the group's composition, they decided to work on a new issue and arrived at family law for Muslims. The accompanying change in the collective entity's name sheds light on the evolving nature of its identity and intragroup relationships. When the group started in 2005, they referred to their collective body as a "coalition"; this was later replaced by "women's rights network."

*Projectivized Activism*

The word "project" neatly categorizes the initiative as a development intervention. In contrast, even though the CEDAW Coalition received support from a variety of donors, none of the interviewed members of the coalition, even those who pulled out and were critical of it, referred to it by the name of a donor.

The objective of the coalition/network changed twice. The objective formally announced at the coalition's inception was "building a strong network and changing the Personal Status Law."[4] Yousry Mustapha jok-ingly added, "of course, whoever put this as an objective must have been a foreigner" (interview by author, July 2010). Certainly, in light of the con-troversy over the Personal Status Law and the complexity of the actors involved, it is unlikely that the work of any civil society initiative would singlehandedly change the law.

There were challenges to arriving at a consensus among NGO activists and practitioners from very different backgrounds and ideological stand-points on a highly contentious and deeply divisive issue such as the revi-sion of the Personal Status Law. The group was neither homogeneous (e.g., they are not all feminists) nor did they have the same frame of reference (e.g., human rights). Hence, the process of arriving at the lowest common denominator was long and exhaustive. This diversity, however, would not have served as a hindrance had they formed organically and had there been a more legitimate leadership process.

The fact that they chose an issue that was not winnable or politically opportune was problematic on another front: an inability to make inroads would also affect group morale and mobilization. Therefore, instead of proposing an alternative or reformed Personal Status Law, the members of NWRO chose to work on a document that was politically less contentious and required a far more modest level of consensus building. The process of arriving at the Legal Guide shows the extent to which the choice of

---

4. The Personal Status Law has been at the center of the feminist struggle since 1929. Key issues with this law include men's unrestricted right to marry up to four wives, a father's almost unilateral guardianship over his children, and unequal rights to initiate divorce. The first Personal Status Law (Law 91 of 2000) was issued in 1920. Almost a cen-tury later and yet the core of this highly patriarchal legislation remains in force despite amendments in 1976, 1980, 1985, 2000, and 2004. The most recent reforms include the promulgation of Law 1 of 2000, which grants women the right to unilateral divorce (*khul'*) on the condition that they forgo their financial rights. Law 10, promulgated in 2004, allowed for the establishment of family courts that granted personal status lawsuits more privacy, secured more judges to deal with the backlog of cases, and provided more opportunities for mediation and conflict resolution. These changes have been introduced in a top-down manner.

issue and lack of collective ownership posed challenges for the creation of a coalition.

One of the highly divisive issues that arose in discussions about the Legal Guide was the question of obedience: whether wives' obedience to husbands should be removed from the existing law. Feminist-leaning members argued that it must; the idea of women being required to obey their husbands was the premise for instituting gender hierarchy in personal relations and ran counter to the idea of gender equality. Others, wanting to adopt a more pragmatic approach, said that if wives' obedience to husbands was removed from the law, their entitlement to alimony may be threatened because alimony is tied to evidence of the violation of the marriage contract on the part of the husband (i.e., a contract based on financial support in return for obedience).

Another highly controversial issue was the idea of joint ownership of wealth; in other words, if divorce occurs, a wife would be entitled to half the wealth that was accumulated since marriage. Many members were in opposition, arguing that such a measure would again put the principle of men's financial obligations to women at risk. Polygamy was also a hotly contested topic. Some members said that the practice should be left alone because it derives from Islam. Others argued that more enlightened readings of Islamic text suggest that polygamy is in fact conditional and not an unreserved or unconditional entitlement. In the end, they agreed to propose the idea of joint wealth, to call for the removal of the word "obedience," and to make polygamy permissible only through approval by a judge (currently men can marry without any restrictions). Despite the negotiations over wording, what to incorporate, and what to exclude, the Legal Guide represented the "lowest common denominator" of agreement. Although it had the official approval of all organizations, informally, several members confided that they disagreed with some of the content.

When the Legal Guide was publicized in a press conference at the press syndicate in 2010, it did not generate any significant ripple effect. It was released without a timely political event, phase, or opportunity, which may have diminished its importance. The government had been clear that no legislative reform on controversial issues was going to be discussed in parliament in the near future, which made the release of the Legal Guide somewhat moot. Members defended it as a platform for encouraging different stakeholders to create an enabling environment for positive change when the occasion arises for its discussion in parliament.

But the Legal Guide did not bear the same weight as a draft law. "What can people do with a set of guidelines?" a journalist asked at the press event. The idea put forward by network members was that the publication of the Legal Guide (*Daleel al qanouny*) would prompt the government to share its proposed legislative amendments, yet privately many confided that they found it unconvincing that after more than two years of work on this issue, a set of guidelines is all they had to show for it.

## Conclusion

Although the two case studies of Karama–Egypt and NWRO point to donor policy failures, I am not suggesting that any coalition or movement is bound to fail if donors are involved. After all, the CEDAW Coalition was the birth child of UNICEF and the FGM Taskforce had selectively worked with donors. Much of the coalitional work in nearby countries like Jordan also relied on donor funding at their inception (Tadros 2011c). What makes or breaks a coalition is not whether an external actor or donor is involved, but the nature of the role the donor plays. Three key elements of Karama–Egypt and NWRO's practices undermined their prospects of success: leadership that lacked legitimacy, the absence of local ownership, and projectivized approaches to fostering collective action.

In the case of the CEDAW Coalition, the donor responded to an organic need within the community by creating the space for people to come together to deliberate, engage, and coalesce around common concerns. The process of arriving at a common agenda with clear parameters was a slow, long, and arduous one. UNICEF did not select the participant NGOs; all were invited to take part and those that were interested stayed. In both Karama–Egypt and NWRO, an external actor (Hibaaq Osman and GIZ, respectively) selected the members of the coalition. In light of the importance of social repertoires for forging the glue that helps people work together (see chapter 6), this choice undermined prospects of people naturally and organically coalescing into a collective body.

It is also noteworthy that in Karama–Egypt there were no opportunities for institutionalizing legitimate leadership through processes of collective negotiation about how the initiative would be led and run (as per interviews). Emerging from the research is the need for particularly high levels of sensitivity on the part of donors to their positionality (an awareness of how they are perceived by others) and how it affects local ownership. In the case of Karama–Egypt, the approach to the issue was externally imposed (the instrumental approach of the cost of violence against women), and in the case of NWRO, people were brought together to identify the issue, rather than the other way around. Moreover, as a consequence of the donor assuming a central role in running the collective entity, processes of institutionalizing horizontal accountability (i.e., leading members being accountable to each other) were undermined. In the case of NWRO, there was a consensus among all of the participants interviewed that Yousry Moustapha expended tremendous efforts to institutionalize mechanisms for decision-making that made members feel accountable to each other. As for Karama–Egypt, interviewees noted that there were no such prospects, as all forms of accountability were vertically directed toward the founder.

The projectivization of collective action, from conception to monitoring and evaluation, created pseudocollective actors. Before convening meetings to bring people together as part of the CEDAW Coalition, Fatma Khafagy sought permission from the UNICEF hierarchy to divert from the project implementation approach because she was conscious that it would kill prospects of collective action (see chapter 3). In a projectivized approach, collective initiatives are expected to fit within logical frameworks. As Batliwala and Pittman (2010, 23) contend, the logical framework relies "extensively on program implementation in stable organizational settings with well-defined planning structures. However, many development settings are not stable and organizations work in complex and radically shifting environments that do not allow for implementation as planned." Batliwala and Pittman (2010, 24) note the difficult of fitting the long and nonlinear processes of building collective action into logical frameworks because "the focus on activities and outcomes instead of actors limits understanding of the processes and people involved in change and does not account for power relations and individuals' voices."

A projectivized approach not only jeopardizes the emergence of collective entities, but also their sustenance and growth. In the CEDAW Coalition, monitoring and evaluation mechanisms meant that the organization that receives funding on behalf of the other actors was only accountable to the donor (the European Union) and not to the other partners. In the case of Karama–Egypt, at the time of the research, it was clear that the organization was treated by the donor as a project with deliverables as opposed to a collective entity involving mutual accountabilities between actors. This is symptomatic of the broader practice of monitoring and evaluation. Batliwala and Pittman (2010, 10) note that the existing monitoring and evaluation tools were not designed for tracking collective action or their impacts, because they were developed with individual projects in mind.

Collective action lite bears several threats to feminist and gender justice activism. The most obvious is the nonsustainable nature of these initiatives. However, the greater negativity incurred from collective action lite is that it gives the external, false impression of a successful form of collective action. It renders an image of pseudocollectivism in which citizens are mobilizing, power structures are being contested, and positive change is being elicited, when in fact none of these actions have occurred. It deepens the disconnect between what Western policymakers and donors think is happening in civil society and what is actually happening on the ground. This disjuncture in turn provides very few opportunities for contesting the donor structures that have perpetuated this pseudoform of collective action in the first place.

During the 1990s, the era in which the CEDAW Coalition emerged, development-oriented NGOs and women's associations had not yet become so steeped in Western funding. Therefore, the professionalized culture in which activists expect donors to pay for the execution of all activities was not so entrenched. After a decade of foreign-funded activism in Egypt, the NGO culture had changed dramatically. A technocratic approach to civil work had already set in. Some Karama–Egypt interviewees who had left the initiative complained bitterly that the lavish meetings that Karama–Egypt held at the Four Seasons Hotel were a form of excess that gave the initiative a professionalized, glossy feel. And in the case of NWRO, running a collective from a donor office is a constant reminder of its genealogy.

It is true that state repression made building a volunteer base extremely difficult (as I have argued in chapter 2). However, alternative modes of engaging existed, even under the oppressive shadows of the government, and these did not suffer from the same ills as those associated with collective action lite. As mentioned in chapter 2, women citizens were already mobilizing under different banners: Islamist, worker, and democracy movements. Less visible, looser networks of youth-led platforms for expressing dissatisfaction with the status quo were finding an alternative space to mobilize constituencies (electronically via online media). The success of the Tunisian people in ousting Ben Ali in 2010 and the open call for protests on January 25, 2011, had a centripetal effect on drawing various movements, political parties, and forces together (see Ezbawy 2012 for an overview of these movements and their mobilizational strategies on January 25, 2011).

In stark contrast to the struggle for women to engage politically during Mubarak's reign, the Egyptian revolution of 2011 unleashed the energies of thousands of women and men who organized collectively into coalitions, movements, and parties and who participated as citizens in broad-based collective action such as protests, marches, and demonstrations. In that new order, collective action lite modalities of organizing became marginal and insignificant compared with how citizens chose to engage politically. Women and men began to organize organically, forming their own initiatives and coalitions around their own agendas, rather than being systemically inserted into an existing gender and development framework like that established by the two internationally sponsored actors examined in this chapter.

# 6

## THE MORNING AFTER MUBARAK'S OUSTER

After eighteen days of sustained citizen protests in the public squares of several cities and towns, President Hosni Mubarak was ousted on February 11, 2011. This was followed by nationwide celebrations of what became dubbed the January 25th revolution. The youth revolutionary forces and several political parties initially welcomed the interim governance role of the SCAF. However, when they realized the SCAF was dragging its feet on the handover of power to civilian rule and was cementing an entente with the Muslim Brotherhood to facilitate the Brotherhood's ascendency to power, the youth revolutionaries announced that the revolution was ongoing and that the struggle persisted under the new mantra, "Down, down with the military rule!" The country was gripped with revolutionary fervor. The floodgates opened, releasing citizen agency of a scale unparalleled in almost one hundred years, perhaps since the 1919 wave of citizen resistance against British occupation.

Reflecting on the wave of revolts that gripped the Arab world, Professor Rada Ivekovic wrote on March 8, 2011, that the protesters in Egypt, like those in Tunisia, Bahrain, and Algeria, were inclusive, representing all sections of society, and "their ethos is admirably unprejudiced, courageous and unflinching—a historic instance of politicisation in the best sense." Ivekovic noted that the protesters had benefited from fluid structures and the absence of traditional influences such as those of the religious hierarchy and political party leadership.

This iconic image of inclusiveness, egalitarianism, and rejection of all that is reactionary, exclusionary, and oppressive was ironically put to the test in Egypt on the same day in which Ivekovic's article appeared on *Open-Democracy*. A group of feminists took to Tahrir Square on March 8th on occasion of International Women's Day to remind Egyptians not to forget women's rights. Hania Sholkamy, a reputed professor of anthropology who participated in the march, provided an account of the day's events and pointed out that even though almost everyone had set up a booth or taken a corner in Tahrir Square to press for their entitlements, the only group that became the target of harassment, ridicule, and assault were the feminists. "No other demonstrators were heckled, told that their demands are unjustified, unnecessary, a threat to the gains of the revolution, out of time, out of place and/or the product of a 'foreign agenda'! No other demonstrators were told to 'go back home and to the kitchen'! No others were heckled for how they looked and what they were wearing" (Sholkamy 2011).

Hoda Elsadda, a distinguished professor of English literature, committed feminist, and deputy head of the left-of-center Egyptian Democratic Party, provides a similar account of what went wrong for women activists. According to Elsadda (2011), people reflected that the moment was not timely (Egypt was still in the middle of chaos); it was naive to assume that patriarchy would be dismantled with the demise of Mubarak; insufficient attention had been paid to the mobilization of the masses; and the attacks were organized by counterrevolutionary forces with the intention of intimidating women into forgoing public activism. She also notes an important factor overlooked at the time that would taint women's rights work for years to come: the association of gender equality with the first lady and her national machinery, the National Council for Women. As noted in chapter 2, the NCW assumed the role of representing women, and through its leadership by the first lady, it became associated with authoritarian, top-down imposition of a corrupt agenda.

Nehad Abou el Komsan, the director of the Egyptian Center for Women's Rights, openly castigated the revolutionary forces for not lifting a finger to show support, even though they shared the same square—one associated with a revolutionary struggle for liberation. "The youth revolutionaries were not convinced with the idea that women's demands constitute a genuine part of [fulfilling the demands of] the revolution," said el Komsan during a 2012 interview.

Undoubtedly, the number of women activists who congregated in Tahrir Square was very small (estimated at less than 100). Few of the youth revolutionaries, women or men, had joined them. A leading female revolutionary and psychiatrist recalled that day's events during an interview in March 2012. She was already in the vicinity because she was taking part in a sit-in organized by the youth revolutionary forces to express their opposition to SCAF rule. She said that neither she nor any of her friends thought for a minute of joining the women's event. In fact, she found the March 8th protest "provocative": "I told them this was not the time for it, and you will find that many of the women who participated in the revolution did not join them, few of them were there, most of those who participated were feminist organizations and a few of the older women leaders." From her perspective, this was not the time for making feminist or any other demands because first the slate needed to be wiped clean. "You must bring down first [what is of the past] and then afterwards you make your demands. . . . We all have demands, whether women, Copts, Nubians . . . and people should take to the streets with them so that we write our own constitution and so that we build our country without marginalization but back then the time was not right."

Paul Amar's (2013) analysis of what went wrong is similar but not the same. He too believes that the feminist identity underpinning the march was to blame, not because the concerns for gender equality had to wait, but because they did not intersect with the other political platforms around which people were mobilizing. The framing and points of reference did not emanate from an organic feminist trajectory, but rather from international feminism.

The revolutionary and psychiatrist quoted above believes that the march failed in part because participants were inept young women who had no prior experience of engaging in public activism nor had they participated in the revolutionary struggle to overthrow Mubarak. Another feminist activist shared the same views, commenting in an interview that some of the privileged, upper-middle-class women students of gender studies were talking at people in a way that made them stick out. This miscommunication was partly due to the lack of class politics in essentialist feminist discourses, debates, and narratives.

The level of animosity toward the women protesters, which reached the point of them being spat on and violently attacked, stemmed from disdain and possible misogyny toward the very idea of women's rights. But that was not the full story. Public engagement with passersby who simply may not have understood why protesters were raising the women's rights banner did not help to win new converts. According to the same feminist activist, some women held banners that said "down with patriarchy," which, when translated to Arabic, makes it sound as if they were protesting against the authority of their parents. The use of gender jargon that neither touches hearts nor minds is symptomatic of the wider phenomenon of talking at people (almost as if at a research conference) rather than opening genuine lines of communication.

The failure of the March 2011 march/protest has been widely covered in scholarly narratives of the revolution (Amar 2013; Hafez 2014; Singerman 2013), possibly because it is the first explicitly feminist encounter with the January revolution. The incident is a critical part of understanding that particular juncture in history. It was the first signal of a backlash against women's rights in a post-Mubarak Egypt that challenged in a fundamental and groundbreaking way the narrative of men and women united in a struggle for social justice. In essence, it also had strong elements of what Deniz Kandiyoti (2013) astutely called "masculinist restoration": when manifestations of patriarchy instability become particularly threatening to the status quo. The March 2011 protest brought to the fore the crisis in the revolutionary pathway to achieving democracy, highlighting a polarization between those who believe in democracy first, equality for citizens later, and those who insist that all forms of emancipation are intertwined. It exposed the weaknesses of feminist engagement in civil society: the questions of whether women's rights should be camouflaged in a populist discourse or explicitly feminist, and whether broad alliances can be forged or the visions should remain apart. Finally, March 2011 marked the public resurgence of the deeply entrenched Islamist movements and demonstrated their key role in the gender backlash.

The post-Mubarak era changed the landscape of the actors influencing the new political and gender agendas, and it brought new opportunities as well as challenges for collective action for greater gender equality. It was an extraordinarily dynamic environment in which contradictory phenomena unfolded side by side. In the first part of this chapter, I focus on the nonstate actors and their agendas immediately after the rupture. I then explore the different power configurations, how they informed collective action, and what factors enabled and constrained alliance-making among different stakeholders.

### Youth Revolutionary Movements

One of the recurring themes of transition experiences is the importance of participation of women in political movements. "It is through their participation in these movements that women and women's groups have been able to stake a claim to equal representation in political life and institutions" (Rai 2000, 4–5).

Ezbawy's (2012) panoramic overview of the different groups that emerged around the time of the January 25th revolution shows a plurality of movements and initiatives. There are two important characteristics of all of these movements. First, many emerged and evaporated within very short spaces of time. In other words, they were of a transient, temporal nature. Second, there was a repertoire of politically active youth who held multiple memberships in several collective initiatives simultaneously, and they sometimes moved from one to another depending on the political moment (a little bit like musical chairs, but the music they respond to is the political contingency).

Members and activists in many of these revolutionary movements also tended to act simultaneously like bees (cross-fertilization of initiatives) and butterflies (moving from one initiative to another). Women comprised a significant proportion of their founders, members, and supporters, and they took part in the protests, sit-ins, marches, and bloody confrontations with the police. In fact, according to one of the leading women revolutionary figures, women participated in disproportionately higher numbers than men in the 2012 protests that challenged SCAF rule. It is important to examine the interface between the agential and structural dynamics at work at these particular junctures to understand why participation did not translate into power sharing. Few women revolutionary leaders emerged in the aftermath of the January revolution.

Some of the movements that existed before January 2011 continued after the revolution (e.g., Kefaya!); others reconfigured into new platforms.

A significant entity to emerge from the pre-existence of former movements was Etelaf Shabab el Thawra (Coalition of Youth of the Revolution). The coalition comprised the April 6th movement, ElBaradei's campaign, the Muslim Brotherhood youth, Karama Party, Tagamu Party, and the Youth for Justice and Freedom leftist movement. Of sixteen representatives of various movements that composed the leadership of the coalition, only one was a woman.

Here I assess the emerging disjunctions between informal leadership and activism on the one hand, and representation, power sharing, and formal leadership on the other, by examining the political trajectories of three leading women revolutionaries: Israa Abd el Fattah, Samira Ibrahim, and a woman who prefers to be unnamed.

Israa Abd el Fattah is one of the most acclaimed figures associated with the January revolution, though she is perhaps most renowned for her role in outmaneuvering the secret police state of Mubarak and bringing greater Cairo to a standstill on April 6, 2008. She supported the revolutionaries' call for a general strike on April 6th. When the security apparatus became aware of the intended strike, they issued harsh warnings of dire consequences for those who took to the street. El Fattah quickly turned the instrument of contention from protest to subversion. She used social media to reach out to large sections of the targeted population with a simple message: show your support by staying at home. It worked. The squares and streets of greater Cairo (i.e., beyond the city center) were empty on April 6th. She was arrested on the same day and detained for eighteen days, though she was treated well by the authorities, who were keen to avoid an international scandal. The April 6th movement emerged out of the success of shaking the state on that day, but el Fattah is keen to emphasize that she was never a member of the movement and had always been independent. Although she did have two short experiments in joining political parties during Mubarak's reign and its aftermath, she concluded on both occasions that political parties do not enjoy sufficient autonomy to allow them to pursue the kind of politics in which she believed.

As el Fattah's experience demonstrates, the gender bias in the political system, in addition to agential factors, has blocked revolutionary women's recourse to formal political representation. One of the other leading women revolutionaries worth mentioning in this context is a psychiatrist who had many roles at the time, including being a steering committee member of several youth-led initiatives. She notes that women played leadership roles in organizing and mobilizing around the January 25th revolution, "but they are not visible in the media because this is a patriarchal society, be it liberal or leftist or Islamist, it makes no difference, they don't put women in positions of representation" (interview by Mohamed Hussein, March 2012). She herself was the only woman of the sixteen representatives that led the Coalition of the Youth of the Revolution. "It was a two-for-one deal," she joked, in reference to her identity as both a Christian and a woman.

Though many revolutionary women and activists were gender blind in their analysis of the revolutionary rupture and emphasized that men and women stood on par, behind the scenes is a different story. The psychiatrist, for example, noted in a 2012 interview that "women do all the legwork and then the men get shoved forwards to claim all the credit." She said that "they always relegate women to admin roles that involve organizational work while they claim the decision-making roles," and she challenged the justification that they were given, namely that men have superior competences in these areas. Research has shown that even among social movements with the most egalitarian goals, gender power hierarchies prevail (Horn 2013; Kretschmer and Meyer 2013). Kretschmer and Meyer (2013, 397) note that even among movements that express the most egalitarian ideologies, such as the American civil rights movement and the antidraft movement during the Vietnam War, women participated in significant numbers but were sidelined from leadership positions dominated by men.

Nehad Abou el Komsan went further in a March 2012 interview, arguing that not only were the youth revolutionaries gender blind, they were gender insensitive. She pointed out that meetings were sometimes held at very late hours of the night (and ended at dawn), and the lack of safety on the streets meant that many women could not attend or had to excuse themselves at some point, therefore missing out on the final decisions. She also noted that sometimes meetings were held at coffee shops that were not women-friendly places. These logistics did influence access to and partici-pation in decision-making processes and outcomes.

In addition to these internal institutional factors, there was also an increasingly hostile political environment in which the SCAF launched a campaign to tarnish the image of the youth revolutionaries. At its height the SCAF publicly accused them of being trained in Serbia and receiving foreign funding for their activities. However, even the vilification cam-paign was gendered: in the words of the psychiatrist interviewed, "men get accused of receiving foreign funding; women are presented as if they have loose morals." She herself was on the receiving end of an attempt to undermine her image. Shortly after the confrontations in front of Magles el Wozarah in November 2011, in which she and another male revolution-ary appeared on television and testified to being beaten by the authorities, their enemies produced a video suggesting that she had an illicit relation-ship with him and had aborted an illegitimate child. She recounted that she was very upset and wondered how her conservative, upper Egyptian family would react to this widely circulated video. They supported her, but for days on end she was quite shaken.

The third activist, Samira Ibrahim, is a powerful revolutionary figure who was not politically represented in any formal capacity. She became iconic of the Egyptian woman's struggle against military rule; her image was splashed in graffiti all over the walls of Cairo in 2011/2012 and repro-duced in feminist posters against SCAF rule. Though she was involved in the revolutionary struggle for many years, she is perhaps most renowned for speaking out against the virginity tests that she and seven others were subjected to at the hands of an army doctor (Abouelnaga 2015).

To check whether they were virgins, a male military doctor had arrested, physically assaulted, and stripped Ibrahim and several other female activists, and then examined them in a sexually violent way. As painful and humiliating as this was, rather than remaining silent, Ibrahim spoke out, shaming the SCAF. She was supported by international and local human rights organizations and, after losing the military trial, her case against the military is now being examined by the African Commission on

Human and Peoples' Rights.[1] What is striking about Ibrahim's case is its demonstration of the ability of women youth revolutionaries to overcome cultural taboos and inhibitions through powerful leadership. Samira Ibrahim comes from Sohag, one of the poorest and socially, economically, and politically excluded governorates of upper Egypt. The youth revolutionary movements were among her strongest supporters, using graffiti, portraits, and slogans on the streets of Egypt in ways that made her a symbol of resistance. The power dynamics behind her elevation to heroine status are important because they turned the concept of honor (and therefore shame) from being associated with a woman's intimate parts to one of dishonoring the army. In effect, Ibrahim's case challenged the notion of the sacrosanct army being beyond reproach. It also challenged conceptions of middle-class respectability in which women's agency is circumscribed by the notion of her responsibility to protect her body from being touched under all circumstances.

As Ibrahim's story and her involvement with the youth revolutionaries demonstrates, movements are dynamic, transformative, and are transformed themselves by changing political circumstances. A pattern of systematic assault on women emerged in late 2011, and many young men began to organize with women in initiatives to counter the discourses and practices that perpetrate assault on women's bodily integrity in public space (see chapter 8).

## Feminist Collective Organizing

Many leaders of feminist NGOs, initiatives, and coalitions participated in the eighteen days of revolts against President Mubarak and continued to participate in public action in their aftermath. How they situate themselves in narratives of the revolution differs. Some see their long history of contesting the regime has part and parcel of the struggle that led to the ousting of Mubarak. Others believe that the revolution is a wake-up call that challenges them to act and engage differently. The revolution meant

---

1. For details of this case see http://www.redress.org/case-docket/samira-ibrahim-and-rasha-abdel-rahman-v-egypt-.

that, on all fronts, civil society organizations could not pursue business as usual. There was a sense of complete ambiguity regarding the new power configurations. Organizations had to determine who makes the decisions, what parties influence such processes, and the identities and agenda of the new elite ruling Egypt. In light of the changing political reality, organizations needed to rethink their allies and enemies and determine how much of the old rules and institutional setups had really changed with the ousting of Mubarak. These were not only philosophical questions about their raison d'être but also practical ones. Does the state security investigations apparatus still govern? Is the National Council for Women still the main governmental body through which demands to policymakers are to be mediated? How does one engage with the growing power of the Islamists in society and politics? How are organizations going to be more open and responsive to youth engagement? The generational gap in leadership of civil society organizations, be they feminist or otherwise, has been one of the factors repelling youth from engaging with these entities and causing them to either establish their own groups or seek alternative, informal platforms for collective public action (see Abd el Wahab 2012).

One of the first measures that several feminist organizations took was to assume a more overtly political stance. They started engaging more directly with citizens in helping them claim their rights, and they mobilized more openly against the SCAF, whom they believed had hijacked the revolution. However, nothing less than a major overhaul of feminist organizations was in order if they were to seize the revolutionary moment. What was needed was a transformation in internal hierarchies: the way they work, communicate, and build relations. At the time, the same recipe of issuing policy statements, writing press releases, and holding conferences mostly attended by the converted was what formed the staple elements of their work.

One of the first measures that many feminist organizations took was to form new institutional umbrellas that would serve as new platforms for collective action. Previously established ones such as the NWRO and the CEDAW Coalition did not die, but they became derelict as women activists chose to channel their energies through new platforms. Several new feminist platforms appeared:

1. The coalition of Egyptian Feminist Organizations (Tahalof al Mou-nazamat al Nissaweyah) comprised seventeen organizations, the majority of which were the same organizations from the original NWRO.

2. The Egyptian Feminist Union (Itehad Nissa' Misr) was established in 2011 and led by CEO Hoda Badran, who is also the CEO of the Arab Solidarity Women Union. The EFU includes members from more than 100 smaller NGOs across the country; its idea is to revive the first-ever feminist organization, Huda Sha'rawi, which was established in 1928.

3. The Egyptian Women's Union (Etehad el Nissa' Al Misry) was established in 2011 and led by the pioneering feminist writer and physician Nawal al Saadawi. Al Saadawi was active in the revolution, and although she is a controversial figure, she has greatly affected the emergence of a feminist conscience in Egypt and the wider region.

4. The raison d'être of Egypt's Revolutionary Women's Coalition was to counter the exclusion of revolutionary women from decision-making power and representation in the newly formed youth collective fronts. The EWRC was founded by Dina Aboulsoud and played a role in pressing such organizations as the Coalition of the Youth of the Revolution to incorporate women in their leadership. Many of the members of the EWRC were young activists.

Some of these coalitions reproduced the same personalization of institutions that gripped the NGOs: they became known for the involvement of a particular person. The retention of this prerevolutionary style of leadership only perpetuates the practice of working in silos, making it difficult for people to invest in long-term initiatives to which they cannot attribute any success under the organizational umbrella.

All four of these coalitions have very similar missions, though the EFU has the most member NGOs, and the EWU's members comprise more individuals than organizations. The key question is whether the proliferation of these coalitions enriched the political scene or whether it reproduced the same fragmentation that existed before the downfall of Mubarak. Some of these platforms almost entirely relied on the repertoire of relations between individuals and organizations that existed before the revolution and that represent distinct clique circles. In that respect the landscape of feminist activism had not changed much in terms of leadership, followers, and alliance-building patterns. Even some of the feminist organizations established before the Egyptian revolution, which were proudly led by younger people, reproduced similar patterns associated with the absence of rotation of power and the prima donna syndrome at the leadership level. It is therefore not surprising that some feminist organizations prefer not to work via coalitions and collective platforms except if it involves a time- and space-bound campaign. Rabha Fathi, head of the Association of Egyptian Female Lawyers, believes that the reason why collective action has failed in Egypt is because everyone wants to be "the big boss" (interview by Mohamed Hussein, March 2012; although the interview was conducted in Arabic, Fathi used this expression in English). She argues that individual organizations working on their own can sometimes achieve far more because they save time that collectives otherwise spend on in-fighting, endless meetings, and power struggles.

However, as I describe in the next chapter, the institutional environment in which feminists mobilized was so harsh that unless strong collective fronts were forged, claims-making by any single organization would fall on deaf ears. Challenges also came from within civil society: the Muslim Brotherhood, one of the key contenders in shaping the new gender agenda in Egypt, enjoyed strong leadership, internal cohesion, and unity among its ranks.

**Islamist Countermovements**

As noted in previous chapters, the Islamist movements consistently blocked attempts to challenge gender hierarchies in state policies and legislations during Mubarak's era, though they were contained by the red lines set for them by the state security investigations apparatus. Like other Egyptian women, the Muslim Sisters participated in the January revolution, albeit a few days later, beginning on January 28. Although many women leaders in the Muslim Brotherhood have great rhetorical skills and decades of experience in talking to ordinary citizens on the ground, none of the Muslim Brotherhood figures who became associated with the political movement's participation in the revolution were women.

This lack of female representation indicates a significant gap in knowledge about Muslim Brotherhood women's agency during the uprisings and in the *millioniyyas* that followed the demise of Mubarak. It may also reflect the Brotherhood's preference for delegating leadership positions to women who are older or whose children have grown, rather than to young, unmarried women or those with children (the bias against young female leadership is shared by non-Islamist groups).

There are several questions pertinent to understanding the agency of the Muslim Sisters after the revolution. Did the removal of the shackles of repression and the sisters' political involvement in the revolution change their position within the Muslim Brotherhood's internal hierarchy? Did the new configuration of power in Egypt open up new opportunities for exercising political agency in public space? Did they contest the gender agenda as a consequence of their own political empowerment? With whom did they create alliances and coalitions? Here I respond to each question separately.

*Taking the Revolt from Tahrir to the Tanzeem*

There is evidence that many female members of the Muslim Brotherhood began to openly voice their desire for a greater recognition of their leadership. At a Muslim Brotherhood youth meeting of approximately 1,500 members in April 2011, issues around the movement's organizational structures were raised, including the necessity of establishing a structure for the Sisters of the Brotherhood. Shortly after, on July 2, they held a conference with the specific theme of "women from the revolution to renaissance." Supreme Guide Bad'ie, Deputy Guide Khayrat al Shatter, members of the Guidance Bureau, key actors, and some 2,500 sisters attended this high-level conference. Bad'ie praised the roles played by women in the revolution as activists, mothers, sisters, and wives of the protesters, and he paid particular tribute to the mothers of martyrs. The conference was a grand event but did not offer any major structural change either in relation to broadening their roles or to their positioning in the Muslim Brotherhood's internal organizational hierarchy. The discourse could have easily been that of the brotherhood in Mubarak's Egypt. The conference recommendations spoke of enhancing women's political representation in syndicates, political parties, and activism through NGOs and of raising women's awareness of the conspiracies aimed at undermining the family (presumably that of international actors and local feminist organizations).

However, the internal mobilization for women to assume leadership within the hierarchy of the Muslim Brotherhood did not change in any concrete way. The invisibility of the Muslim Sisters within the formal decision-making apparatus of the movement continued. Contrary to some scholars' expectations that once the shackles of Mubarak's authoritarian rule were removed, the Muslim Sisters would gain their rightful place within the Muslim Brothers' internal hierarchy (Abdel-Latif 2008), this did not materialize. There are no women members of the Shura Council or the Guidance Bureau of the Muslim Brotherhood. Some young women members, empowered by the experience of participating in the Egyptian revolution and realizing afterward that there were few opportunities for influence within the Brotherhood, were compelled to leave.

Another important element of the Muslim Brotherhood's experience is that their renaissance was short-lived, lasting only three years before their leadership was ousted and they were subjected to an intense crackdown (see chapter 10). Hence, it is not possible to test the hypothesis that had they continued to be in power for decades, the pressure on them to internally reform would have increased. Within the short period in which they rose to power, an organizational transformation did not occur because the old guard continued to retain power and were resistant to changing the hierarchy of the Muslim Brotherhood.

*New Opportunities for Political Agency*

After the Egyptian revolution, the Muslim Sisters seized the newly opened political spaces to engage fully in the social, political, and economic life of the nation. Although the Brotherhood's power structure remained impenetrable for women, there were more spaces for their participation and assumption of formal leadership roles in the political arm of the Brotherhood, the Freedom and Justice Party (as founders, leaders, and members of several committees). They also won seats in parliament, and after the Muslim Brotherhood won the presidency, they were delegated to several political positions in government. The political party in effect opened opportunities that were blocked within the internal party structure. However, none of the young, revolutionary Muslim Sisters occupied such positions, which were typically retained by the older generation (see chapter 7).

The political agency of Islamist women flourished. They participated in *millioniyyas* organized by the Islamists and played a key organizational role with respect to women (who tended to be segregated from the men). They had extensive and expansive skills in outreach and constituency building, which they had established through years of welfare provision from charitable organizations and through building bridges with women in universities and educational institutes. In 2011, against the backdrop of a new political climate that allowed them to engage in formal political spaces, the Muslim Sisters played an instrumental role in transforming the social base into a political constituency. For example, each year on Mother's Day, every Egyptian province celebrates a woman deemed to be a "model mother." Nehad Abou el Komsan, director of the Egyptian Center for Women's Rights, said that in her governorate, Giza, women activists from the Freedom and Justice Party paid a visit to this model mother, gave her a Qur'an, and invited her to become a member of the party (Nehad Abou el Komsan, interview by Mohamed Hussein, March 2012).

*Reclaimed Citizenship and the Gender Agenda*

It is difficult to fathom whether the removal of authoritarian repression, the flourishing of the movement, and the successes of the leading women members of the Muslim Brotherhood propelled an internal revision of the interpretation of jurisprudence and the Brotherhoods' doctrine on gender issues. There are many factors that may have hindered such a process. The leading (and most visible) women of the Muslim Brotherhood tended to be from the old guard and of the older, more conservative generation (though of course there are exceptions). Hence it is unlikely that they would have formed a collective to rethink the agenda that they themselves have championed for many decades. In addition, there has always been a kind of comfortable disconnect between proclaimed ideological and policy positions and personal and professional trajectories, which has in effect created maneuvering space without rocking the boat.

Some of the most powerful women to have assumed key leadership positions in public life were (at the time I interviewed them) the fiercest advocates of women's primary responsibilities being in the household. If the Muslim Sisters had gained some level of institutional autonomy from the Muslim Brothers, they may have had the space to develop their own interpretations on matters of jurisprudence; however, the hierarchal hold remained rigid, leaving little room for thinking outside the box. Many of these women had been politically engaged for years in international fora through the International Islamic Committee for Woman and Child, through which they championed their agenda on women, children, and families. With the new political openings available to influence national agendas, they were eager to show their party and movement that they could make strides toward revoking the old regime's gender policies. As I will show in the next two chapters, the sisters of the Muslim Brotherhood became the most vocal champions of reversing gains made in expanding women's choices in terms of family law and bodily integrity.

*Ideological and Political Alignments*

As far as individual women in the Muslim Brotherhood, there is diversity in perspectives and personal trajectories as in any movement. To understand the political choices of the Muslim Sisters, it is important to first understand them as members of the Muslim Brothers and not as leaders in a parallel, autonomous movement of religious women. Their prospects of building coalitions and alliances with other women's groups must be understood through that prism. In an international policy-making arena such as the United Nations, the Muslim Sisters find that alliance building with American right-wing evangelical Christians makes more sense than aligning with Egyptian delegates from the CEDAW Coalition (see chapter 4).

On a national level, the opportunities for joint work (even if transient) have been more viable between members of the Muslim Sisters and their Salafi counterparts than among the revolutionary women or the women activists working for NGOs, coalitions, or non-Islamist political parties. Non-Islamist feminist actors who wish to partner with the Muslim Sisters to benefit from the latter's constituency should be reminded that the

Muslim Sisters view their agency as promoting a higher good—the establishment of an Islamic state—and not for the sake of achieving their full potential as individual women. In terms of ideological disposition and overall goals, the points of convergence between the Muslim Sisters and the female members of the Salafi movement are likely to be far greater in number than those between them and the feminist movements.

After the January 25th revolution, the political and security restraints were removed, allowing Islamist movements to flourish. A number of Islamist movements appeared publicly and chose to engage politically: the Muslim Brotherhood, the Salafis (who until then had chosen to adhere to a strictly *da'wa* role), the Gama'at Islamiyya, and several militant groups who set up base in Sinai. The previous electoral law, which had prohibited the establishment of political parties of a religious nature during Mubarak's reign, was replaced with another law in which the interpretation of "religious nature" was more relaxed. The Muslim Brotherhood established the Freedom and Justice Party, the Salafis established the Al-Nour Party, and the Gama'at Islamiyya established the Construction and Development Party. Hence, the role of Islamist groups in Egypt was amplified as they claimed a formal role in politics via political parties and expanded their informal role in society via their social and political movements.

The competition for visibility, influence, and power among the Islamist movements was at times intense, to the point where one group would condemn the other as being un-Islamic. However, at other times ideological, organizational, and political differences were put aside and they united ranks (such as the constitutional referendum of March 2011). Where the differences were most striking was on an organizational level. The Muslim Brotherhood by its nature had a highly sophisticated institutional pyramidal structure that had survived and evolved over eighty years, with clear lines of command and division of labor. Conversely, the Salafi movements did not have a unified leadership nor elaborate hierarchies and chains of command. They had a more horizontal structure with supporters following various leaders who were neither united in stance nor in how they wished to engage politically.

The Muslim Sisters and the women belonging to the Salafi movements had much more in common than women activists of non-Islamist orientation. Ideologically, they both held a common aversion for feminist movements, ideas around gender empowerment, and the West and its bilateral and multilateral agencies (which, according to them, included the United Nations). Organizationally, both the Muslim Sisters and the Salafi women were deeply engaged in the provision of charity, social services, and religious teaching (in particular for women), and they had built strong social networks and constituencies through their activities. However, the Muslim Sisters were part of a movement that had its own organizational structure with various levels of command, and the women belonging to the Al-Nour Party had no such structure. Whereas the Muslim Sisters were allowed to assume formal political leadership in parliament and other legislatures, the women belonging to the Al-Nour Party were not.

## Conclusion

This chapter began by problematizing the interpretation of women's presence in protests as a sign of transformed politics. It contested the notion that the ethos of the new social and political movements was "admirably unprejudiced" (Ivekovic 2011) and argued that the narrative of celebrating unity in diversity deliberately obscured divisions and power differentials.

The revolution may have appeared gender inclusive in its participation but it was gender blind in its power dynamics. Like other social movements, the youth coalitions and initiatives, though horizontal in structure, were still patriarchal in essence. Concurrently, women's rights activists had isolated themselves in a gender bubble that disconnected them from a broader context in which multiple struggles required a nuanced and intersectional approach to engaging with inequalities. In an environment in which the catchcries of the revolution—bread, freedom, and social justice/dignity—were as distant from realization as during Mubarak's era, there were new forces to contend with: a breakdown in the security force's maintenance of rule of law and public safety, a severe economic downturn, and an intense backlash against women and minorities (among other groups).

In this chapter I examined why a feminist collective or bloc did not emerge immediately to counter the backlash and I identified a number of intertwining factors that inhibited the formation of intergroup and intragroup alliances. Different theories of change (democracy first, inclusion second, or both simultaneously), negative constructions of the other, elitist policy engagement versus street politics, and contending visions of friends and foes contributed to some real divisions.

Although I began this chapter with a critical juncture at which mobilization around gender justice was at its weakest, I have chosen to end it twelve months later, on the same day as the ousting of Mubarak, with a very different political scene.

Faced with a real threat to women's rights and the elevation of that threat to the agendas of multiple stakeholders, the opportunity for engaging in collective action emerged around the celebration of International Women's Day on March 8, 2012. The numbers exceeded any other march that women's organizations had ever organized on International Women's Day in Egypt. The accounts of women from revolutionary backgrounds, activists from feminist NGOs, and women involved in political parties all pointed to common reasons for the success on March 8th. Azza Soliman recalled that at the planning stage for the event, "we sat with all the movements, and it was for the very first time that we sit and engage and coordinate together" (interview by author, July 2012). These organizations included the Coalition of the Youth of the Revolution, a wide array of political parties, and several informal, youth-led gender justice initiatives against gender-based violence in public space (see chapter 8).

Women from revolutionary backgrounds believe that the success of the event was attributable to the youth revolutionary forces' mobilization of women and men. They also believe that the articulation of the message in a language that captures the imagination of ordinary men and women and that uses gripping images and slogans made women's rights seem like an issue that they can claim as their own. There was no gender and development jargon or feminist rhetoric being used, and for this reason there was no dilution of the strength of the message on women's rights.

Nehad Abou el Komsan thinks that the mobilization was successful because of an awakening to the reality on the ground. She believes that one year after the ousting of Mubarak there was a growing consciousness of the real threat to women's rights, and that the idea of putting the house in order and then tackling inequalities had been proven fruitless. El Komsan said that by March 2012, the gap in people's consciousness between democracy and women's participation had been addressed (interview by Mohamed Hussein, May 2012). "After a year they discovered that this was a big hoax (or deception), that we are neither putting our house in order nor is anything being resolved and that women's issues were being used to cover up for the real problems exactly the same way that the Mubarak regime did. Instead of talking in parliament about the reform of the educational system, there was talk of segregating boys from girls. Instead of talking about providing respectable housing for people so that they can marry and start a new life, there was talk of lowering the age of women's custody [of her children]."

Though women were still sexually assaulted on International Women's Day 2012, the event was declared a success by all participating forces. The success was attributed to the strength of that collective action: the bringing together of the skills, resources, and people around a common cause in a coordinated and synchronized way.

# 7

## WHOSE DEMOCRACY WISH LIST(S)?

In June 2011, four months after the ousting of President Mubarak, the euphoria around Egypt's democratic takeoff was at its apex. UN Women, together with the Institute of Democracy and Electoral Assistance (IDEA) and Pathways of Women's Empowerment, hosted a major conference on women and democratization at the five-star Marriott Hotel in Cairo. The focus was how to ensure gender issues were integrated in Egypt's transition and how to learn from other countries' experiences of incorporating gender equality in their democratization processes. Michelle Bachelet, speaking in Cairo, shared reflections from the Chilean experience and emphasized the importance of women's empowerment being at the heart of any democratization. She highlighted that "it is crucial to understand that the processes of social struggle and the transition to democracy are unique moments for mending broken ties with the community, shaping institutions, and thinking about the country in the coming decades" (Bachelet 2011).

In the same conference, and during the many conferences that followed in the months after the ousting of Mubarak, invited participants issued recommendations for how Egypt should democratize. But while people gathered in the Marriott Hotel to learn about what must be done to engender Egypt's democratic transition, the situation outside the hotel was not very promising. In March 2013, members of the army police had sexually violated women who were peacefully protesting in Tahrir Square (see chapter 6 for more details on the virginity test lawsuit). A UN staff member blew the whistle on the SCAF and was killed shortly thereafter in broad daylight, in what was believed to be an assassination. On February 15, 2011, Mohamed Tantawy (representing the SCAF) announced the formation of a new committee tasked with amending the constitution. The committee was headed by Tarek el Bishri, a former head of Conseil d'Etat, and comprised another seven members: Atef el Banna, Hassanein Abd el Al, Mohamed Bahi, Sobhi Saleh, Maher Sami, Hassan Badrawi, and moderator Hassan Begato. The committee members were all judges and professors of law except one participant, a Muslim Brotherhood lawyer. There was not a single woman on the committee despite the fact that Tahany el Gebaly was the deputy head of the Supreme Constitutional Court and in spite of the large cohort of distinguished women professors of law in Egyptian universities.

A transitional government was appointed with minimal representation of women. There were rumors that Essam Sharaf, who presided over Egypt as prime minister from March 3 to November 22, 2011, had pledged to establish a women's ministry—an idea that once again did not materialize. The political situation deteriorated even further as youth revolutionary forces battled the army, accusing it of usurping power and encroaching on civil liberties. The state-owned and affiliated media and press began a vilification campaign against the youth revolutionaries (Amar 2013). The Islamists also contributed to the demonization of the revolutionaries, portraying them as "not real men" and agents of the West. As for women, the image of the emancipated woman camping in Tahrir Square began to be associated with loose morals and questionable character and was replaced with an emphasis on "the mother of the martyrs": pious, veiled women in black who sacrificed their sons for the nation.

Faiza Abou el Naga, then minister of international cooperation, spoke at the UN Women conference of the importance of recognizing women's role in development and nation-building. El Naga showed a great deal of enthusiasm for Egypt's democratic transition but less than six months later launched a callous assault of shocking proportions on civil society organizations. The scale and intensity of the crackdown on international and local human rights organizations far surpassed any single act of assault on such a group during Mubarak's reign. Forty-three NGO workers were sentenced to prison and several organizations were forced to shut down (Reuters 2013). However, as long as Egypt was holding elections, many international policymakers still considered the country to be on the track of democratic transition. The government and international community's narrative of such a transition was strikingly at odds with the youth revolutionary narrative of "the revolution is ongoing."

**Playing Institutional Politics**

None of the feminist organizations had any illusions that if gender issues were going to be taken into consideration in the new institutional power politics, they would have to influence the policies and processes at a very early stage. Much of the feminist literature on women's movements and transitions considers the point at which regime change occurs as critical for promoting and strengthening women's collective mobilization because it affords what social movement theorists identify as political opportunity structures. Ray and Korteweg (1999, 53), drawing on the work of political sociologists such as McAdam and Tarrow, identify political opportunities as "changes in access to power or shifts in the ruling alignments that enable those outside the polity to gain access to it."

Beckwith (2007, 319) reflected on the importance of regime change for forging a gender-just new order: "Changes of regime, forging of new constitutional arrangements, state reconfiguration and revolutionary contexts are major examples of shifting opportunities of which organized women, among other collective actors, may take advantage." Feminist scholarship has recognized that although such critical junctures affords opportunities for influence, they also become suspect to capture by groups with counteragendas. Professor Georgina Waylen's (1994a) pioneering work on comparative experiences of women's role and gender hierarchies in Latin American and Eastern European transitions showed that whether a new political order assumes a gender-equal agenda is linked to the nature of collective mobilization around gender issues (among other factors). In examining the experience of regime ruptures and gender outcomes in Latin America and Eastern Europe, Waylen notes that women participated in the overthrow of regimes in both regional contexts, but in the former, women's movements pre-existed and were well organized in a manner that allowed them to leverage the negotiation processes so that women's rights featured as part of the democratization agenda. In countries of Eastern Europe, however, the absence of women's organized activism meant that when the new political order was envisaged, there was no collective actor to advocate for women's rights. As a consequence, in many contexts, they lost pre-existing rights in the political, economic, and social realms (Waylen 1994a).

Studies of gendered readings of transitions have also highlighted the importance of institutional design following regime rupture (Rai 2000). There are several overlapping factors that undermine the prospects of influencing institutions to be more gender-responsive to inequalities on the basis of class, gender, age, and religion. Comparative studies of engendering transitions show that there are some common structures of constraint (uncivil civil society and patriarchal institutions, policies, and laws) and similar enabling factors (organized feminist movements, recognition of women's role in ousting dictatorships, and positive international influences). Nonetheless, in each country there is always a particular constellation of factors that influence political trajectory and gender outcomes. Such factors emanate from contextual interfaces and historical experiences.

Political opportunities afforded by the new configurations of power in Egypt often became areas of contestation in which women's rights activists were not necessarily well positioned to make political wins. These areas were (1) claiming a national women's machinery as the channel through which to influence policy-making processes, (2) the constitution, (3) parliament, and (4) institutional design with respect to governance structures. I discuss each of these areas below, except for the constitution, which I examine in the next chapter.

### Finding a Common Platform

One of the common features of the scholarship on engendering processes of regime transition is the need for feminist advocates to shift their activism from the street level to the policy level. In Egypt, feminist activists found themselves having to engage equally on both levels. The theory of change behind the international literature is that, following regime rupture, there is a democratic transition that will lead to consolidation. However, in the case of Egypt, many believed that the country was in a state of ongoing revolution, and hence it was natural for protests, demonstrations, and street activism to be sustained, and it was crucial for feminist activists to be present in that space.

Conversely, because the new status quo acted as if the country was in a postrevolution state, it was crucial for feminist activists to engage in that policy space so as not to find themselves excluded from done deals. A strong, organized feminist front was needed to exert influence not only on the visible configuration of power (what gets discussed) but also on the hidden aspects of governance (what gets kept off the negotiating table and by whose influence).

In the case of the South African nation-building project after the demise of the apartheid regime, women as citizens and through various organizations and movements played a central role in the downfall of the regime. However, none of the parties/actors, no matter how well organized, could yield the political weight on their own to enforce their policy recommendations. They formed a Women's National Coalition to organize the formation of a tripartite alliance of women academics, activists, and politicians. The African National Congress Women's League (ANCWL) realized early on that without alliances, it would not have the political weight to influence. Thanks to the combined efforts of the Women's National Coalition and women parliamentarians, they were able to make several important institutional inroads, including the insertion of an article on nonsexism in the interim constitution and the formation of an institutional body designed to make recommendations to parliament for addressing gender issues in legislation (Waylen 1994a).

It was clear in South Africa at the time that the Women's National Coalition, which was formed when the country was making a transition toward a postapartheid era, played an important role akin to that performed by national women's machineries (though one had yet to be established). A national women's machinery already existed in Egypt and was responsible for policy engagement and influence: the National Council for Women. It is telling that the very factor that empowered the NCW—its close association with the ruling party and regime—became its curse in the physical and political sense. The building in which the NCW was housed was torched and remains (at the time of writing) a sooty remnant iconic of the downfall of Mubarak's party and regime.

One of the justifications of the backlash against women's rights in Egypt is the movement's association with the first lady and the NCW (Elsadda 2011). When Mubarak fell and the revolution did not reap its intended fruits (bread, freedom, and social justice/dignity), many ordinary citizens blamed Suzanne Mubarak for the country's predicament. A common narrative was that Suzanne Mubarak was the one running the country and she brought her husband's ruin; if it had not been for her, the country would not have collapsed. Suzanne Mubarak was commonly referred to as *el Hanem* (the lady), which was used in a derogatory manner to refer to her supreme position (see Abd el Fattah 2015). Political analysts close to the ruling regime provided evidence of Suzanne Mubarak's interference in the governance of the country (see Mustafa Bakry's 2011 account of Suzanne Mubarak's increasing powers during her husband's last ten years in office). However, the actors and forces behind Mubarak's downfall were many (not least himself), and the focus on Suzanne Mubarak as being the source of all evil is, according to Farkhonda Hassan, her secretary general, reflective of a longstanding tradition of blaming Eve for Adam's downfall (Hagras 2014).

In a deeply polarized and fragmented society such as that of post-Mubarak Egypt, the one common thing everyone could agree on was hating the NCW. The youth revolutionaries saw it as a symbol of the corruption of the regime; ordinary citizens thought of it as the first lady's toy; feminist organizations regarded it as the nemesis of feminist civil society activism; and for the Muslim Brotherhood and other Islamists it was a symbol of the regime's import of Western imperialist values to ruin Egyptian Muslim families. How to move forward was a dilemma. There was consensus among youth revolutionaries, feminist activists, and women political figures that a national women's machinery was indeed necessary, and that without it, there was a serious political vacuum.

The first option was to abolish the NCW altogether and establish a new entity. The Muslim Brotherhood was keen on the dismantlement of the NCW and its replacement by the National Council for Family Affairs. The Brotherhood had the support of the Islamists on this proposal. The new institutional umbrella would frame women's rights as "protecting motherhood" and "supporting the family." Camillia Helmy, a leading political figure in the Muslim Brotherhood, strongly advocated for the abolition of the NCW on account of its role in corrupting the Egyptian family and society. She considered the NCW a foreign body that did not reflect a need of the Egyptian people and held it responsible for the increase in divorce based on its support of laws that destroy families (el Agouz 2012).

The Council for Childhood and Motherhood (CCM), which predated the NCW (see chapter 1), was dissolved in 2011 and brought under the fold of the Ministry of Health and Population. An informant within the CCM confided in June 2011 that, under pressure from certain Islamist factions, they were told to stop their media campaign against female genital mutilation (see chapter 4). The CCM removed their public billboards and ceased to broadcast their television ads against female genital mutilation. Consequently, the early political signals suggested that should the NCW be dismantled and replaced with a Council for Family Affairs, it was likely to lead to the negation of gender equality and rights.

The second option was to reform the NCW in its entirety—mandate, structure, and modes of operation—to make it fit for purpose. Advocates for its reform presented contending visions for its restructuring. One of the most robust and comprehensive proposals was put forward by Fatma Khafagy, a veteran gender and development expert with many years of experience in institutional reform. Another initiative was put forward by Nehad Abou el Komsan, a seasoned political activist with many years of experience in initiating successful campaigns; however, women activists I spoke to said they had not seen either proposal. Abou el Komsan said in an interview in March 2012 that she submitted the proposal directly to the prime minister. She had been called for consultation with Essam Sharaf (prime minister from March 3 to November 22, 2011) and Kamal el Ganzoury (prime minister from November 24, 2011, to November 26, 2012). She made suggestions for potential NCW board members, though the list was finalized internally by the SCAF and government. Most women activists advocated such a reform option but there was no unified stance on how to proceed, which allowed the regime to capitalize on the fragmentation and introduce minimal change.

The third option, which the government accepted as its course of action, was to restructure the NCW so as to remove the ancient regime leaders and substitute them with new blood. However, the issue was so deeply politicized that it led to a deep fragmentation among gender equality advocates, which enabled the Sharaf interim government to divide and conquer, therefore getting away with minimal change. The SCAF, in lieu of the president, became the party responsible for choosing the members of the board. Mervat Tallawy, a veteran femocrat who served as minister of social solidarity and secretary general of the NCW under Mubarak, was appointed chair. The appointment of a former Mubarak minister did not exactly yield the impression of fresh blood. Tallawy's commitment to women's rights is typical of femocrats; however, she is believed to hold much disdain for civil society and under Mubarak had introduced one of the most draconian NGO laws ever, which was later declared unconstitutional by the Supreme Constitutional Court.

The composition of the restructured NCW did include some token members of the old regime, rather than a council representing the new individual and collective actors whose voices were critical for promoting gender justice in post-Mubarak Egypt. Perhaps the most conspicuous characteristic of the new council was that it was predominantly composed of individuals forty years old and older. There was only one member of the youth revolutionary movements represented, Bassem Mohamed Kamel, and no women revolutionary leaders. The council comprised roughly one-third men, and some of the men had virtually no record of engaging with women's rights. The council did count Amna Nosseir, a renowned Islamic scholar, and a number of other Islamic scholars in its ranks. There was some fresh blood such as Neveen Mosaad and Hania Sholkamy, both highly respected professors and public figures, yet the latter stepped down a few months later on the basis that the decision-making process was not participatory or open (interview by author, September 2012). Hoda Elsadda, another renowned scholar, found her name announced among the new members but she declined to accept. She cited concerns about its nondemocratic character (interview by author).[1]

1. For the full composition of the board, see http://www.us.sis.gov.eg/Ar/Templates/Articles/tmpArticles.aspx?ArtID=44685.

Nehad Abou el Komsan was nominated by the board to serve as secretary general. At first, she defended the decision:

> Maybe it was not the best thing but in my opinion it is reflective of the people to a large extent. I am responsible for the negotiations [over the names] though the final selection was not up to me but I was happy that it had youth, that there were Copts and men in it. (interview by Mohamed Hussein, August 2012)

However, several women declined the invitation or accepted and then resigned shortly thereafter. What is striking is the way in which selected members were not even individually notified and instead learned about their invitations from the media. This was indicative of the former regime's manner of working, in which members of civil society are supposed to feel privileged that the authorities are looking down on them and bestowing the honor of membership.

Camillia Helmy and other members of the Muslim Brotherhood expressed the Freedom and Justice Party's disappointment over the fact that only one member of the Brotherhood, Reda Abdallah (an MP for Sharqiyya governorate), was appointed to the board. They expected a much higher representation of their members because they had won a clear majority in parliament. Helmy commented that although a third of the council were remnants of the old regime, the rest were "liberals and secularists" (el Agouz 2012).

The new institutional setup of the NCW reproduced to a large extent the previous one. Instead of the first lady, her former secretary general was assigned the head of the institution. Instead of having downward accountability toward its constituency, it continued to be upwardly accountable to the government (though this was temporarily broken during Morsi's tenure). Feminist civil society organizations continued to claim that there was no sense of ownership over the institution and that it lacked the broad-based legitimacy to enable it to speak on behalf of Egyptian women.

In an environment in which political culture was flourishing for perhaps the first time in more than seventy years, many feminists who had been active in civil society organizations instead channeled their energies into political society organizations, including movements, political parties, and coalitions. The position of many leading feminists in political parties allowed them to advocate for engendering the party platforms with their own feminist agenda. When women did constitute a bloc in a political party and were in leading positions in the general hierarchy, they succeeded in securing 30-percent representation in all decision-making positions within the party structure (such as in the Egyptian Social Democratic Party). However, their powers to influence were limited by having to work through women's committees/wings of the party. Although a few women assumed leading positions in the upper echelons of the party hierarchy, many became leaders or participants in the women's wings. As with conventional political practice in other contexts (Goetz and Hassim 2003), they were often ghettoized and sidelined. Strategically, instead of pressing for support via the women's committee, more efforts were needed to build allies with the top leaders of the political parties (while engaging in backstage liaising with the women's committees).

Another factor that undermined feminist NGO leaders' bargaining power when entering political parties was the weakness of their constituency. Because these NGOs did not have extensive outreach and had not built a constituency of citizens who endorsed their work, feminist leaders did not have a community base (potential voters) to leverage when negotiating with the party leadership. In other words, they could not claim a political constituency as a bargaining chip.

It is important to note that feminist activists were functioning in a highly polarized political context at this time. As a microcosm of the broader political scene, feminist NGOs (and many youth revolutionary movements) were internally divided regarding the political forces that represented the greatest threat to the revolution. Although not articulated as such, the stances were influenced by some hard choices in terms of what would be most detrimental to democracy and to women's rights: the boot of the army or the sandals of the ultraconservative Islamist. This was also part of a broader debate within youth revolutionary forces. As with the April 6th movement, some youth revolutionaries had forged strong relations with the Muslim Brotherhood and had openly endorsed its candidate for the presidency in 2012; other youth revolutionary groups (such as the Revolutionary Populist) had remained skeptical.

Hala Kamal, professor of English literature and gender studies at Cairo University, member of the Woman and Memory Forum, and member of the coalition of Egyptian feminist organizations, recalled that the political situation was opaque and the choices of who to endorse and who to contest were very much on the agenda of the coalition (interview by Mohamed Hussein, March 2012; see chapter 6). She believed that there was a great deal of hysterical hype about the dangers of the Muslim Brothers. In 2011, she argued that the process of creating Egypt's new constitution would be far less oppressive under the Muslim Brothers than under the SCAF: "If you ask me personally, I prefer to work in a constituent assembly under the shadow of the [Muslim] Brothers than SCAF. Of course some of my colleagues may hold a different position. New political circumstances make us unable to assume a unified political position."

Nevine Ebeid, a leading activist, member of the New Woman Foundation, and a member of the coalition of Egyptian feminist organizations, saw the situation differently: "Sometimes I differ with the direction of the coalition generally when I see them convey an enmity to the military much weaker than that towards the [Muslim] Brothers because I am of the view that political Islam is no less dire and dangerous a threat than the army" (interview by Mohamed Hussein, May 2012).

**The Democratic Wedding**

Egypt's first parliamentary elections following Mubarak's ousting were considered by Western media, analysts, and many academics to be a major milestone in the transition toward democracy. There was much talk in Egypt of the country's "democratic wedding" (*'orse dimoukrati*) when referring to the parliamentary elections. However, the engagement period was a thorny one, which terminated with some parties choosing to exit the relationship. The youth revolutionary forces, which did not represent a political bloc, preferred that the elections be postponed until the security situation improved and the newly formed political parties had a chance to prepare. Their argument was that there already was an unfair playing field because the Muslim Brotherhood had had eighty years to build a constituency on the ground, whereas newly formed political parties had just been established. The other argument put forward was that the elections should not have been held under SCAF rule.

Nevertheless, many youth revolutionary forces and the newly formed political parties participated in discussions about the development of a new electoral law. Despite the intensity of the disagreements, there was one policy that all negotiating parties could agree on, whether they were of the left or right, Islamist or non-Islamist, revolutionary or reactionary: the annulment of a quota setting aside sixty-four seats of parliament for women.[2]

The background of the instatement of what was dubbed the "first lady quota" is of particular importance. In 2009, the Egyptian parliament passed a new law that added sixty-four seats to the 554-seat parliament for which only women were permitted to compete. Although there was some international praise for the Mubarak regime for introducing affirmative action, feminist activists and leading women politicians decried the law as being designed in such a manner as to expand the ruling National Democratic Party's dominance of parliament under the progressive veneer of expanding women's representation (Tadros 2010b). This foresight as to the regime's use of the quota for political ends proved to be well placed: of sixty-four seats, only one was not occupied by a woman running under the ruling party banner. Although the quota had indeed achieved its aim of increasing women's representation from 2 to 13 percent, both its gender credentials (adding new seats rather than reconfiguring power) and its tailored nature (an electoral district that is much larger than that set for nonquota candidates and is almost impossible for any candidate to cover; see Tadros 2010b) added to the list of grievances against it.

Yet when the new political forces in post-Mubarak Egypt decided to drop the quota, the decision was not entirely motivated by the desire to eliminate all traces of the former regime. For example, for fifty years

2. In the debates that took place in 2011/2012 about the electoral law, the Muslim Brotherhood representatives showed very little resistance to the idea of introducing a woman's quota (especially if it was not a high percentage).

a quota was in place that allocated 50 percent of parliamentary seats to workers and farmers. This quota was not abolished even though one of the arguments against the women's quota was that it was against the concept of equal opportunity. After the abolition of the women's quota, it was not replaced by any other form of affirmative action to redress the structural constraints that undermine women's opportunities to gain seats in parliament. The new electoral law did stipulate that at least two women must be placed on the party proportional list, but it did not specify where. Not surprisingly, political parties of Islamist and non-Islamist backgrounds relegated women to the bottom of their lists.

The resistance to recognizing the need for endorsement of women's political leadership was very strong, even among some of the progressive revolutionary youth forces. In an interview by Mohamed Hussein (2012), Abou el Komsan described an intense negotiation with a leading member of a revolutionary youth group in which they tried to reach an agreement of mutual support to endorse each other's agendas. She recounted that some of the youth coalitions wanted the law to prescribe a 30-percent quota for young people, but they were not willing to have the quota equally split between women and men. They refused any kind of gender quota.

> The youth [revolutionaries] had a demand that there be a 30-percent quota [in parliament]. I said, we will strongly endorse your demand and will lobby for it with all our strength, but are you prepared that out of this 30-percent quota, 15 percent go to women and 15 percent go to men? They said no. I asked them why not? They said that because women's political experience is still nascent. To be honest, the experience of one of the people who said this cannot be described as nascent, but simply nonexistent!

The disconnect between women's political agency during the revolution and their performance in parliament was particularly acute. Women's representation in parliament fell from 13 percent in 2010 to 2 percent in 2011 despite the fact that the number of women who nominated themselves for office had doubled (for further details see Tadros 2014).

The youth revolutionaries were also marginally represented in the first post-Mubarak parliament. They touched a chord with millions of citizens when they rose against Mubarak and called upon the people to join them. However, their chances of building political constituencies that allow them to win electoral seats are dismal. Revolutionary mass support does not translate into electoral political constituencies. Moreover, some of the youth movements had boycotted the electoral process as an expression of their rejection of the legitimacy of SCAF rule.

Not a single woman revolutionary figure made it to parliament, which shows how the intersection of age (young), ideology (revolutionary), and gender (woman) worked against them. Their lack of representation was partly a reflection of the political scene at that juncture and partly a reflection of the intensity of the backlash. There were agential factors as well. When a leading revolutionary woman figure was asked whether she would nominate herself for parliament, she replied in the negative for two reasons. First, even though she had years of experience in street activism, she felt unequipped to venture into parliamentary competition. Second, she did not recognize the parliamentary elections because the revolution was still ongoing (interview by author, May 2011). Her sentiment was shared by many women and men youth revolutionaries; if the revolution was ongoing, it was not the time to participate in the political system. Perhaps if Egypt was truly ruled by civilians, then they might consider running for electoral office.

Another leading revolutionary woman figure[3] emphasized her independence from any particular political party or force. Her attitude toward political parties as repositories of corruption and personal gain kept her from involvement in old or new parties. Instead she formed an informal group that engages in informal politics; in other words, politics outside the formal legislatures and government. She too has rejected nominating herself for a parliamentary seat because she believes that the parliament does

---

3. It was not the intention to have faceless names mentioned in this chapter. The names of these revolutionary figures were mentioned in the original manuscript; however, because of the publisher's requirement of written permission for their voices appearing in the book at a time when accessing them was very difficult, the names were removed. Permissions to interview them were obtained at the time of the original interviews, but new ones were needed for publication in the book.

not meet the aspirations of the revolution. When I interviewed many revolutionary women in 2012, they expressed hope that one day they would be able to run for office when Egypt is governed as a civilian country. It was a vicious circle: for them to exercise power and influence politically, they had to be part of the political process, but their engagement was necessarily in the informal sphere on account of their commitment to an ongoing revolution.

In contrast, a select number of women leaders in the Muslim Brotherhood were strongly backed by their political party (the Freedom and Justice Party) in their election campaigns. Similar to the demographics of Muslim Sisters in leadership positions, they were all highly educated, white-collar professionals that were middle-aged or older, most were wives or daughters of key Muslim Brotherhood figures, and they had decades of experience in social work (Tadros 2014). Unlike Salafi women who were put on the bottom of their party list, some of the Muslim Sisters were put in strategically high places. Four of the eleven women who made it to parliament were Freedom and Justice Party nominees.

Nine women MPs were elected and two were appointed. (The SCAF, in lieu of the president, had the right to appoint ten MPs.) Of the nine who won on their party lists, four belonged to the Muslim Brotherhood's Freedom and Justice Party, three belonged to the right-wing, non-Islamist Wafd Party, one belonged to the left-of-center, non-Islamist Egyptian Democratic Party, and one belonged to the centrist, non-Islamist Reform and Development Party. The two appointed women did not have a long history of formal political engagement; however, they were active within their respective churches (evangelical and orthodox) and were nominated by church leadership. It is likely that the SCAF accepted their nominations because they were both Coptic and women, the two underrepresented groups in Egyptian political life.

Once the Muslim Brotherhood and the Islamist parties assumed a clear majority in parliament (71 percent), a debate emerged among women's rights coalitions as to how to engage with the new political order (keeping in mind that the youth revolutionaries had opted for a boycott, nonengagement approach). The impossibility of building a collective front through a women's caucus became very apparent early on. Although over-all women's representation in parliament amounted to no more than 3 percent, the strength of the Muslim Sisters in that percentage was visible because their party was the largest one in parliament. Some of the Muslim Sister MPs became the greatest champions of legislative changes that would in effect diminish women's freedoms.

According to the Egyptian Center for Women's Rights (ECWR), Azza Al Garaf (who preferred to be addressed as Um Ayman, in reference to her position as mother of Ayman) proposed a draft law to amend Article 242 in Penal Code Law 126 (2008) that criminalized female genital mutilation. She advocated that FGM should be performed only in hospitals by doctors rather than be completely prohibited as per the existing Child Rights Law (Diaa 2013). The Muslim Sisters were also strong advocates of annulling an amendment to the Personal Status Procedural Law of 2000, commonly referred to as the *khul'* law. The *khul'* law gave women the right to arbitrarily divorce their husbands via the court without their husbands' permission, but on the condition that they forfeit their financial rights under conventional divorce (Diaa 2013).

However, in the short period in which parliament convened, the Muslim Brotherhood did put forward—and pass—a law that met one of the key demands that feminists had advocated for on behalf of female-headed households. In May 2012, parliament issued a law recognizing female-headed households' rights to medical benefits.[4] The recognition of the welfare needs of vulnerable women certainly represented a concrete positive measure on the part of the new government. What concerned many interviewees, who were speaking from a feminist perspective, was that the wording of the law enforced the idea of a paternalistic state engaging with the vulnerable through a needs-based rather than rights-based framework. They were concerned that although benefits were supposedly being extended to female-headed households, other laws would be put forward

4. For further details on the law that was promulgated in parliament, see http://www.ikhwanweb.com/article.php?id=30028.

**Table 1. Women Members of Egypt's First Post-Mubarak Parliament, 2011–2012**

| Name | Birth Year | Party | Electoral District | Political History | Profession |
|---|---|---|---|---|---|
| Hanan Abou el Gheit | 1974 | Wafd | Kafr Saad, Damietta | Member of local council | Agriculturist |
| Suzie Adly | 1962 | Appointed | N/A | None known | Professor of law, Alexandria University |
| Reda Atwa | 1964 | FJP | Sharqiyya governorate | Graduate of Koranic Studies Institute | Inspector at the Ministry of Irrigation; engineer by training |
| Marguerite Azer | 1961 | Wafd | Madinet Nasr, Cairo | None known | Senior civil servant in Ministry of Education |
| Seham el Gamal | 1965 | FJP | El Dakahleya governorate | None known | Human development trainer with degree in education |
| Azza Al Garaf | 1965 | FJP | Imbaba, low-income district in Cairo | Daèya (engaged in proselytization) | Freelance journalist; human development trainer |
| Hoda Ghanneya | 1968 | FJP | Greater Cairo district of Shubra el Kheima (Qalubiyya governorate) | Member of several civil society organizations and of the women's committee of the physicians' syndicate branch in Qalubiyya | Physician by training (specializes in epidemiology) |

| Magda el Noweishi | 1955 | Wafd | Islamiliya | Won parliamentary elections of 2010; long history of political and women's rights activism | Senior civil servant in Islamiliya governorate |
|---|---|---|---|---|---|
| Sanaa el Saaeed | 1966 | EDP | Asiut | Former MP in 2010 parliamentary elections; long history of political activism | Accountant in the local development bank |
| Fadeya Salem | 1977 | Reform and Development | South Sinai | Member of local council | Lawyer |
| Marianne Magdy Shenouda | 1984 | Appointed | N/A | None known | Lawyer |

*Source:* Developed by author based on interviews and the Directory of the MPs for Parliament 2012 (Rabie 2012a).

*Note:* FJP indicates Freedom and Justice Party; EDP, Egyptian Democratic Party; MP, member of parliament; N/A, not applicable.

that would reinforce patriarchal power relations and negatively affect all women, including the poor and vulnerable (e.g., laws affecting mobility, sexual and reproductive rights, divorce, etc.).

The suspicions held by many non-Islamist feminists that the Muslim Sisters would seek to revoke the modicum of rights that were secured through Egyptian women's century-long mobilization for emancipation proved to be well founded when, in the deliberations over the constitution of 2012, the Muslim Sisters defended an article that would make women's equality to men conditional upon its compliance with Islamic precepts (see chapter 8).

Opportunities for alliance-building are always premised on finding common ground for collaboration or political bargains that involve providing one concession in return for another. There was little that non-Islamist feminist blocs could offer women MPs belonging to the Freedom and Justice Party in return for endorsing their agenda. The non-Islamist political blocs did not seem at the time to have large constituencies on the ground nor substantial street mobilizational power.

In the absence of opportunities to build a collective front to support women's rights, many feminist activists resorted to engaging with head policymakers. In March 2011, the women's coalitions, in alliance with the women's committees in political parties, went to meet with the deputy head of one of the committees in parliament, Ashraf Thabet, to convey their demands. It is noteworthy that Thabet is also the deputy head of the Salafi Al-Nour Party, whose political positions on gender issues were the most uncompromising in their rigidity. "We went to see who is responsible for decision-making. We went straight to the legislative committee to discuss with them our demands, not go build alliances with women who are not the decision-makers when it comes to these laws" explained Hala Kamal, referring to the decision to sidestep the Muslim Sisters (interview by Mohamed Hussein, September 2012).

In light of the growing strength of the Muslim Brotherhood and Salafi movements in political life, what many women's rights activists could wish for at the most was to block proposals for revoking legislation that had been issued during Mubarak's tenure and that, although imperfect, had granted women a modicum of rights. But six months after its inauguration, parliament was declared null and void on technical grounds (candidates affiliated with political parties were running for seats assigned for independents, according to an electoral law that violated the constitutional amendments of 2011). Hence, very few laws were passed during this period.

The polarization between Islamist and non-Islamist was also experienced on a grassroots level. In focus groups I organized in March 2013, women affiliated with Islamist movements deployed a discourse that spoke of unprecedented freedoms that Egyptian women enjoyed since the Islamists came to power (though President Morsi had yet to become president). They pointed to the political freedoms that women had as a consequence of the ousting of the old regime and of their liberation as apparent through their participation in the elections and protests. They argued that this was a golden era for women who could now express themselves without fearing the repressive apparatus of the Mubarak regime. They recognized that the country was experiencing an economic downturn and a lack of security for citizens, but claimed that both were the work of the old regime trying to bring down Islam (these views were particularly conveyed by focus groups in Fayoum and Beni Suef, two governorates renowned for being Muslim Brotherhood strongholds).

Non-Islamist women who participated in focus groups shared a different narrative. They complained that public space was becoming more hostile to their presence not only because of the security breakdown (presence of thugs, increased sexual assault, theft, etc.) but also because they were being harassed by men and women who publicly scolded them for not being covered enough (regardless of whether they were nonveiled or wearing the regular veil). In many focus groups, women expressed a genuine fear that their daughters would be discouraged from continuing their education and that women would be under pressure not to work in public.

The Muslim Brothers took no measures to restrict education or work in public space nor did these matters feature in any of their official discourses. However, to accuse these women of a hysterical, unfounded fear of the rise of the Islamists to power is to fail to see reality through their eyes. Although there were no policy changes on the education or work fronts, the Islamist discourse in public space (e.g., markets, mosques) and on Islamist satellite television became increasingly open in its call for women to return home. The challenges that the majority of women faced were related to economic hardships, which were associated with political economy factors and not linked to the agency of the Islamists. However, there were new gender-related forms of emotional strain that were directly related to the political ascendency of the Islamists. In focus groups in Giza and Qena, women complained that during the Friday sermon in some mosques, men were being encouraged to take on second wives from among the Syrian refugee population in Egypt as a kind of social solidarity with the Muslims suffering because of the war.

Within the non-Islamist constituency in focus groups, it seemed that those who feared the Islamists most and most frequently shared accounts of increasing encroachment were the Coptic Christian women. Like other Egyptian women their top grievances were increasing economic hardship and security breakdown. However, also topping their list was an increase in religious intolerance toward them as members of a religious minority. Their experiences of sectarianism were gendered. Most middle- and working-class Muslim women are veiled (though not necessarily among the upper classes); therefore, as Christian women who do not don the veil, their deviance from the increasingly conservative norm is conspicuous in public space. Several of these women from focus groups in rural and urban areas complained of being beaten up and told to veil voluntarily rather than be forcefully veiled later. They also complained of increasing harassment from women in the all-women carriage of the subway, who took it upon themselves to press Coptic women to cover their hair and dress more conservatively. They said that they did not experience this during Mubarak's reign and identified the growing powers of the Islamist movement as the reason behind this exposure to religiously mediated forms of assault.

### The West's Version of Egypt's Transition

After the Egyptian revolution, there was a strong sentiment of anger toward Western actors for their role in supporting the Mubarak regime over the course of thirty years. With the rise of political Islam to power, Western support for the Muslim Brotherhood regime became more conspicuous

(Abou el Fadl 2013). Feminist activists perceived that the Western interest in engaging voices of the opposition, in particular from women rights activists, had disappeared.

After the political ascendency of the Islamists, Western donors put increasing pressure on feminist organizations and other civil society actors to engage with them. In November 2012, I shared with a Western donor my intention to hold a workshop with one of our local partners (CEWLA) for informal youth-based groups working on sexual assault in public space. I was stunned that the only concern he raised was "have you invited members of the Freedom and Justice Party and Al-Nour Party?" The event was targeting a particular group: youth involved in addressing sexual assault in public space. Why would we want to invite leaders from political parties, and why would we want to single out the Islamist-leaning ones? I thereafter discovered that many local feminist organizations were also being pressured in the same direction: the involvement and inclusion of women from Islamist backgrounds in workshops, conferences, roundtables, and all other events.

Although engaging diverse actors is certainly relevant, the Western donor's underlying motive did not seem to be ensuring inclusive representation of different categories of women. For example, no one asked, "Do you have adequate representation from marginalized Coptic women? Are poor rural women adequately represented? What about women and men who work on gender equality issues in upper Egypt?" The intention behind urging civil society organizations to deepen their engagement with women from Islamist backgrounds was the belief that common ground was discoverable through deliberation.

Herein lies the contradiction in donor policy. On the one hand was the "engendering transitions" discourse (e.g., during the June 2011 UN conference in Egypt). On the other hand, donors expected to achieve this aim through support for actors (Islamists in parliament) who championed an agenda committed to maintaining a patriarchal hierarchy in which power relations are not challenged. In short, they deployed democratic channels (parliaments) to advance antifeminist aims cloaked in gender language.

At the root of this contradiction was a deeply problematic, essentialist understanding that all women share the same political agenda of expanding and enhancing women's rights. The key recommendation suggested by many international donors at the time was to get more women into politics. Speaking at the UN event in June 2011, Secretary General Vidar Helgesen (International IDEA) noted that the Arab region had the lowest average representation of women in parliament (11 percent) compared to the global average of 19 percent. "Let us hope that that figure will be much higher in one year's time after elections have been held in Egypt and Tunisia. Let us also hope that it will be even higher in ten years' time" (Helgesen 2011).

There was no discussion in Helgesen's speech or in any other made during that event (or during most of the other international events held on helping Egypt to democratize) on whether a critical mass of women is desirable or whether a more gender-progressive set of policies or outcomes is what is needed. There seemed to be an inflation of the two, or an assumption that one would naturally lead to the other. In Egypt in 2011–12, there was an *inverse* relationship between having more women in parliament and advancing a gender-progressive agenda. Some of the women who succeeded in politics championed overtly antifeminist agendas. Yet the Western narrative on engendering Egypt's democratization continued to be underpinned by the use of a blueprint premised on other countries' transitions and by reified conceptions of women as if they were a uniform category with a common set of interests.

The new political reality in Egypt prompted Western donors to introduce a new "recipe" using the same old cookie-cutter approach to their programming. Many Egyptians involved in the debates and discussions around building a new country said in interviews that the exposure to different country experiences and an understanding of their political trajectory was useful. However, the blueprint approach—and the politics behind it—made them feel that the same prescriptive approach was being pursued.

The revolution may have changed the political scene in Egypt, but it seemed to have no impact on international ways of working (Mustapha 2012). No paradigms were questioned, no practices were altered, and no theories of change were critiqued.

## Conclusion

This chapter examined the opportunities and challenges of incorporating gender equality issues in Egypt during the period of SCAF rule and with the political ascendency of the Islamists to power, formally and informally. In it I argue that although there were similarities between the postrupture experience of Egypt and that of other countries in which authoritarian regimes were overthrown, there was a deep disjuncture between the international and national discourse about Egypt's democratic transition and the revolutionary forces' stance that the revolution is ongoing and its aims have yet to be achieved.

This disjuncture in perception led to the international prescription of measures that were associated with liberal procedural democracy (such as elections) and democratic transitions in Latin America and Eastern Europe. In practice, it meant that Western donors relied on frameworks for analyzing "gender in transitions," set key milestones and benchmarks for measuring progress, and based their plans on a linear process involving a move from constitution-writing to parliamentary, presidential, and local elections. Yet these plans failed to engage with the power configurations on the ground, and they were peripheral to the unfolding political scene for all parties concerned.

Because the instigators of the revolution did not assume power afterward, those endorsing a women's rights agenda faced a dilemma from the outset. Do you support the revolutionaries in their stance rejecting the new status quo in its entirety and insisting that the revolution is ongoing? Or do you engage in institutional politics, which are deeply flawed but represent the governing reality on the ground? Advocates of women's rights were divided in their agenda and therefore multiple strategies were simultaneously pursued. A constellation of factors affected the prospects of influencing the new configuration of power.

Congruent with the experiences of many other countries with regime ruptures, there was a backlash against women's rights that was made more acute with the political ascendency of the Islamists. The prospects of a gender-equitable political settlement were further hindered by the association between the women's rights agenda and the first lady. However, it was not only the structures of constraint that blocked opportunities for influence. On the agential front, the lack of a broad-based constituency for the feminist movement and a weakness in the alliances (at that time) with political parties compounded the disabling environment in which advocates of women's rights found themselves. Moreover, the absence of a unified collective stance among the various feminist actors did not put them in a strong negotiating position nor allow them to seize small openings to elicit the kind of policy outcomes to which they all aspired. At such a critical juncture without a unified stance, they lacked the political clout to influence, and in the absence of consensus over leadership and strategy, the powers that be were able to take advantage of their divisiveness to evade making any commitments. This was evident in the reform of the National Council for Women. Conversely, when feminist actors did mobilize collectively, their political weight was substantial enough to force the powers that be to listen to them, as with the hearing session organized with the deputy parliamentary speaker.

# 8

## TOWARD A NEW SOCIAL CONTRACT?

The assumption of Dr. Mohamed Morsi to the presidency was intended to herald the beginning of a new era in Egypt's history and a new nation-building project. Naturally, there were contending visions of what a new Egypt should look like and how it should be governed. The Muslim Brotherhood's rank and file expected that a president who was one of their own would pursue a kind of restorative justice, ensuing moral and political (and financial) compensation for the years of hardship and repression that they endured since the movement's inception eighty years ago. The Guidance Bureau of the Muslim Brotherhood that had nominated Morsi also expected to assume a governance role to put into practice its policies and vision. The extent to which President Morsi enjoyed the freedom to pursue his own policies in an autonomous manner, independent of the intervention of the Muslim Brotherhood, is highly questionable. He was also pulled in many opposing directions by different political forces that had entered into ententes with him during the presidential race.

### Ententes Gone Bust

The political ascendency of President Morsi was met with celebration from the Islamist factions, cautious optimism from various non-Islamist social and political forces, and strong opposition from others. The Egyptian population was deeply polarized. Some believed that the new president was a triumph for Islam and for the Muslim *ummah*; others believed he would bring prosperity for the Egyptian people. Still others believed that Morsi was the beginning of the end and that the country would go downhill under his leadership. Egyptians referred to people in the middle as the "lemon squeezers"[1]: those who overcame their discomfort with the Brotherhood coming to power to avoid the reproduction of the old regime in Ahmed Shafik. Lemon squeezers were willing to give the Muslim Brotherhood a try and had very high expectations for them to deliver on their promises.

Before Morsi became president, several leading non-Islamist political forces and the Muslim Brotherhood established an informal entente known as the Fairmont Agreement. After the first round of presidential elections, in which Morsi faced competition from Ahmed Shafik, a former minister from Mubarak's era, these groups called a meeting in the five-star Fairmont Hotel. The meeting was attended by leading figures of the Muslim Brotherhood, including Morsi himself, representatives from non-Islamist political parties, members of other parties such as Misr al Qaweya (Strong Egypt Party), and leading figures from youth revolutionary forces. After substantial negotiations, leaders from across the spectrum of participants announced in a press conference that they would endorse Morsi's candidature (and not Shafik's) to avoid reproducing the old regime and to give the Brotherhood an opportunity to rule Egypt in an inclusive manner. The agreement stated that in return for the endorsement from revolutionary forces, political parties, and some leading intellectuals, the Brothers would commit to power sharing if they came into office.

The Fairmont Agreement led to a situation in which Morsi was pulled in several directions from the very beginning of his presidency. The new regime in Egypt was in a highly dubious situation and the expectations from different political factions seemed almost irreconcilable. In addition, the new regime's legitimacy was quite precarious. Morsi did not win with a sweeping majority (only 2 percent more than his opponent) and he lacked the charisma and the political career credentials that would make his leadership uncontested. He had promised to be a president for all Egyptians rather than for a particular faction, namely, the political movement to which he belonged. From the outset, it became clear that

---

1. The expression comes from the practice of squeezing lemon on food that one does not like to make it sufficiently palatable.

the Supreme Guidance Bureau of the Muslim Brotherhood was yielding much influence on (and some suggested governing) the presidential post. Hence, the maneuvering space available for President Morsi to pursue alliances with the opposition was limited by the informal decision-making processes in place.

The Salafis and various Islamist movements that had supported Morsi in the run-up to the presidency expected that he would deliver on the implementation of the Shari'a in a full and systematic manner. The rank and file of the Muslim Brotherhood also expected that after years of waiting, their ascension to power would mean enjoying the bounty of having won the battle. The political factions that signed the Fairmont Agreement with President Morsi had high expectations that the principle of power sharing would inform the president's every policy. The youth revolutionary movements expected that the catchcry of "bread, freedom, and social justice" would materialize after their long struggle for a civilian government.

In addition to the political expediency of members of the Fairmont Agreement, various interest groups (youth, workers, farmers, the poor, etc.) as well as wide sections of the Egyptian population had high expectations that the new government would deliver on its promise for a material improvement in their lives. In addition there were the *feloul* (remnants of the Mubarak regime), some of whom were opposed to the Muslim Brotherhood rule and were intent on sabotaging their governance strategy. The *feloul* included employees working in various governmental institutions and ministries as well as leading members of the former regime's National Democratic Party.

**Women in the 100-Day Honeymoon**

The president had promised the delivery of a 100-day program of action that would reinstate security for citizens, clean up the cities, and ease the fuel crisis (in particular, make cooking gas canisters more accessible). These were colossal tasks to achieve, especially within a time frame of less than three and a half months. Not surprisingly, the situation had changed very little by the end of Morsi's first 100 days in office. Some youth movements organized large-scale protests to hold the government accountable for failing to deliver on its promises (Akram 2013). Others urged for

President Morsi to be given more time and pointed to a Western, secularist conspiracy to bring down a pious Islamist ruler.

There was little clarity in the specific plans of the Morsi regime. The widely publicized Renaissance Project (*Al Nahda*) had set out in vague terms the broad parameters of national policy. It included goals as diverse as the restructuring of the deep state in Egypt, support for citizens' political participation, the promotion of human development, the cultivation of Sinai, and security system development. The short document spoke of the Muslim Brotherhood's commitment to "*mousharaka la moughalaba*" ("participation not domination") as its approach to governance and of its commitment to supporting citizenship rights for all, including youth, Christians, and women.

On women's issues, the Renaissance Project document (*Akhbar al-Youm* 2012) said that the Freedom and Justice Party pledges "the empowerment of Egyptian women and making space for them to participate in the social and political life of the nation and its national and developmental priorities, out of our faith that women are equivalent to men in status and they complement men in work and duties." This brief statement reflects many of the key ideological underpinnings of the Muslim Brotherhood's vision on gender relations. The discourse of women being equivalent and complementary to men rather than equal is reflective of an ideological commitment to the idea that women and men are born with different roles in life that are marked by biological differences. The complementarity is in work and duties (or responsibilities) rather than rights, because rights in and of themselves are mediated by religious qualifiers (Tadros 2012f).

In the Renaissance Project document the above statement is followed by reference to the Brotherhood's commitment—not by rhetoric but by deeds—to remove all obstacles to women participating in all aspects of life while bearing in mind the need to balance work with family responsibilities. It also states that the Brothers are committed to protecting women from harassment on the streets and are against all forms of discrimination that prevent women from taking on public positions. Finally, the document promotes women's involvement in economic activity, particularly microenterprises for female-headed households (*Akhbar al-Youm* 2012). One advantage of such microenterprises was that they were commensurate with the Brotherhood's overall neoliberal policy, which was premised on a market economy. If some economic activities could be undertaken in the home, society could be reordered with greater gender segregation and a stronger association between women and the domestic sphere.

In the months following his assumption of the presidency, Dr. Mohamed Morsi convened a number of consultation meetings with individuals and groups to listen to their wish lists and policy recommendations. The consultation with women's rights activists came considerably later than with other groups. Mervat Tallawy, representing the National Council for Women, Hoda Badran, representing the Egyptian Feminist Union, Mona Zulficar, the renowned legal expert on gender issues, Mona Makram Ebeid, a former MP, and three more women went to the presidential palace to meet with the president. Badran's account of that encounter is insightful:

> We sat in one row and on the opposite row were the MB [Muslim Brotherhood] women including Pakinam Sharkawy. It seemed that we were pitted one against the other from the outstart. President Morsi lectured us for almost half an hour about how much women enjoyed their rights in Egypt and how much women in America have their rights violated. Mervat Tallawy spoke first, commending the president for his government's commitment to female-headed households, and then raised concerns about the threats to women's existing legal rights, and gave him many examples. I spoke next about how America is not my reference point but Egypt with its 7,000-year civilization and how we don't want to go back in time but progress forwards. The other women did not have a chance to talk because he was called in for another meeting and excused himself. We realized we were not going to influence policy and were fighting a lost battle. (interview by author, April 2014)

The seating arrangements alone showed the difficulty of working with women political leaders in Morsi's government. Deep polarization informed the power configurations on the ground. It is telling that Pakinam el Sharkawy seated herself on the side of the Muslim Sisters rather than in a more neutral spot. Pakinam el Sharkawy is a professor in the Faculty of Economics and Political Science at Cairo University, and she did not have a renowned public profile at the time. She was appointed as counselor to President Morsi on August 27, 2012, and she later assumed several other positions and capacities. As counselor to the president, sitting next to the Muslim Sisters would have only enforced the impression that she is one of the Muslim Brothers and is not there in an impartial capacity to mediate between the presidency and the political forces.

For President Morsi to invite a delegation of women activists only to lecture them at length is indicative of his exercise of a *power over* relationship rather than attempted bridge-building. The content of President Morsi's lecture shows the extent to which ideology rather than concrete policy drove his take on gender issues, and it was underpinned by a conflation of gender equality with Western culture. Finally, the fact that the meeting ended not with assurances of taking their concerns on board nor practical suggestions for pursuing the conversations on gender policy indicates the emptiness of such meetings. These invited spaces were devoid of any prospects of policy influence, consensus building, or even building the trust and goodwill that would create a fertile ground for further deliberations and negotiations.

**The Constitution: The Wiles of Majoritarianism**

One of the conditions agreed to in the Fairmont Agreement was that if the Muslim Brotherhood came to power, they would endorse a constitution premised on inclusive representation of all political forces rather than predominantly the party in power. The constitution was their first litmus test of applying the principle of *mousharaka* (participation) not *moughalaba* (domination).

The new constitution was also the first challenge that President Morsi faced in steering the country toward a new legacy. It would represent a new social contract between state and people. The struggle over the timing, sequence, and content of the constitution as well as the composition of the constitution-drawing assembly and the leadership within its internal committees shaped the political trajectory of the country in powerful ways between 2011 and 2013. After the first round of presidential elections on May 28, 2012, the two contenders appeared to be Ahmed Shafik and Mohamed Morsi. On June 12, 2012, the April 6th movement announced its endorsement of Mohamed Morsi. On June 14th, the Supreme Constitutional Court announced the dissolution of the parliament on grounds of its unconstitutionality. In the absence of a parliament, the next president of Egypt would have the executive and legislative powers concentrated in his hands (including, e.g., the right to declare war). The absolutist powers of the next president increased the anxiety of some leaders, who conveyed their concerns to the Supreme Council of the Armed Forces. The SCAF responded on June 18, 2012, by issuing a constitutional decree that severely undercut the rights of any future president. Groups such as the April 6th movement and the Muslim Brotherhood saw this as a power grab by an army intent on retaining power from behind the scenes and obstructing the transition to a fully civilian state, and they protested against the SCAF's declaration (Hussein 2012).

The constitutional decree gave the SCAF five principle powers: legislature in the absence of parliament; declaration of war; declaration of state of emergency; internal governance of all matters associated with the military and all levels of leadership including its commander; and reformulation of the members of the constituent assembly responsible for the drawing of Egypt's new constitution. There was pressure from within the Muslim Brotherhood and from some of its supporting allies in Egypt (e.g., the April 6th movement) to withdraw from the presidential race in protest. On June 24th, Morsi's victory over Shafik was announced. Morsi was under extreme pressure from all political forces, Islamist and non-Islamist, to retrieve the powers that were usurped in the constitutional decree of June 18th. The only option for him was to annul this constitutional decree as president and replace it with a new one.

On August 12th, President Morsi announced a new constitutional decree that annulled the SCAF's decree. He removed Field Marshal Tantawy, commander of the SCAF, dissolved SCAF itself as a mode of governance, and appointed General Abdel Fattah el-Sisi as minister of defense. This action, however, turned the non-Islamist political forces against Morsi. They accused him of concentrating power in his hands in an absolutist manner via a constitutional decree that he unilaterally drew. President Morsi found that the only way in which he could claim these powers as legitimate was to have a constitution drawn that would define and bestow upon him the rights to rule. For these reasons the inauguration of a new constitution was an urgent matter for the new president.

Between 2011 and 2013 Egypt witnessed three attempts at arriving at a new constitution. The first constituent assembly was initiated in 2011 but declared null and void a few months later by the Supreme Constitutional Court for its lack of inclusivity. The second constituent assembly produced a new constitution in 2012 and early 2013 that subsequently fell with the ousting of President Morsi. The third constituent assembly put a new constitution in place in December 2012 and January 2013. This quick turnaround of constitutions is unsettling in many ways and is reflective of the deeply unstable political state of the country.

Technically, President Morsi did not have a direct political role in informing the process of drawing Egypt's new constitution; the task was assigned to a constituent assembly. However, he could veto the constitution by not signing the document. Should he withhold his signature, the constitution would not be put forward to the people for referendum. The downfall of the Muslim Brotherhood regime can be partly traced back to the constitution and the political strategies deployed by those in power to secure its promulgation.

The selection of the 100 members of the constituent assembly in 2012 was a two-tiered process. First, the different political forces arrived at an agreement whereby the Islamists would take 50 percent of the 100-seat constituent assembly and the non-Islamist political forces the other 50 percent. This seemed on the surface a fair compromise for all. A spokesperson for the Muslim Brotherhood and a member of its Supreme Guidance Bureau argued that because the Islamists occupied 77 percent of seats in parliament, their compromise was not to insist on the same scope of representation in the constituent assembly. The non-Islamists argued that they had sacrificed the notion of a rainbow representation, whereby equal weight is given to all different political forces, and had instead resigned to a two-camp system of Islamist and non-Islamist.

The second part of the assembly selection process involved "filtering" the lists. Members of parliament and the Shura Council would vote on the final selection of names from the proposed list. In effect, the formula above still led to a majority Islamist representation in the constituent assembly because the parliament and Shura Council were dominated by Islamists (75 percent) who vetoed proposed names that they did not like and endorsed those considered more acceptable (Essam El-Din 2012).

Despite these hidden power differentials informing the process of selecting the 100-member constituent assembly, the accounts of all interviewed members of the assembly prior to its dissolution suggest that there was sufficient goodwill at the beginning among all parties to predict that the process had a good chance of succeeding.

### The Politics of Negotiating Gender in the Constituent Assembly

One of the most contentious aspects of the constitution-drawing process and outcome was related to gender matters. Here I argue that the negation of gender equality in the constitution was an outcome not only of ideological considerations, but also of political power-sharing deals between stakeholders. The demarcations were not always set between Islamist and non-Islamist; there were instances in which many members from both groups united against matters pertaining to gender equality. However, there was one distinctive variation: the stance of non-Islamist political forces in their diversity was unpredictable, but belonging to Islamist political forces (as opposed to independent Islamist figures) was an important predictor of a particular position on gender equality.

Yet issues of gender equality were not only areas of power struggle among members of the constituent assembly. They became catalysts for the collective mobilization of a broad spectrum of actors against the regime, including non-Islamist political forces and parties. The first part of this chapter engages with the politics behind negotiating gender in the constitution-drawing process and its outcomes, and the second part addresses the new government's engagement with gender matters on national and international policy levels.

The representation of women in the constituent assembly was problematic from both descriptive and substantive points of view. There were only seven women in the constituent assembly, representing 7 percent of the total membership. In terms of advancing women's interests, the situation was significantly worse. Of seven women representatives, only one had any track record of promoting women's equality. Among the seven were three women from the Islamist camp: Hoda Ghonia of the Freedom and Justice Party; Omayma Kamel, the women's advisor to the president; and Amany Abou el Fadl, a prominent Islamist. The remaining four women were Manal El Tibi, a champion of the rights of the Nubian people and head of the Egyptian Center for Housing Rights; Manar el Shorbagy, an academic and member of one the newly formed political parties who specialized in international relations and was not involved in women's rights advocacy; Shahira Doss, a member of the Wafd Party who, according to all those interviewed, never turned up for the constituent assembly meetings and was virtually invisible; and Soad Kamel Rizk, dean of the Department of Management and Information Systems at the French University in Egypt, who was not known to have any previous engagement with gender justice issues or in politics generally, and who did not make her presence felt in the constituent assembly meetings.[2] Suzie Adly joined the constituent assembly when Manal El Tibi pulled out, but again, she had no credentials of women's rights work nor was she in contact with women's rights initiatives.

The contrast between the performance and capacity of the four politically savvy women from the Islamist camp in the constituent assembly and those from the non-Islamist camp was striking. The Islamist women were very well versed in gender matters, and they had a clear agenda to take forward in contrast to the non-Islamists (El Tibi excepted). When one of the four non-Islamist women was questioned about affirmative action, she proceeded to ask what it meant; when she was asked about the differential impact of Shari'a law on Muslim and Christian women, she was speechless. It is fair to argue that just because they are women does not mean that they would have a particular normative understanding of women's rights or even engage with women's issues in the first place. However, the lack of representation of plurality of agendas and interests in the constituent assembly on gender matters is problematic. In other words, while the Muslim Sisters advocated for a gender agenda commensurate with their movement's stance, there was no counterrepresentation in the

2. All efforts by journalist Robeir el Fares to reach Doss, Shorbagy, and Rizk for interviews failed.

constituent assembly of a feminist stance except for El Tibi, who as one individual in a group of 100 had minimal influencing power.

The position of the women representatives from the Muslim Brotherhood was to espouse the agenda that they had championed and lobbied in national and international fora for years: a rejection of any articles that challenge men's *qawama*[3] and that remotely relate to the rights enshrined

3. *Qawama* as viewed by the Muslim Brotherhood "is merely a matter of leadership and directing in exchange for duties that should be performed. For it is the husband who pays the dowry in marriage, it is he who provides the house, its furniture, and all its needs and it is he who provides for the wife and children. He cannot force his wife to pay for any of these expenses even if she is wealthy. In most cases, the husband is older and it is the husband who is usually the breadwinner of the family and mixes more, with a wider range of people. Every type of group including the family must have a leader to guide it within the limits of what Allah has ordained for there can be no obedience for a human being in a matter involving disobedience to the Creator. It is the husband who is qualified for that leadership" (Tadros 2012f).

Leading women members of the Brotherhood such as Camillia Helmy have framed men's *qawama* over women in terms of a defense of women's human rights. "We raise the banner of men's *qawama* as a right for woman and not for man," Helmy affirmed in a 2012 interview, explaining that it is men who are required and obligated to earn a living and provide for the household and not the woman. The fact that a woman is not required to earn her bread is for Helmy one of the privileges afforded to women as a result of men's *qawama*. In practical terms, although Helmy talks about men's obligation to provide for the household as a woman's right, there are a plethora of personal and economic factors that would prevent a man from being able to provide for his family (such as unemployment) and for which it would be difficult for women to hold them accountable. In such a context, a man's *qawama* over women in terms of a power relationship does not change unless a woman wishes to apply for a divorce.

Although the principle of *qawama* is applicable to both the domestic and public spheres according to the *fatwa* of 1981, the current official Muslim Brotherhood position is that *qawama* is only applicable to marital relations. "The boundaries of men's *qawama* over their wives is restricted to marital partnership only and it is a *qawama* of sincerity and mercifulness and consultation in return for responsibilities born by the husband" (Muslim Brotherhood 2006). This is also the position taken by the leading figures in Muslim Brotherhood political thought, such Qaradawy, El Bahnasawy, and El Wa'i. Narrowing the sphere of men's *qawama* over women to marital relations in effect denies the claim of universal *qawama* of all men over all women; therefore, theoretically, women are not

in CEDAW and a gender blindness toward inequalities on the ground. They systematically mobilized for the introduction of new qualifiers to women's rights, and they thwarted all proposals for their expansion. In interviews with the Muslim Sisters, they vigorously defended the new constitution on three grounds: women would benefit from the expansion of rights made to all citizens; the most vulnerable would benefit from provisions for female-headed households, and the clause on the protection of the family would benefit women.

The constitution, according to a leading woman figure of the Muslim Brotherhood,[4] enhanced rights for all and therefore meant an expansion of women's rights. She cited new rights that would benefit women and men, such as the right to a clean environment, right to information, and right to housing. The Muslim Sisters and the Islamist bloc also defended the new constitution by saying that it introduced a new clause that recognized the state's commitment to providing support for female-headed households and the neediest via welfare and health insurance. The last line of Article 10 stipulated that "the State shall provide special care and protection to female breadwinners, divorced women and widows." This constitutional commitment is in line with the legislation supporting female-headed households passed in parliament earlier that year (see chapter 8).

Islamists also heralded the article in the new constitution regarding the state's commitment to the family. Article 10 stipulates that "the family is the basis of the society and is founded on religion, morality and patriotism. The State is keen to preserve the genuine character of the Egyptian family, its cohesion and stability, and to protect its moral values, all as regulated by law. The State shall ensure maternal and child health

---

prohibited from assuming leadership positions in politics and society. However, in practice, the regulation of marital relations in the private sphere via *qawama* has implications for women's participation and leadership in the public sphere. On account of *qawama*, a husband may deny permission for his wife to work or run for office.

4. The original text included the person's name; however, due to difficulty accessing her for written permission after the crackdown on the Muslim Brothers, I have had to remove her name.

services free of charge, and enable the reconciliation between the duties of a woman toward her family and her work." Many interviewees argued that because the constitution recognizes religion as the foundation upon which the family is built, it will serve to safeguard women's rights. Although this article existed word for word in the 1971 constitution, it never provided the pretext for the promulgation of progressive laws or policies, and therefore it was unclear how the Muslim Sisters intended to use it this time around for the advancement of women's rights.

The constitution did not only fall short of the expectations of a post-revolutionary social contract that would recognize women's rights; it represented a dilution of the modicum of rights that were enshrined in the previous constitution. At the heart of the constitutional assembly's dispute on women's rights was Article 68 from an earlier draft of the constitution, which stipulated that "the State is committed to taking all measures to establish equality between women and men in political, cultural, economic and social life and all other fields as long as it does not violate the provisions of the Shari'a." The Islamist lobby, in particular the Muslim Sisters, assured skeptics that the insertion of the Shari'a qualifier was simply to acknowledge that in matters such as inheritance and divorce, equality between men and women is not absolute. Another leading Muslim Brotherhood female member of the constituent assembly argued that the addition of the qualifier, "what does not violate the Islamic Shari'a," to the original article in the 1971 constitution was in recognition of the fact that "full equality is not compatible with issues of inheritance, marriage, and divorce." The qualifier, she explained, was so that "we don't have a case where a lawsuit is filed because a man took up another wife when Islam allows polygamy" and for other issues pertaining to civil life such as inheritance (interview by Robeir el Fares, November 2012). A renowned Muslim Brotherhood female MP argued from the same standpoint, saying that the principle of equality needed to be balanced with recognition of the principle of *qawama*, whereby men are financially responsible for women. She elaborated as follows:

> We have a fear of the word 'equality' and its interpretation in international treaties, which have causes, threats, and infringements, which is

what happened in Tunisia when they annulled polygamy on the basis that the taking up of other wives causes psychological harm to the [first] wife and during the discussions some fear of leaving the article as it is [without the addendum] so it needs a reformulation. (interview by Robeir el Fares, November 2012)

However, many interpreted this qualifier as aimed at denying women all kinds of rights, including those associated with leadership, under the pretext that women cannot rule over men according to some Islamic interpretations. It is this article in particular that was most recognized by interviewed non-Islamist members of the constituent assembly as threatening to women's rights. Many held no illusions of the potential of this clause being used to block women assuming particular leadership positions such as judges and strategic ministerial portfolios or to restrict women's reproductive and sexual rights.

In the end, the clause was removed from the constitution in its entirety, rather than strictly the qualifier. The move was supposed to appease the Salafists as well as assuage the fears of women rights activists. A representative of Ghad al-Thawra Party from the constituent assembly defended the draft constitution vigorously after the removal of Article 68:

We removed Article 68, which spoke of equality of men and women as long as it does not contravene the precepts of Islamic Shari'a and therefore our constitution does not make any word or condition/exception that differentiates between men and women, female and male . . . citizens are all equal. There are articles that allow women to nominate and elect women and that allow women to occupy positions in parliament. I think this is a very good situation. (interview by Robeir el Fares, December 2012)

It was not only what the constitution included in its articles that signaled a lack of political will to endorse women's rights, but also what was left out. The level of mistrust toward the Islamists and especially the Salafis was so deep that their opponents assumed a backstopping stance by seeking to have as many rights inscribed in the constitution as possible so they would be more difficult to revoke later through legislation. Naturally, there was resistance from the Islamist bloc. There was extensive lobbying among feminist circles to introduce a clause that would commit the state to protecting women from all forms of violence. This clause was rejected on several grounds. One of the women members of the constituent assembly argued that the decision not to incorporate a clause on violence was because the assembly condoned violence. She publicly announced her resignation from the assembly and cited the anti-women's rights stance as one of the reasons. In retaliation, members of the Islamist bloc began to spread rumors that El Tibi was championing gay rights and abortion. Most interviewees mentioned in their recollection of Manal El Tibi's participation in the assembly that she never commented on abortion or gay rights. Such a rumor was deliberately circulated to undermine her credibility in an environment in which patriarchal and homophobic norms are widely prevalent. The only interviewee who said that El Tibi was claiming such an agenda was a member of the constituent assembly associated with the Islamist movement. This Islamist woman member said that El Tibi asked for the right to abortion; the women then questioned, "How could she ask for reproductive rights in an Eastern state?" She also accused El Tibi of asking for gay rights, adding that "Egypt, which is home to Al-Azhar and the Coptic Orthodox Church, will never permit the recognition of the rights of gays not ever, not in twenty or fifty years' time" (interview by Robeir el Fares, December 2012).

Women's rights activists pressed for the constitution to stipulate a minimum age of marriage. This motion was rejected by an Islamist female member of the constituent assembly on the grounds that marriage age is a matter that is best dealt with in legislation rather than in a constitution. She explained that "the constitution did not specify the age of marriage because it is a matter pertaining to laws and the laws change *and at the moment* the law has set the age of marriage at eighteen" (interview by Robeir el Fares, November 2012; emphasis added). The above statement helps explain why feminists attempted to introduce as many clauses in the constitution that affirmed women's rights as possible. They were concerned because laws are transient and amenable to change via parliaments, whereas the constitution is a social contract with the people that requires a referendum for its articles to be modified.

The Islamist constituent assembly member's words suggest that the eighteen-year-old stipulation may be subject to change. In view of the fact that many within the Muslim Brotherhood and the Salafis believe that the age should be reduced (the Salafis suggested it should go down to nine), it is not surprising that feminists sought to make the legislation immune from Islamist influence. In a deeply suspicious environment, feminists feared that they needed to guard against future tinkering with the laws and change them through "democratic paths" (i.e., majority rule in parliament).

Women rights activists' struggle for a gender-sensitive constitution was a particularly difficult one because of the political dynamics governing the negotiations among members of the constituent assembly. In response to the majoritarian dynamics influencing the writing of the constitution, different factions had to fight for their set of interests/issues and therefore were not willing to champion other causes that may not swing the pendulum in their favor. This meant that beneath the Islamist versus non-Islamist demarcations, there were other, more opaque lines being drawn. For example, informants said that Ayman Nour's party (Ghad al-Thawra) was closely collaborating with the Muslim Brotherhood, an alliance that was unilaterally denied by his party representative in the constituent assembly.

In contrast, the debate over whether there should be a quota for women was primarily driven by political considerations rather than ideological stances. A leading member of the Muslim Brotherhood argued that the idea of a quota was not acceptable because there was no quota for Copts or for youth. He pointed out that the presence of a quota would create contradictions in the constitution because the constitution is premised on the idea of equality for all. The existence of a quota reflects a broader philosophical debate that is not specific to the Egyptian, Arab, or Eastern context. Higgins (1997), speaking of Western legal traditions, suggested that for many decades there has been a disjuncture between feminist statist scholarship and mainstream constitutional theory. Whereas feminist theory has emphasized the constraints on women's choices emerging from inegalitarian power relations and structures of inequality, mainstream constitutional theory tends to emphasize equal citizenship, sovereignty, and legitimacy emanating from equality of status, rights, and duties.

In fact, there was a consensus established among many political parties across the liberal/Islamist divide over the principle of dropping any kind of affirmative action. A right-of-center, non-Islamist member explained it as follows:

> We agreed on a set principle, which is that there be no discrimination in favor of any creature on the face of the earth and that the constitution does not discriminate in favor of any human being: not workers, nor farmers, nor women, and we agreed that the electoral law [to be developed] would be balanced. (interview by Robeir el Fares, November 2012)

The opportunities of influence for feminist groups were not only affected by who among the non-Islamist groups were willing to endorse their cause, but also by who among the Muslim Sisters were willing to engage with them. Interviewees said that of all the sisters of the Muslim Brotherhood, Omayma Kamel was the most approachable and most keen to allow for an exchange of ideas. Through Kamel's liaising, Mohamed el Beltagy, the speaker for the (later devolved) parliament, convened a session to listen to the views of women's rights' activists on the proposed constitution. Many leading women's rights organizations, including those with legal expertise, contributed to the session. The NCW and the EFU sustained the pressure for women's rights throughout.

After the session, Beltagy was relegated with the responsibility of sharing the recommendations with members of the constituent assembly. In the end, most of their concerns were not taken on board and were never put forward to the constituent assembly to discuss in the first place. When asked what happened to the recommendations, an Islamist woman member of the constituent assembly explained that the suggestions of the NCW and the EFU were dropped "because the committee delegated with formulating the wording of the articles of the constitution felt they were more appropriate for consideration at a legislative rather than constitutional level" (interview by Robeir el Fares, December 2012).

The decision on what to include at a constitutional level and what to relegate to legislature was not a technical matter, but one largely reflective of power dynamics. Articles, qualifiers, and addendums that were commensurate with the Islamists' vision were added to the constitution, whereas insertions that clashed (or had the potential to clash) were rejected on the basis that they were best dealt with at a legislative level. The power dynamics at work were not only on a visible level (e.g., the stances and positions made by members in the constituent assembly) but on a hidden level as well (e.g., which proposals made it for discussion, which were excluded, which were seen as important enough for a constitutional level, and which ones were seen as more suitable for legislation).

Feminist voices, though marginal, sought to build alliances among the non-Islamist forces to remove the qualifier for women's rights (Article 68 of the draft). Feminists won the battle with the qualifier, but they lost the war. They were outmaneuvered by the last-minute insertion of a clause that effectively empowered the Islamist constituency to redress all existing rights by introducing new qualifiers affiliated with Islamic jurisprudence. Article 219 was purposely kept at the end of the constitution to deflect attention. It stated: "The principles of Islamic Shariʿa include general evidence, foundational rules, rules of jurisprudence, and credible sources accepted in Sunni doctrines and by the larger community." The Salafis proposed the clause and various Islamist movements supported it. It was vehemently opposed by many representatives in the constituent assembly who had thought that there was agreement to drop it. Yet on the very last night, Islamists voted in majority in its favor and it passed.

In effect, Article 219 meant that should conservative Islamist political parties assume a dominant presence in parliament, they could choose the most regressive interpretations in Islamic jurisprudence and base legislation upon them. In light of the fact that Al-Azhar University has adopted a consistently reactionary stance on women's rights, such legislation would get its blessing. The reaction to Article 219 among feminists exceeded disappointment and spilt into feelings of being cheated. It was sufficiently strong to catalyze women activists from different backgrounds—development NGOs, feminist NGOs, political parties, and nonpoliticized citizens—to join ranks and make a unified stance demanding their rights.

The loss of faith in the process of constitution-writing experienced by many feminist actors represented a microcosm of what was happening within the wider scene of non-Islamist actors. The Muslim Brotherhood–led government experienced a major blow when all three leaders of the Coptic Christian churches in Egypt took a united stance of withdrawing from the constituent assembly. This action was followed by a string of withdrawals by representatives of key political forces and actors in Egypt: Al-Azhar University, several renowned intellectuals, the representative of the April 6th movement, and representatives of key left-of-center political parties, among others.

When a key member of the Muslim Brotherhood was asked about how the walkout of major political factions was received in the assembly, he said it did not bother him because the rule of democracy is to go by the majority and not the minority. He also shared that he saw their walkout as a form of blackmail (they either got their way or walked out), especially since the process had been going on for five months. He believed that the Islamists cared more for the good of the country whereas the others were more exploitative and bad-willed toward an Islamist president. A leading member of the April 6th movement who later pulled out of the constituent assembly criticized the fifty-fifty principle guiding the composition of the assembly on the basis that there are at least four different political forces in Egypt, not two. He said that he later realized that the fifty-fifty formula was a cover-up for majoritarian politics and not intended to give equal weight to the plethora of political orientations that have a presence in Egyptian political life.

The Muslim Brotherhood and champions of women's rights were to engage in another conflict (around gender-based violence) less than two months after the constitution-writing saga. This time, however, it was to assume international proportions, forcing the Muslim Brotherhood to recognize the importance of creating a parallel institutional mechanism to the existing national women's machinery that was inimical to their reign.

### The Brotherhoodization of Gender Policy and Its Limits

President Morsi had promised that in his first 100 days in office his government would strive to improve security for citizens, create economic opportunities, and address the waste disposal problem. There did not seem to be an improvement on the streets with respect to daily incidents of socially motivated harassment. According to Farah Shash, a psychologist with El Nadim Center for the Rehabilitation of Victims of Violence, politically motivated sexual harassment had gotten worse. Although she conceded that incidents of politically motivated sexual assault had been documented during SCAF rule, such incidents increased in frequency and severity when the Muslim Brotherhood entered government (see chapter 7).

Informal youth initiatives working on gender-based violence in public spaces put pressure on the Morsi government by exposing the scale and intensity of women's exposure to assault and by holding the government accountable for their failure to protect such women (see chapter 7). Although these initiatives were uniformly committed to defending women's rights to unhindered access to the streets, they held differing positions on how to engage the Morsi regime. Some adopted a method of nonentanglement in the power struggle between Morsi and his opponents, preferring to focus exclusively on addressing gender-based violence. Others believed that the struggle to address gender-based violence was part of the broader struggle to resist a regime whose legitimacy was being called into question.

The Morsi regime's stance on gender-based violence in general and on harassment in particular added fuel to the fire. At the 57th session of the Commission on the Status of Women in March 2013, the commission issued a set of "agreed conclusions" on the elimination of all forms of violence against women and girls. The agreed conclusions reiterated many of the principles highlighted in CEDAW and reinforced the message regarding a zero-tolerance policy toward both private and public forms of gender-based violence. This was a golden opportunity for the Morsi-led government to show the international community that an Islamist regime recognized and endorsed women's bodily integrity. Instead, the Muslim Brotherhood issued a statement condemning the agreed conclusions on account of their incompatibility with the specific needs of Muslim women and their destruction of family values.

Most members of the Shura Council endorsed the Muslim Brotherhood's stance against the CSW declaration on gender-based violence. However, unlike the political stance they took on quotas, members of the constituent assembly were not unanimous in their view of the CSW's gender-based violence declaration. Misr Al Qaweya (Strong Egypt), the Islamist-leaning political party led by presidential nominee Abd el Moneim Abou el Fotouh, rejected the declaration and stated that Egypt, the country home to Al-Azhar University, would never accept any international documents that violate Shari'a principles that raise the status of women (Moubasher 2013). Al-Azhar and the Salafi political figures agreed with this policy. Representatives of the non-Islamist political parties did not rush to declare their support for the CSW document, but at least one head of a non-Islamist political party did come out in favor of it. Amr Moussa, another former presidential nominee and head of the Conference Party, endorsed the declaration, called upon Egyptian society to support it, and warned against the use of religion to justify discrimination against women.

The reaction of the Islamist political forces to the CSW's call for a condemnation of gender-based violence challenged ideas integral to understanding the political scene in Egypt. The first was the notion that there are a variety of positions on gender issues across the spectrum of progressive, moderate, and conservative Islamist political forces (El Mahdi 2010). The fact that the political party that was most associated with the progressive, moderate Islamism rejected the elimination of gender-based violence indicates a consistent rejection of all policies that expand women's rights. Although there are different shades of ideology, when it comes to gender matters, political forces always coalesce into a political bloc that stands against any fundamental challenge to the gender hierarchy.

The second notion that was challenged via political society's reaction to the CSW was that there is no difference between Islamist and non-Islamist political parties because they all hold the same reactionary stance on women's rights (see Hatem 2013 for an explanation of this stance). It is true that all political parties across the Islamist and non-Islamist political spectrum are deeply patriarchal, but non-Islamist political parties do not consistently hold the same policy/position on gender issues nor do they act as a unified bloc. Amr Moussa's endorsement of the CSW declaration is a case in point. In terms of building alliances and pathways of policy influence, because not all non-Islamist political parties hold the same position on women, the possibility of finding strategic supporters is there.

President Morsi chose to send his political advisor, Pakinam el Sharkawy, to head the Egyptian delegation to the CSW in New York instead of Omayma Kamel, the presidential advisor on gender issues, possibly because the former is considered to be feistier.[5] For the first time ever, the opponents of the official delegation did not come from conventional circles (local and international civil society) but from among its own leadership. At the CSW, the tensions between Pakinam el Sharkawy and Mervat Tallawy, the head of the National Council for Women, became conspicuously evident.

The president delegated to El Sharkawy, not Tallawy, the task of delivering the official speech, a political signal that indicated a lack of trust in the leadership of the NCW. In her speech El Sharkawy used the "cultural specificity" argument to justify reservations to the CSW document. She stated that violence against women should be combatted based on "balance between the values shared by humanity, and the cultural and social particularities of countries and peoples" (Tolmany 2013). The national and international political cost of this speech for the Muslim Brotherhood regime was immense. They had continuously stressed that they did not run the show in government, but the fact that El Sharkawy went to the CSW to champion the Brotherhood's stance on gender-based violence exposed the overlap between the presidency and the Muslim Brotherhood as a movement. In addition, the Muslim Brotherhood's transnational alliances in the CSW did not seem strong enough to counter the transnational feminist mobilization against them. The international feminist and human rights groups blasted the Muslim Brotherhood for their stance and made them the object of negative public opinion. Amnesty International's Women's Action Network, for example, issued a statement calling the Muslim Brotherhood's stance as "alarming" and appealed for mobilization against it (Amnesty International 2013).

Internal dissent among the ranks of the Egyptian delegation to the CSW only served to undermine further the Muslim Brotherhood's

---

5. One month later Pakinam el Sharkawy was promoted to deputy prime minister and minister of international cooperation.

position. In New York Mervat Tallawy explained that although she consulted with El Sharkawy regarding the official speech, there were elements that they agreed on and others on which they differed. Tallawy said that she concurred with El Sharkawy's opinion that the regional office of UN Women should remain in Cairo and not be moved to Amman, but they disagreed on the extent to which Egypt's constitution recognized women's rights. She explained that El Sharkawy ignored her plea not to refer to Egypt's constitution because she rejects the current constitution. Tallawy told the *Al-Ahram* newspaper:

> I see that the content [of the constitution] did not safeguard women's rights and will force us later on to beg the President or his wife. We really wanted definitive rights for us as citizens within the Constitution and not be bestowed upon us as a gift or reward from any system, whether political participation or economic and social rights, or a fixed percentage in parliament, and this, unfortunately, does not exist in addition to the [absence of] prevention of trafficking in human beings and a commitment to international conventions and so on and then for us to say that this is the best constitution in the world is not reasonable. (Hellal 2013)

When asked in the interview about how Egyptian women fare with respect to violence against them, Tallawy's answer was to talk about the incidents of sexual assault in Tahrir Square and the international courts that prohibit the use of sexual violence against women in conflict. She then said what can only be interpreted as a covert threat to the regime: "My sincere advice to those responsible is not to take lightly the violations occurring in Egypt that are considered by the international community as crimes against humanity which may drive them to go to the International Criminal Court and we would find ourselves then faced with an international scandal" (Hellal 2013).

Informants from Egyptian civil society who attended the CSW said that Tallawy's open criticism of the Egyptian government's policies toward women and her exposure of the extent to which women's rights were threatened was received sympathetically by the international community. Because of her former role in the Foreign Ministry, Tallawy had strong allies in the upper echelons of the UN apparatus and the CSW. These allies looked favorably on her role as defender of women's rights from within the Egyptian government. In this international space she could exude more political influence than Pakinam el Sharkawy, the Muslim Brotherhood's representative. The international damage to the Brotherhood's image was considered sufficiently embarrassing as to merit presidential intervention (see below).

The Brotherhoodization of state policy vis-à-vis gender issues was evident in a two-pronged strategy adopted by the Muslim Brotherhood. First they created a select corps of women whose agenda was congruent with that of the Muslim Brotherhood, even if they were not organizationally part of the movement. These women were to lead in all policy spaces by essentially playing political musical chairs. In effect, they were substituting the first lady's entourage under Mubarak with the Muslim Brotherhood's female corps and other women with Islamist sympathies. For example, Omayma Kamel was a parliamentary candidate, a member of the constituent assembly delegated with the responsibility of drawing up the constitution, and a presidential aide to President Morsi.

The second part of the strategy was to co-opt one of the institutions close to the state so that it would be compliant with the Brotherhood's political agenda on gender matters. Shortly after the CSW President Morsi announced a new initiative at a conference in the presidential palace that was committed to elevating the position of Egyptian women. He announced that the government plan of action to enhance the situation of Egyptian women would be led by the Center for Sociological and Criminological Studies. Little of his speech announcing this initiative tackled women's issues per se; its content mostly focused on reprimanding opponents who had resorted to political violence against the Muslim Brotherhood and his government at a time of rising tensions.

The intention behind the conference at the palace was not only to save public face on women's issues, but also to pull the carpet from beneath the NCW as *the* key national institution delegated with addressing women's issues in Egypt, and which clearly was resistant to co-option. Mervat Tallawy was invited to the conference but was absent on account of being "sick." This was a move by Morsi's government to replace one resistant institution that could not be co-opted with another one that was more amenable to yielding to the political will of those in power. A postconference workshop to examine gender-based violence issued recommendations for the security apparatus on how to better handle assault in public spaces, but nothing came of such recommendations. The idea of a new action plan to enhance the status of Egyptian women was quietly buried, possibly because of a lack of genuine political commitment, but also because the government was forced to prioritize the growing internal dissent toward its rule.

The losses that women's rights activists experienced on a policy level galvanized a collective spirit of resistance, which brought on board activists and advocates whose earlier stance was to give the Muslim Brotherhood a chance. Simultaneously, the political exclusion of a wide array of groups encouraged the building of alliances across varied causes, which were now bound together by opposition to the regime in power. The new alliances between feminist activists and other political forces were a microcosm of a broader political process emerging on the ground: a countercoalition to the regime. The countercoalition's formation was further catalyzed by President Morsi's issuance of a presidential decree in November 2012 that gave him sweeping powers and subdued parts of the executive, legislative, and judicial branches of the state to his authority. One of the underlying goals of the constitutional decree was to allow the president to circumvent the possibility that the Supreme Constitutional Court may once again rule that the constitution is unconstitutional on procedural grounds. The second article of the decree stipulated:

> Previous constitutional declarations, laws and decrees made by the president since he took office on 30 June 2012, until the constitution is approved and a new People's Assembly [lower house of parliament] is elected, are final and binding and cannot be appealed in any way by any entity. Nor shall they be suspended or cancelled, and all lawsuits related to them and brought before any judicial body against these decisions are annulled. (Tadros 2012e)

Even Mubarak at the apex of his power had to concede to the Supreme Constitutional Court, which was one of the few state institutions that retained a certain measure of autonomy from the executive powers in Egypt. Morsi's presidential decree was met with an intifada in front of the presidential palace that involved not only the revolutionaries and political parties but thousands of citizens. Supporters of President Morsi gathered in the vicinity to "protect legitimacy" (in the person of the president). Violence ensued and some youth groups abandoned the pacifist nature of their protests, torching buildings belonging to the Muslim Brotherhood.

Hence, the constitution was an indirect catalyst to the demise of Morsi's regime. After the constitution passed, the Muslim Brotherhood's narrative shifted from Egypt's democratic transition to a phase of democratic consolidation. This widened the gap between them and the political forces that were excluded from power-sharing and had walked out on the constitution-writing process. The revolutionaries and sympathizers took up the slogan, "Down with the rule of the Guide," referring to the Supreme Guide of the Brotherhood (*Yaskut Yaskut Hokm al Morshid*), whom they accused of exercising power behind the curtains.

# 9

## THE CHANGING FACE OF GENDER ACTIVISM
## IN POST-MUBARAK EGYPT

B y 2012, Cairene citizens passing through the city center had become accustomed to the sight of young men and women who were wearing fluorescent jackets bearing messages against women's harassment and patrolling the squares and crowded streets. Citizens were most likely to encounter these individuals on days of planned protests, 'eid (feast) days, and other days in which crowds were expected. An entirely new social phenomenon emerged in post-Mubarak Egypt that bore the potential to integrate the women's equality agenda. This phenomenon held the promise of contributing to the emergence of a new gender justice (distinct from feminist) movement. The walls surrounding Cairo's squares and major streets said it all. Graffiti images were everywhere: displays of famous women loved by all Egyptians (actresses, activists, and singers) and accompanied by simple messages about women's dignity and the shame of harassers. The graffiti was not just an act of resistance against sexual violence. It was a clear message to the Islamists who were widely and loudly proclaiming their discourse of women's voices being 'awra (shameful).

The intensity of the backlash against the modicum of rights that women enjoyed, together with a post-Mubarak, revolutionary, and intensely political culture generated a new resistance movement. They comprised a broad range of nonstate actors who rose to the occasion. Though their primary sites of engagement were women's everyday exposure to sexual violence and the more targeted harassment of women protesting in public spaces, their movement galvanized efforts around redressing the growing encroachment on women's freedoms.

The focus of this chapter is the emergence of informal forms of collective action around gender-based violence, how they materialized, their strategies of engagement, and their impact. Such forms of collective action may be transitory but they may reinvigorate activism around gender issues by challenging conventional wisdom regarding ways of "being" and "doing" gender justice.

## In Perspective: Sexual Harassment in Egypt

Sexual harassment on the streets had increased in the last years of Mubarak's rule but was historically entrenched in Egyptian social practices. Almost on a daily basis, the newspapers published reports of women being kidnapped and raped on their way home from work or while leaving schools. In 2007, the sexual assault of women in downtown Cairo during the 'eid days assumed high-profile status as the video images and witness accounts showed women of all ages, irrespective of how they were dressed (even if they were fully covered), subjected to such assault without protection from the police. Women's exposure to sexual assault became the subject of much public debate about the economic and social roots of the phenomenon as well as about the role of the police and judiciary.

In the years that followed, security presence increased during the 'eid festivities in downtown Cairo, which helped reduce the incidences of assault. Generally, though, the broader phenomenon of women's increased exposure to sexual harassment remained unchecked. After the January 25th revolution, sexual harassment increased dramatically, both in intensity (more molestation and groping) and in frequency (in particular in urban areas). According to a HarassMap report on sexual harassment released on April 1, 2013, 60 percent of sexual harassment acts happened on the street, and half of all incidents took the form of groping (Kortam 2013). The HarassMap report stated that approximately half of the harassers were young adults between eighteen and twenty-nine years old, and almost another 40 percent were children under eighteen years old. Only 14.5 percent of harassers were adults thirty years of age or older. The study also noted that approximately 27 percent of incidents of harassment were perpetrated by more than one harasser. Women respondents reported that more than half of the victims who faced mob harassment did so alone and without other people around. Most of the perpetrators in incidents of mob harassment were men. In 45.8 percent of harassment cases, it was possible to identify the age of the harassers.

In April 2013, UN Women released the results of a nationwide survey that showed that 99.3 percent of Egyptian women have experienced some form of sexual harassment and that the most prevalent form (96.5 percent) was touching (El-Dabh 2013). This and other research on what accounted for the increase in sexual harassment of women after the revolution[1] pointed to security laxity. The police retreated from the streets after the ousting of President Mubarak, and thugs, gangs, and criminals began to act in an unrestrained manner. People have since perceived an increase in theft under force, assault on women, and break-ins on private property.

Although most women generally identified the absence of security as the main reason behind increased harassment, social and political factors also played important contributing roles. From a socioeconomic perspective, according to many actors, there is a disproportionately high percentage of unemployed youth in Egypt who come from economically marginalized groups and take up harassment as a pastime. From a political perspective, religious leaders and Islamist political parties, including the Freedom and Justice Party in power, have propagated a discourse that lays the blame of harassment squarely on women's presence in public space, attire, and behavior (see Tadros 2012a).

The post-Mubarak environment in Egypt continued to worsen on many fronts such as unemployment and increased economic hardship, and absence of safety in public space was one of the most cited problems faced by citizens. The harassment of girls and women in particular had a far-reaching impact on all aspects of their lives: girls could no longer walk with their friends to nearby schools and instead had to be accompanied by a parent; many young women were forced to stop going to university

1. Such research included informal interviews with activists, secondary data analysis, and sixteen focus groups that I undertook in 2011 for the Swiss Development Cooperation with women living in low-income areas in Egypt.

because the journey and the campus were no longer safe; women could not run errands in the evening alone and had to be accompanied by their husbands; and social calls to family and friends, one of the few ways in which working- and middle-class women spend their leisure time, were kept to a minimum.

Although domestic violence has affected a large proportion of Egyptian women (see chapter 4), by 2012 the most pressing form of gender-based violence affecting women was their exposure to sexual harassment in public space, be it the streets, transport, marketplace, schools, or universities. Politically motivated sexual assault in protest spaces also became more vicious and widespread in 2012–13 and was intended to intimidate women so they would abstain from public activism (see Tadros 2015). Feminist scholarship has sought to address the underlying power dynamics beneath this epidemic of violence. Nadje Al-Ali (2014, 122) suggested that

> It is important to look beyond the systematic gang attacks and tackle wider forms of sexual harassment, linking it to domestic violence, marital rape, female genital mutilation and honour-based crimes and killings. In addition to 'looking inward'—and many Egyptian feminists have already made this connection for many years—we need a more long-term and holistic strategy against harassment that includes a campaign for a fairer economic redistribution, against neo-liberal economic policies, and, crucially as well, a campaign against the systematic marginalisation of women in decision-making processes, both within governmental institutions and many opposition and dissident contexts.

The two women's rights issues around which there was the most mobilization during 2011–13 were gender-based violence in public space and the promulgation of a gender-just constitution (see chapter 8). Mobilization around gender activism transformed the nature of gender activism in three fundamental ways. First, in agential terms: the active involvement of men in initiating and sustaining collective action around violence against women suggested that a nascent gender justice movement may have been in the making that was distinct in composition and leadership from the conventional feminist movement. Second, whereas typically the work on gender equality was pursued through advocacy in the policy domain or through development interventions in poor communities, the strategies used by the groups working on gender-based violence engaged the broader Egyptian public in highly unconventional ways. These strategies were neither informed by the Women in Development paradigm nor by the Western liberal tradition of advocacy. Their inspiration came from the revolutionary ethos characteristic of that political phase of the country's history. Third, the new forms of activism around gender-based violence shifted the targets of intervention; the government became increasingly marginal to what the activists did, sometimes for better, sometimes for worse.

In 2012, actors considered influential in gender-based activism in post-Mubarak Egypt agreed to interviews with the Social Research Center at the American University and a mapping workshop held by the Institute of Development Studies, University of Sussex, in partnership with the Center for Egyptian Women's Legal Assistance. From the workshop as well as interviews with socially active men and women, we were able to identify eleven actors whose work was creating a ripple effect. Of the eleven actors, three formed in 2011, six in 2012, one in January 2013, and one formed one month before the January 25th revolution. Not surprisingly, none were registered with the Ministry of Social Solidarity as NGOs or coalitions at the time. Much of the collective action that emerged in post-Mubarak Egypt was in a public space that was less controlled by the government and was looser in structure and organization. Some of the actors focused exclusively on sexual harassment as their raison d'être whereas for others harassment was only one area of their work. Most adopted street action strategies but some worked virtually via networks and Facebook pages. The eleven actors reflected my normative values, namely that collective action should seek to enhance women's freedoms and choices. This meant that Islamist movements, for example, which addressed gender-based violence by blaming women (promoting more conservative attire and encouraging women to stay at home), were not selected as part of this group. See Table 2 for an overall profile of the eleven initiatives.

**Table 2. Characteristics of Youth-Led Collective Initiatives on Gender-Based Violence in Public Space**

| Initiative | Establishment/Reason | Objectives | Distinctive Activity | Role of Men | Collective Action |
|---|---|---|---|---|---|
| Arab Women Uprising | October 2011<br>To document women's experiences during the Arab revolutionary revolts | Serve as e-platform for reporting, sharing, and discussing women's predicament during the revolution | Discussion of taboo issues and gender-based violence on Facebook | Contribute messages and participate in debates | Uses Facebook to raise awareness of other initiatives |
| Baheya ya Misr | February 2012<br>To defend social justice issues, in particular women's citizenship rights | Lobby against the constitution and raise awareness on women's rights | Graffiti and storytelling as awareness-raising strategies | Serve as volunteers and leaders (particularly in graffiti initiatives) | Participates in other initiatives to raise awareness of gender-based violence |
| Bassma (Imprint) | July 2012<br>To work on sexual harassment, street children, and other societal issues; formed in response to a founder's own experience of sexual assault | Patrol public areas to rescue victims and help them file police complaints; raise awareness of sexual assault | Security patrols | Founders of the movement; play the leading role in security patrols and all activities | Synchronizes with other actors working in security patrols |
| Fouada Watch | June 2012<br>To follow President Morsi's performance with regard to the gender agenda | Monitor and document the government's performance on gender matters | Documentation and commentary on government policy; engagement with the media | Involved in art and media engagement, though not as founders | Collaborates with Shoft Taharosh and others to document and publicize cases of harassment |

| HarassMap | December 2010 To document where harassment is happening and give victims a chance to report it | Use technology to flag locations of harassment; create safe zones for women | Use of social media as a tool for women to identify incidents of assault | Head of the outreach team; many male volunteers in community activities | Works with other initiatives (e.g., Baheya ya Misr and OpAntiSH) to produce flyers and banners on sexual harassment |
|---|---|---|---|---|---|
| Kat' Eidak (Cut Off Your Hands) | January 2013 To prevent sexual harassment | Lobby for an all-women cabin in train station; catch and shame harassers; raise awareness | Use of violence against harassers | 12 of 20 of the founding group | Keen to work with Bassma and with other initiatives that provide psychological and legal support to complement their activities |
| Nefssi (I Wish) | May 2012 | Respond to women's aspirations for a better life; address sexual harassment | Use of a silent human chain in public spaces | Involved in the chains and graffiti | Participates in many of the awareness-raising campaigns on sexual harassment through the wide dissemination of banners and flyers |
| OpAntiSH (Operation Anti-Sexual Harassment) | November 2012 In opposition to group-organized sexual harassment | Rescue women being harassed in demonstration spaces and deal with their immediate needs | Belief in women's involvement in male-led rescue operations | Dominate rescue activities; members of core group | Synchronizes with other initiatives (e.g., Bassma, Shoft Taharosh) |

**Table 2. Characteristics of Youth-Led Collective Initiatives on Gender-Based Violence in Public Space (*Continued*)**

| Initiative | Establishment/Reason | Objectives | Distinctive Activity | Role of Men | Collective Action |
|---|---|---|---|---|---|
| Shari' Wai (Alert/ Aware Street) | September 2012 | Deal with issues of equality, including gender matters | Use of art and drama to support other initiatives | Founders; actively engaged in man-to-man peer education and use of puppets and music for awareness | Called upon by other initiatives to deliver messages in entertaining ways |
| Shoft Taharosh (I Saw Harassment) | October 2011 To protect women in crowded public spaces | Create a coalition to raise awareness of sexual harassment on the streets and save victims | Combination of awareness raising and rescue operations | Founding members; particularly active in the rescue operations in Tahrir | Emerged organically from a campaign involving various partners |
| Tehmarboutah | May 2011 | Sensitize Egyptian society to the need to recognize and include women in all levels of policymaking | Graffiti and catchy slogans | Active in the graffiti component | Supports other initiatives raising awareness of sexual harassment |

## Gendering the Face of Collective Action on Women

The overwhelming majority of the new initiatives formed in direct response to an impending threat associated with a particular political moment. There was a trigger met by an individual or a group mobilizing to respond through collective action. For example, the establishment of Arab Women Uprising was in direct response to the pressing need felt by the organizers to document women's experiences during the Arab revolutionary revolts. What prompted the formation of Bassma (Imprint) was the subjection of one of its founders to sexual assault in Tahrir Square, which, when shared electronically, galvanized others to step in and demand collective action. In the case of Shoft Taharosh (I Saw Harassment), the trigger was the need to protect women in crowded spaces in downtown Cairo during feast days. Fouada Watch was formed on President Morsi's inauguration day as a watchdog to follow his performance on the gender agenda.

The capacity of these initiatives to respond to such triggers was based on several factors that facilitated collective action. The deeply politicized culture during the early post-Mubarak years made many urban youth, even those who did not participate in the January 25th revolution in 2011, become more interested in politics, even if it was not formal politics. The Egyptian revolution that began on January 25, 2011, had a profound impact on citizen agency (Tadros 2012c). People participated in protests for years before the revolution, and the frequency of such protests increased tremendously between 2008 and 2010 (Ali 2012). Nevertheless, citizen participation in *millioniyyas* (calls for one-million-person protests) created a new energy around the expression of voice. The ousting of President Mubarak also removed the fear barrier for many who then dared for the first time ever to join in demonstrations, sit-ins, and marches. With respect to collective agency on gender-based violence, this had a dual impact. Many youth who did not have backgrounds in political engagement were attracted to the new movements. In addition, the youth who had already been active in revolutionary politics were responsive to the calls for collective action on this front. All of the eleven actors coalesced through networks of friends, comrades, and colleagues, and all of them were successful in mobilizing large numbers of volunteers and supporters through social media and/or street activism.

One of the most distinctive elements of these new movements was the involvement of men. Men's involvement, for the most part, was driven by their personal empathy with the problem of sexual harassment. Many men who joined or formed initiatives felt shock, pain, and especially anger when their colleagues, companions, sisters, friends, and female relatives were exposed to sexual harassment. Others personally felt the weight of having the mobility of female family friends constrained as a consequence of increased harassment. One man who participated in Nefssi (I Wish), one of the informal youth-led initiatives, said that he wished he did not have to escort his sister every time she had to leave the house. In other instances, men were mobilized to act because they believed that a fundamental right that had flourished during the uprising against Mubarak—that of women protesting side by side with men—was being seriously violated, and they felt personally and politically committed to fight that violation. It is this personal element that drove most men to mobilize around sexual harassment as opposed to, for example, a campaign on women's right to political office (in which men's involvement has been virtually nonexistent).

In five of the eleven initiatives reviewed, men played a pioneering role as founders. All five initiatives with men as founders also have non-feminist names, such as Nefssi (I Wish), Shoft Taharosh (I Saw Harassment), Kat' Eidak (Cut Off Your Hands), Bassma (Imprint), and Shari' Wai (Alert/Aware Street). It seems that when men are involved as founders, the organizations choose names that reflect the cause rather than the gender identity of the founders.

Men's activism was concentrated in certain activities: first and foremost, the patrol and rescue operations, and secondly, graffiti work, art, and media production. Some of these activities may be commensurate with traditional "manly" roles, but many volunteers put their masculinity at risk in their roles. The young men who joined Nefssi, the group that organized silent human chains in crowded spaces in Cairo and held posters and banners with messages on women's dignity and freedom, were often subject to verbal abuse. Some passersby would shout that they were not real men, that they were not masculine, that they had become just like the "girls" whose rights they were endorsing, and that they just wanted an excuse to hang around pretty girls. The slurs were so abusive at times that fights almost broke out, and members of Nefssi had to intervene to remind male participants that theirs was a peaceful demonstration. Even men who framed their championing of women's freedom from exposure to violence in terms of social justice were subject to social stigma from peers who thought it embarrassing and unmanly to be advocating such things in public. Hence, in many ways, men who were founders and active members in these movements and who invited others to join them were clearly defying social norms and values of appropriate masculine behavior and were doing so at great personal cost.

In the eleven organizations reviewed, it was clear that there was a positive correlation between a gender-inclusive movement and men's participation. The more the initiative represented and identified itself as one working on citizenship, social justice, and sexual harassment on the streets, the greater its appeal to a broad spectrum of men (compared with initiatives that explicitly identified themselves in feminist terms and as women's groups). In other words, these eleven youth initiatives are distinct from feminist movements in the composition of their leaders and members. Batliwala (2012, 6, emphasis in the original) suggests that some of the key distinguishing characteristics of a feminist movement are "(1) a critical mass of women form the movement; (2) use of a gendered analysis of the problem or situation; (3) feminist values and ideology; (4) systematically built and centered women's leadership in the movement; (5) seeks to transform *both* gender and social power relations; (6) use gendered strategies and methods; (7) women feature at every stage of the process; and (8) create more feminist organizations."

Batliwala's criteria touch on the identity, processes, and outcomes of the movement, and they do not apply to half of the eleven actors examined here. In all eleven cases, activism directly contributes to feminist outcomes because they are confronting violations against women's bodily integrity. Nefssi, Tehmarboutah, and Arab Women Uprising are feminist in identity, process, and outcome, but these initiatives have relatively fewer members who are active in the streets compared with other initiatives like OpAntiSH (Operation Anti–Sexual Harassment), Shoft Taharosh, and

Bassma. The perspectives of the latter group of initiatives are less explicitly feminist and they have roughly the same proportion of women and men in leadership and membership. In other words, women do not necessarily represent a critical mass, nor do they use explicitly gendered strategies and methods. Their aspiration is certainly not to create more feminist organizations. These new initiatives could be described as more in tune with gender justice. They are not feminist in identity and process, but they believe strongly in the unjustness of social and political orders that deny women fundamental rights.

The difference between feminist and gender justice movements is that their acts are not driven by women's empowerment but by the belief that society as a whole is negatively affected by women's exposure to violence and that the demobilization of female protesters is an attempt to undermine the revolution. Movements can be described as gender just insofar as they emanate from a publicly conceived sense of opposition to how women are being treated in society and a need to redress this injustice. Although the eleven movements have not described themselves as gender-just initiatives, their actions speak to one element of Goetz's (2007, 29) conceptualization: "Ideally, the issue of the meaning of gender justice would be established as a practical project—through democratic debate. Organized constituencies of women and men would express outrage about unjust social practices that discriminate against women or circumscribe men's roles." This approach to defining gender justice best describes these initiatives: they emanate from a practical project involving much democratic debate and organize through constituencies of women and men that have risen against the status quo.

The leaders of the collective actors are distinct from those leading women's NGOs during Mubarak's era because they are young volunteers and they comprise both women and men. Of the eleven initiatives only two do not have men as founders. Many of the NGO leaders were professional, middle-aged, and above all, women. All of the founders of the new movements are elites and they enjoy class and socioeconomic privilege. Most of them are professionals (mostly white collar, though Shari' Wai is an exception). The founders of Shari' Wai have backgrounds closer to that of the general population. In terms of age, all of the initiatives are predominantly youth led (younger than thirty), even when older women and men join. All of the founders are highly educated (at least undergraduate degrees, with some members having doctoral degrees), and they are all volunteers who have strong values of promoting and supporting a culture of volunteerism. However, the membership of these groups does include men and women from the working class, and such members have actively volunteered in the initiatives' activities.

The above profile of the leaders and founders of these new initiatives is very different from the profile of the most renowned NGOs working on women's equality in Egypt. The professionalization of the sector had choked out volunteerism, and the NGOs often were known by the names of their woman leaders rather than by their real names.

### Different Way of Doing Gender Activism

The youth initiatives working on gender-based violence in public space emerged at a historically critical juncture, one characterized by the country being in a state of revolution but also one where heavy-handed tactics were used to deal with civil resistance. The new actors that emerged were not an extension of the civil society that existed before the revolution. They were neither registered NGOs nor foundations that complied with the Ministry of Social Solidarity regulations and laws. They were not nonprofit civil companies doing conventional NGO work under a different legal umbrella. The individuals who coalesced around common agendas chose to work through informal collective entities, some describing themselves as initiatives (*moubadarat*), some describing themselves as coalitions, and others as movements. The informal nature of all eleven actors surveyed has worked to their advantage in the sense that it kept the structures fluid and allowed them to avoid government intervention. However, being informal also meant that they could not take advantage of some of the benefits associated with formal structures, such as applying for funds.

Many of these informal youth actors were the offspring of the revolutionary phase of civil activism, and therefore they mobilized on gender issues in new and different ways. There was a clear paradigm shift from engaging through conventional development practice to the use of revolutionary politics. In the 1990s and 2000s, organizations did gender work through community interventions that helped women meet their basic needs, awareness raising and legal aid, or advocacy for policy change targeted at the government. In the post-Mubarak phase, new actors did much of the work on gender through street politics. Protests and marches became some of the most popular ways of making gender claims. Graffiti, art, public songs, and catchy slogans exploded on the scene, forcing ordinary citizens to take note of the messages being conveyed. Male peer-to-peer dialogues and human chains deghettoized the gender agenda as activists engaged with the citizenry on why these issues are pertinent to their everyday lives and that of their families. Works of art and gripping messages used a nonelitist, colloquial language that spoke to people, and previously untapped constituencies such as school and university students were mobilized.

One of the key factors behind the success of youth initiatives on gender-based violence in public space was their ability to make gender issues relevant to people's lives through appropriate framing, a task that pre-existing NGOs and coalitions had not particularly mastered. They framed messages in street language that used popular idioms, sayings, and expressions and often appealed to people's sense of dignity, fairness, and mores. They often conveyed messages not only in words but in images (e.g., pictures or graffiti). When applied to sexual harassment, these messages created empathy among citizens with the victims of assault; they portrayed victims as *your* sister, *your* mother, or *your* daughter.

The security patrols and rescue operations organized by the youth vigilante groups were not just involved in making claims vis-à-vis policymakers but also in street activism. Key to the success of the vigilante groups' interventions was the role of men. Men's involvement deghettoized sexual harassment from being a woman's problem to being a people's issue; in addition, men have successfully prevented the harassment of women activists. They have served as positive role models, challenging the notion that it is the masculine norm to harass women.

There were several ideological differences when it comes to gender issues among the various youth initiatives. Some movements (e.g., Shoft Taharosh/I Saw Harassment) believed that there was a direct link among the regime in power (led by the Muslim Brotherhood), the Muslim Brotherhood movement, and the backlash against women's rights. When advocating for women's rights during protests, they would shout, "Down, down with the Supreme Guide's rule!" Conversely, some movements (e.g., Bassma/Imprint) deliberately chose to avoid taking a political stance against the Muslim Brotherhood or the Islamists, believing instead that a nonpartisan position would attract a wider following of people who want to avoid partisanship. Whereas some movements believed that women should have the choice to be involved in the security patrols, others unequivocally rejected women's involvement on the basis that it would deter the group from achieving its purposes. Some members of the movement strongly linked women's exposition to sexual violence to an inegalitarian society where male privilege goes uncontested. Others were more exclusively focused on fighting sexual harassment on the street as a socially reprehensible phenomenon.

In spite of these different political stances, there is evidence of a sufficiently clear common vision and set of goals across these initiatives that enabled a high degree of collaboration. There is consensus among all of the groups interviewed that public space should be made free of harassment. They all have a shared belief in an unqualified rejection of harassment against women, irrespective of what women are wearing, who they are with, or at what time of the day they are out. The predominant narrative that pervaded the ascendency of political Islam in 2011–12 emphasized that women were responsible for their own harassment. These youth initiatives insisted that it was never the women's fault and that there was no circumstance in which women deserve to be assaulted.

The success of these youth-led groups should be assessed against the backdrop of a highly volatile political context in post-Mubarak Egypt. There are several key indicators of their success. First, people on the street often stop members of the groups to ask if they can join them or simply to share a word of encouragement and appreciation. While I sat in a coffee shop in Cairo with founding members of Bassma, a group of young women and men haphazardly approached them and said that they saw them on television, they have seen their work, and they would like to be involved. Such an encounter is an indicator that at least on the level of urbane Cairene middle-class circles, these groups have won recognition and respect and are still drawing people to them.

The second indicator of effectiveness of the youth-based initiatives engaging with sexual harassment is that they have generated a large number of volunteers who are prepared to give of their time and abilities in various ways. Some have volunteer lists of more than one hundred applicants who want to join. The third indicator is that they have become an authoritative source of information, verification, and evidence on what is happening with respect to gender-based violence on the streets of Egypt. During the worst waves of sexual assault during the protests in Tahrir Square, which reached their climax in January and June 2013, OpAntiSH and Shoft Taharosh became authoritative sources of information on the number of incidents, where they occurred, and how they had been treated. They successfully conveyed this information to both the national and international media. The fourth indicator is the role of the security patrols: although they were not always successful in preventing sexual assault, they were able to intervene to rescue victims. In some cases they succeeded in rescuing women before they got assaulted; in other cases, they managed to retrieve women from the mobs of men assaulting them, or they arrived in time to provide postassault assistance in the form of urgent medical and psychological care.

The final indicator of the youth initiatives' success, which is far more difficult to assess, is the change in social norms and beliefs toward gender-based violence. Their impact outside Cairo is very limited because most of the initiatives operate in the city center.[2] Within Cairo, it is difficult to measure the impact of graffiti on passersby or that of pop songs about not harassing women that are widely played in public spaces and sung by the youth. It is also challenging to discern whether the attitudes of the people they engaged with through peer-to-peer encounters have changed. However, there are signs of shifts in normative values in some circles. For

---

2. Some of the interviewed actors mentioned their visits to governorates outside Cairo to raise awareness; however, upon further investigation, these visits were usually one-off events with limited outreach and impact.

example, Egyptian national television, a highly conservative establishment, featured several documentaries on sexual assault that were sympathetic to the work of the youth groups and to the plight of the victims. Some interviewed men who were active in these movements were converts to the cause as a consequence of their interaction with the groups. In other words, as a result of coming into contact with the men in the youth-led groups, these converts experienced a shift in their attitudes, turning from latent empathy to public activism and in some cases becoming change agents themselves.

The question of policy influence is a complex one. The most salient way in which the youth groups sought to engage with policymakers is through protests and marches. Engaging policymakers required a political stance on the legitimacy of the government. In December 2012 a faction of the groups agreed to present President Morsi with a bill for addressing sexual assault; another faction refused to join them because doing so would recognize Morsi's legitimacy and that of his government. In the end, they did not submit the bill, and it was a source of great friction among the groups. In that sense, the way the youth initiatives engaged in policy influence seemed far more radical than that of the pre-existing women's NGOs and coalitions during Mubarak's era.

During that time, there were several attempts to engage government officials, members of the National Council for Women, and actors close to state officials. Policy influence was part of the advocacy and campaigning agenda that donors funded and expected of women's human rights NGOs. The revolutionary climate characterizing the post-Mubarak period led to a more contentious stance on engaging with the government, one that became increasingly weary and conscious of the power of people mobilizing on the street. Avoiding engagement with the government may also have been a politically savvy and pragmatic choice: the Supreme Council for Armed Forces and the Morsi-led government were not particularly responsive to policy recommendations on gender equality.

There was another prickly matter to deal with when it came to engaging the government. Some members of the youth groups believed that the police were implicated in many of the sexual assaults against women protesters in Tahrir Square. For all of their vigilante work, good intentions, and organization, the security patrols could not substitute for a police force equipped in dealing with mob violence and assaults. The state of mistrust between the youth groups and the police was highly problematic. Without the police, the violence could not be contained. Without security sector reform, the youth groups were mistrustful of the intentions and behavior of the police.

## A Revolutionary Chapter or a Nascent Movement?

During their two years of mobilization (2011–13), the informal youth-led initiatives managed to sustain collective action. Two critical questions remain: Will these initiatives fade out with time? And, if they do survive, could they develop into a gender justice movement?

It is likely that some of the initiatives will disappear while others will continue and expand or metamorphose into something else. One of the key elements that sustained these forms of collective action is the nature of the cause around which they have mobilized. Sexual harassment is widespread and Egyptian society as a whole has suffered from the scale of its harm. It is a problem that is unlikely to go away. Will these movements lose steam if other, more pressing issues emerge?

One of the weaknesses in some current initiatives is that they are essentially time-bound campaigns on very specific issues. They need to reinvent themselves and set new goals if they are to survive as actors. Moreover, the way in which founders and members keep moving from one initiative to another, depending on energy and urgency, means that sometimes initiatives will quietly die.

Some of the initiatives (e.g., Bassma, Tehmarboutah, Kat' Eidak) are keen on registering as foundations with the Ministry of Social Solidarity to assume a legal character. Becoming a foundation or NGO is a double-edged sword. On the one hand, it may contribute to the organizational sustainability of a collective actor; on the other, it may lead to the erosion of the volunteer culture and create new disconnects between the NGO and the street as the organization assumes a professional character.

Many of the interviewees spoke of invitations they had received from well-established women's NGOs to join them and come under their institutional umbrellas. Some have resisted, believing that they would lose autonomy and have no possibility of leadership or transformation of the institutional culture. Other initiatives that have worked under existing NGO umbrellas have found that such an arrangement offers financial and technical support.

The survival of some youth-led initiatives will also be influenced by the extent to which the new authorities allow them to operate freely without co-option or repression. Some may be forced to come under the umbrella of existing organizations to protect themselves, whereas others will establish their own initiatives and others still may choose to abandon the initiative as a way of escaping state control.

One of the key determining factors regarding the sustainability of these new initiatives is funding. In 2013, when the founders were interviewed, nine of eleven initiatives were self-funded and relied on the benevolence of volunteers. Some were seriously in need of funds but did not have the institutional framework (a registered organization), contacts, or the knowledge of soliciting funds to approach Western donors. These initiatives were not very likely to be funded by Arab or Islamic donors who tend to focus on charity and community development interventions. Some of them might discontinue if they do not find sufficient resources to undertake their work. Conversely, an injection of large funds may also kill initiatives if it creates competition over resources and if the management of funds becomes too overwhelming and time consuming (see chapters 3 and 4 for evidence of how donor practices undermined collective action). Until 2013, there was no evidence that donors' funding policies toward Egyptian civil society had changed in recognition of the new post-Mubarak reality. In the spirit of business as usual, the same funding practices continued with the same donor darlings.

Evidence on the ground suggests that collective action on gender-based violence stands a good chance of continuing with respect to the larger, more established initiatives. These larger initiatives have shown great agility, shifting their focus from one site of sexual violence to another (from Tahrir during Morsi's reign to the subway and crowded inner city streets after June 30, 2013). The perceptions of interviewees, as well as the evidence, suggests that the size of the initiative is a very important determinant of the quality of the intervention itself. Initiatives such as OpAntiSH,

Shoft Taharosh, and Bassma tend to have greater visibility when working in the street because the groups are larger. Furthermore, initiatives with large numbers tend to have better outreach in the street because they cover greater territory. Such large initiatives (e.g., HarassMap, Bassma, OpAntiSH, and Shoft Taharosh) organize into several fronts/areas of work because they develop a more elaborate division of labor. This in turn increases their weight and ability to influence through different channels. Also, the larger the initiative, the greater its bargaining power in seeking collaboration and coalitional work with political parties and other actors.

As for the prospects of building a gender justice movement, this will rely in part on the extent to which young men continue to be engaged. The role of men in movement building has been key in terms of internal organizational dynamics as well as impact.

However, collective action has been undermined by power struggles between different groups/cliques over visibility and attribution of success to their individual initiatives rather than to common efforts, a trait that will worsen if they receive foreign funding. So far, the challenges of creating internal cohesion within the initiatives have not, for the most part, threatened their existence. Most initiatives relied on their repertoire of friends, contacts, and acquaintances to mobilize support and establish contacts with the media and various political parties and movements. However, creating a sense of common mission and stance across the initiatives may be more challenging. To move toward a cohesive movement, legitimate leadership that has consensus (as with Marie Assaad's role in the FGM Taskforce) is needed. Such legitimate, inclusive leadership would provide a unified front that takes advantage of the resources inherent in a common movement in terms of numbers, resources, skills, and networks.

The challenge for these initiatives is to provide platforms for collaboration that go beyond a specific intervention. In 2012–13 different groups cooperated and worked well together when they had to plan for an intervention in Tahrir Square. Beyond those events, the will to collaborate has been constrained by several factors. Among such factors is the dilemma of "attribution not contribution," which underpins each initiative's desire to gain visibility as being the most influential and successful in the field. The fear of ideas being stolen and the entrenchment of clique groups has stymied opportunities for collective movement building, though the challenges ahead may serve to unite them. The diminishing threat of politically motivated sexual assault in Tahrir Square after the ousting of President Morsi also means that the raison d'être of some initiatives (e.g., OpAntiSH and Tahrir BodyGuard) is called into question. Finally, as will be shown in the next chapter, the June 30th rupture has created deep polarization within and among groups over whether the outcome is a throwback to the revolution or a necessary step forward.

## Postscript

Through research undertaken in 2015 (Tadros 2015), I found that the political context surrounding these initiatives provided both opportunities and constraints. On the one hand, the space for organic activism involving street-based activity such as protests, human chains, graffiti, and theatrical performances was severely circumscribed because permits had to be obtained from the Ministry of Interior before stepping onto the pavement in a collective capacity. These permits were extremely difficult to obtain. Moreover, the spirit of civic activism and sense of optimism that the youth had in transforming political culture, which characterized the period after the overthrow of President Mubarak, had waned significantly. On the other hand, the government had issued for the first time ever a fairly harsh (though severely flawed) sexual harassment law. It had also established a special women's unit in the police to address sexual harassment in public spaces. There was a political will to tolerate a certain level of public action around gender equality, as compared with other issues pertaining to political freedoms such as detentions and incarcerations (and as long as such action did not approach matters like sexual assault in prisons and other security premises).

As predicted, some initiatives were inhibited from pursuing their activism on account of their raison d'être. Organizations such as OpAntiSH seemed to have limited or waned their activity, according to several interviewees engaged in work on sexual harassment in Egypt. However, many initiatives survived, finding highly innovative ways of navigating the new political context without compromising their mission. Their strategies are intended to circumvent the heavy-handed reach of the Ministry of Interior by finding parallel and alternative public spaces in which to engage.

HarassMap and Bassma acknowledged the highly differentiated and bureaucratic structure of state governance, in which different parts of the country and even the streets themselves are under different jurisdictions, and they took advantage of that structure to sustain public activism. HarassMap recognized that certain governorates have slightly more relaxed security arrangements, and they sought permits to work in the streets in those governorates. Both Bassma and HarassMap deepened their work in universities, which they saw as alternative public spaces in which to recruit volunteers and engage with a large and diverse student body. HarassMap obtained permission from the governor of Alexandria to work inside public transport vehicles and depots because these came under the governor's jurisdiction. They chose not to work on the pavements/streets because they were under the jurisdiction of the Ministry of Interior. These innovative strategies of engagement ensure that initiatives do not become co-opted or elitist. They continue to do work that is deeply relevant to the Egyptian context, and they continue to develop their strategies to respond to the pulse of the street as it changes in its perceptions and practices toward sexual harassment. However, maintaining the morale of the teams continues to be a challenge for these initiatives. They seek to create safe spaces in which volunteers can share and reflect: a parallel though not disconnected community.

Although there was some level of intragroup collaboration, by 2015 there were few signs that a movement against gender-based violence was forming through joint action. It was easier for two or three organizations to work together than for a coalescence of initiatives to collaborate. A collective front comprising many organizations may be strategically more vulnerable to security infiltration or encroachment. Without a collective front, though, opportunities of influence on a policy level may be severely circumscribed, a theme that I return to in chapter 11.

# 10

## THE MORNING AFTER MORSI'S OUSTER

The mass uprising against Morsi's rule that erupted around June 30th and the much smaller but highly visible protests in support of the president marked the second major rupture in Egypt's history, both of which occurred within the same two years. There was large-scale mobilization of women in the June 30th uprisings, and the outcome of the revolts—the ousting of Morsi via military intervention—created new fissures in the countercoalition that emerged. This chapter discusses the polarization that the outcome of the rupture (in terms of labeling it as a coup or revolution) has created among revolutionaries, activists, and feminists, as well as the broader polity and its implications for building collective action around a common gender justice agenda. In it I also examine the process of arriving at a new constitution after two former attempts were declared null and void. I then reflect on the question of whether we have reverted back to the same old political scene during Mubarak's tenure. Are we back to mobilizing behind old red lines?

### The June 30th Rupture

Women were some of the biggest supporters of the Muslim Brotherhood and actively contributed to their ascendency to power in parliamentary and presidential elections (Diaa 2013). However, they were also some of the most vehement opponents of the Brothers and they participated in large numbers in the June 30th uprisings. The Western media and policy analysts widely covered and publicized the role of Egyptian women in the January 25th revolution in terms of celebrating their political agency, their participation, and the multiple roles they assumed (mobilization of the crowds, makeshift hospitals, resisting the security apparatus, etc.). But although women rose in greater numbers and assumed an even greater role in the June 30th mass revolt, this time there was neither an acknowledgment nor a celebration of their political agency. Admittedly, in the January 25th revolution, the women who participated in counterprotests in support of President Mubarak hardly amounted to a few hundred, whereas the women who rose in support of President Morsi were in the thousands. Even higher were the numbers of women who revolted against the Morsi regime on June 30th.

The diversity in the population groups who participated on June 30th was far greater than that witnessed on January 25th. During the eighteen days of revolt against Mubarak in 2011, the protests were by and large encapsulated in Cairo, Suez, and Alexandria. In 2013, citizens went out in the thousands in at least fifteen of the major governorates of Egypt. Citizens living in the governorates of upper Egypt (with the highest levels of poverty and political exclusion) had minimal participation in the 2011 revolution. Yet on June 30th, the squares of Asiut, Minya, Sohag, Qena, and Aswan were packed with ordinary citizens. The wealthier governorates of the Delta that had not participated in the 2011 revolts joined in the 2013 protests in the hundreds of thousands. Consequently, women who had largely been absent from the January 25th revolution, such as rural women, women in the provinces, and women in upper and lower Egypt, all participated on June 30th. Moreover, rural populations who historically have not participated in uprisings and who represented the core constituency for the Muslim Brotherhood rose against the regime this time. Women and men from all backgrounds poured into the urban squares to join in the chants of "leave."

The millions of women who rose against the Morsi regime in 2013 were not explicitly driven by their gender identity. However, unlike the January 25th revolution in which grievances were conveyed in broad terms (bread, freedom, and social justice), on June 30th slogans were used (particularly in Tahrir Square and its vicinity) that explicitly mentioned women's rights. For example, the slogan *"sawt al mar'a thawra mish 'awra"* ("a woman's voice is a revolution not a depravity") was heard in urban squares in Cairo.

In Egypt there was an agreement among all of the different political forces not to raise their own separate identity banners. However, there was evidence of mobilization of parts of the crowd on clear identity terms, such as the workers. This was not the case with feminist activists in the January 25th revolution. Yet in the revolts of June 30th, there was an explicitly feminist presence emanating from the mobilization of several collective initiatives that were pressing people to rise against the regime. This time, unlike the march on March 8, 2011 (see chapter 5), the feminist presence blended in, and the messages, slogans, and banners were relatable for ordinary citizens.

Because images and accounts of women sexually assaulted in the mass demonstrations that took place in Tahrir Square on the second anniversary of the January 25th revolution were widely circulated in the media, there were doubts whether women would dare join in the June 30th revolts and whether their families would forbid them. Although some women spoke of wanting to join and being prevented, others went out with their families in large numbers. Nevertheless, some of the worst acts of sexual violence were reported during those days of mobilization against the Morsi regime. According to a feminist research and advocacy organization, Nazra for Feminist Studies, there were 101 incidents of sexual assault in the vicinity of protest spaces between June 28th and July 3rd (Nazra for Feminist Studies 2013).

When General Abdel Fattah el-Sisi announced the ousting of President Morsi and the appointment of the head of the Constitutional Court as the interim president on July 3, 2013, he did so in a public conference that was attended by representatives of all of the factions who had been politically marginalized during the SCAF's and Morsi's rule. Representation from the National Salvation Front, the judiciary, Al-Azhar University, the Coptic Orthodox Church, Tamarod, and the Salafi movement was intended to signal a political settlement that was all encompassing (the Muslim Brotherhood declined their invitation). Sakina Fouad, a renowned non-Islamist female writer, was also present. It is likely that her attendance represented women, as she was later appointed Adly Mansour's (the interim president) councillor for women's affairs.

Although a countercoalition calling for President Morsi to step down from office (whether through an ouster or early presidential elections) had emerged, uniting non-Islamist activists together on June 30th, Morsi's removal from office via military intervention fostered deep polarization within the ranks. A rift emerged among revolutionary women, feminist activists, political party figures, and informal youth initiatives over whether to consider the rupture a revolution and recognize the interim government as legitimate or to conceive of it as a coup and its consequent regime a military junta. This rift was so deep that women's rights gains in the constitution were of inconsequential weight to the coalition when assessing the democratic potential of the country.

Opponents to the regime linked the return of the heavy-handed security apparatus and the fate of Egyptian women, pointing to the increased violence perpetrated by the regime against the Muslim Brotherhood as a bad omen for what was awaiting human rights and other civil society organizations that assumed a watchdog role (see Kittleson 2014). Supporters of the new regime insisted that the new political order had removed some of the principle sources of oppression against women and that the violence from the Muslim Brotherhood toward unarmed citizens was being omitted from the narratives about the situation on the ground.

**Same as the Old?**

Some leading feminist academics, such as Professor Mervat Hatem, have argued that the coup led to a counterrevolution that will reinstate the old pattern of state governance of gender politics. Hatem (2013, 11) suggests that el-Sisi reverted to "classic, Mubarak-style tokenism" in relation to the participants at the press event in which he announced the ouster of Morsi on July 3rd and the appointment of three "token" women to the cabinet. Reflecting on Morsi's appointment of el-Sisi as minister of defense, Hatem notes (2013, 16), "It turned out that Morsi and al Sissi shared ideas about gender. . . . It is a logical inference, for example, that al Sissi was the anonymous source who defended the army's egregious 'virginity tests' to intimidate and humiliate women marking International Women's Day on March 9, 2013. These young women 'were not like your daughter or mine,' this source said. 'There were girls who had camped out in tents with male protesters.'"

However, the complexity of the situation needs to be unpacked. The initial response of the SCAF generals in March 2011 when women were arrested, incarcerated, and subjected to virginity tests was to deny that such violations ever happened. El-Sisi was the first army general to actually admit to their occurrence. According to Amnesty International's (2011) account, "Major General Al-Sissi said that 'virginity tests' had been carried out on female detainees in March to 'protect' the army against possible allegations of rape, but that such forced tests would not be carried out again. He also added that the army would avoid detaining women in the future." That el-Sisi justified the occurrence of the virginity tests on account of protecting the army from future allegations of sexual assault is indefensible; however, he is the only army general who displayed a commitment to desist such violations. Amnesty International's (2011) account of the meeting also stipulates:

> In relation to abuses by the security forces during the uprising and in the past thirty years, Major General al-Sisi told Amnesty International at Sunday's meeting that there was a need to change the culture of the security forces, and gave assurances that instructions had now been given not to use violence against demonstrators, and to protect detainees against ill-treatment.

The conclusion that el-Sisi was the anonymous source who defended the army's virginity tests is incommensurate with other evidence that suggests that it was Major Ismail Etnan who made these comments, a fact that was widely circulated in the news at the time (Dion 2012). It is also important to note that the attack did not happen on International Women's Day; Samira Ibrahim, who was subjected to virginity tests after being arrested by the military police, did not participate in the March 8th women's event. The army's violent assault on protesters was on March 9th (when the virginity tests took place), and it had nothing to do with International Women's Day. Although this slip in Hatem's account may seem trivial, it is crucial to the storyline intended to convey an image of el-Sisi as intolerant of women's rights.

Hatem (2013, 17) concludes her description of el-Sisi by saying that he "embodies the return to personalized authoritarian politics that the national consensus prior to the January 25 revolution rejected." Yet it may be worthwhile to examine why so many citizens who endorsed the January 25th revolution also supported el-Sisi's role in ousting Morsi. This is in no way a vindication of el-Sisi or his policies on gender or human rights. Rather, it is a plea for understanding the pulse of the citizenry and its dynamic nature in 2013/2014.

At the time prior to publication of this book (December 2015), there are very few signs to suggest that the revolution's aspirations for political freedoms have been fulfilled or are likely to be fulfilled in the near future. To the contrary, there are signs of the return of authoritarian patterns of rule, the most important of which are the resurrection of the security apparatus and its policing and surveillance roles and the growing repression of voices of dissidence, even when they have pursued nonviolent forms of engagement (though many have not). But it may be too simplistic to read the current situation as simply a reversion to the past. People have revolted, the fear barrier has been overcome, red lines have been transgressed, and all of this has done something to people's characters and their thresholds for tolerating injustice. The question has become a cognitive one: which injustices under what conditions will be perceived as surpassing citizens' threshold of endurance?

In interviews with many of the women activists in 2012 who played a key role in organizing for the protests, they bet firmly that although women face a severe backlash, there comes a point when they will rebel and revolt. "Once you have gone out, you can't be forced in again" was a definitive assessment of the political situation that was echoed over and over again. Their belief that there is no going back seemed to me overhopeful at the time; however, they were proven right, and women went out in the millions on June 30, 2013, even if not under a feminist banner.

An understanding of gender politics post-Morsi requires a more nuanced reading. The Muslim Sisters have suffered as part of the security crackdown against the Muslim Brotherhood and so have women dissidents who dare to defy the protest law and are now subject to extreme forms of violence at the hands of the security apparatus. However, in terms of gender outcomes of the June 30th revolution, the situation for the majority of women has improved compared with previous years. There are several indicators of this improvement: a constitution that grants them a wide array of rights in the political, social, and economic arenas; the disappearance of Islamists' harassment of women on account of their attire on the streets of Egypt; the disappearance (for the most part) of a highly reactionary discourse in Islamist satellite television; and the disappearance of organized group forms of politically motivated sexual assault in protest spaces. The suffering of low-income, rural, Coptic women at the hands of the Islamists has certainly waned, not on account of direct state policy to attend to their plight, but on account of the general repression of Islamist forces. However, this analysis applies only to the one year after the ouster of Morsi, and it may be very different when applied to a later phase.

**Gendering the New Constitution**

Although the descriptive representation of women in policy spaces remained poor, their substantive representation improved dramatically. The constituent assembly that was formed to arrive at a new constitution for Egypt included five women in the fifty-member body. Of the five, at least four women were strong advocates of women's equality. Two of them were from the national women's machinery: Azza El Ashmawy was a representative for the National Council of Motherhood and Childhood, and Mervat Tallawy was the head of the National Council for Women. The other three women were Mona Zulfiqar, one of the most influential lawyers defending women's rights in Egypt and a representative for the National Council for Human Rights, Abla Mohey El Deen, a representative for the industrial chambers committee, and Hoda Elsadda, a professor of English literature, founder of Woman and Memory, and a feminist activist.[1]

There were no women revolutionary leaders, farmers, or workers, and no women of leftist or Islamist orientation in the constituent assembly. What accounts for this homogeneity in representation? Coalitions and NGOs had pressed each stakeholder (political parties, unions, syndicates,

1. For a full profile of members of the constituent assembly, see http://www.daily newsegypt.com/2013/09/01/constituent-assembly-member-names-out/#sthash.F6 gl6PJp.dpuf.

etc.) to nominate 50 percent men, 50 percent women; however, there was no political interest or pressure to do so. The intersection of class, religion, and political ideology in the selection of women would have given the constituent assembly a more inclusive profile. There was a clear trade-off between inclusive representation and substantive outcome. All five women were from privileged, white-collar backgrounds and were middle-aged or older, and at least three of them were very well versed on examining constitutions through a gender-sensitive lens. All of the women representatives were politically astute with sophisticated competencies in navigating the policy-influencing terrain, striking deals, and pushing their political weight to get other parties to listen to them. These were skills that were certainly inherent in many women from different backgrounds, but others may have lacked the repertoire of networks that enable behind-the-scenes negotiations to happen and deals to be struck.

In terms of substantive representation, these five women not only represented a bloc that pushed for an expansion of women's rights, but one of them, Hoda Elsadda, was head of the Freedoms Committee, one of the most important and influential committees working under the umbrella of the constituent assembly. According to Elsadda, the presidency put forward the composition of the constituent assembly members as follows: three Al-Azhar representatives, three representatives from the Coptic Orthodox Church, four youth figures (including a member of Tamarod), and six representatives from political parties. The cultural sector was represented by four members, the labor sector by two members, professional syndicates by four members, and farmers by two members. National councils would be represented by five members, and unions and federations by five members. The armed forces and the police would each choose one person to represent them, and the cabinet would nominate ten public figures to join the assembly (Taha 2013). In terms of political orientation, the Muslim Brotherhood was not represented; however, the ultraradical Salafis were, and so were a number of renowned Islamist thinkers, in addition to Al-Azhar.

Some have argued that the constituent assembly did not sufficiently comprise members from Islamist movements. Like its predecessor, it reflected the power configuration on the ground, which had been reversed the year before: Islamist political forces had become unpopular among the public and they were now a political minority. It is unclear, however, who the new majority was; no single political party could claim to represent Egyptians. Although the reconfigured power dynamics opened opportunities for negotiation over women's rights (in return for endorsement of other groups' rights), this did not mean that a shift from Islamist to non-Islamist necessarily created a bloc favoring gender equality.

The process of creating consensus on these "gains" for women was not an easy or straightforward one. Some members of the constituent assembly were willing to support some women's rights but not others. In other words, feminist advocates could not count on support for the indivisibility of human rights. For example, some members were willing to concede an article prohibiting violence against women but completely rejected the idea of quotas. Quotas were a particularly divisive issue. Elsadda confided that the issue of quotas was often subject to negotiations and bargaining between different factions rather than ideological positions. Those who endorsed having a quota for workers and farmers recognized that the bloc favoring a quota for women would not accept their demands unless they equally recognized the women's quota.

Opposition to recognition of women's rights came not only from the Islamists but also from those considered liberals. Elsadda said that there were some distinguished liberals who unexpectedly launched the most vehement blockage to women's rights in the constitution. What helped, however, was that the group of five women in the constituent assembly consistently and categorically championed women's rights in the constitution. They also created alliances across some parties (including liberals) and various institutions so that in return for their endorsement of each group's interests, those groups would support an agenda that enhances women's rights.

In informal conversations with some Egyptian feminists and activists, they reflected that Islamists and liberals show the same contempt and misogyny for women's rights. The Egyptian case study suggests that although all political forces are patriarchal and resistant to reversing gender hierarchies, there are two intertwined, qualitative differences. The first is that the Islamists were unified in their rejection of any articles that challenge gender hierarchies, whereas there was a diversity of viewpoints among the non-Islamists, depending on the article and individual and political preferences. This difference may not necessarily apply to individual Islamist thinkers or to movements and parties outside of Egypt, but it does apply to the Egyptian case study. The second qualitative difference, which builds on the first, is that because of consistent rejection of challenges to gender hierarchies, advocates of women's rights have not found opportunities to build alliances with any Islamist political parties. There are varied positions among the non-Islamists, though, so such alliances with women's rights advocates (even if very temporary) were sometimes possible.

If the new constitution is read through a gender-sensitive lens, women are conceivably some of its most notable winners. For the first time ever, the constitution stipulates that the state is committed to women holding public and senior management offices, to the appropriate representation of women in legislative bodies (thus endorsing the principle of affirmative action), and to women's appointment in judicial bodies and authorities without discrimination. The clear stipulation of women's entitlement to hold judicial positions without discrimination not only consolidates the gains they had already made in becoming judges but it effectively forces certain judiciary bodies such as the Council of State, who had refused to appoint women, to change their course of action.

Also for the first time, the state committed to protecting women from all forms of violence (Article 11 of the constitution). This is one of the battles that feminists had fought and lost in the previous constitution. Moreover, the same article stipulates the rights of Egyptian citizens to pass on their nationality to their children, irrespective of gender. The decree prohibiting women from passing on their nationality to their children was overturned during Mubarak's era (albeit some qualifiers still applied), but by enshrining it within the constitution any reversal of the law was made far more difficult. In addition, Article 180 sets aside a quarter of seats in the local council for women (another first).

Article 2 stipulates that Islam is the principle source of legislation. Conservatives could use this article to undermine the idea of unqualified rights; however, any removal of that article would have been met with complete opposition from large segments of the constituent assembly. Article 93 stipulates the state's commitment to international conventions that it has ratified, which is instrumental for women's rights in view of Egypt's ratification of the CEDAW and will leverage the constitutional premise for the state's observance of women's rights.

The removal of Article 219 from the 2014 constitution jettisoned the major threat of conservative readings of Islamic jurisprudence being used to justify the denial of women's rights. To satisfy the Salafis, the preamble stated that it will be up to the Supreme Constitutional Court to determine the interpretation of the Shari'a. The record of the Supreme Constitutional Court is a mixed one: at times it has produced enlightened readings; at others, more regressive ones. The only way to ensure that the odds are against conservative readings justifying regressive policies would be to revert Article 2 to its previous phrasing, in which the Shari'a is *a* source of legislation, not *the* source. This change was not broached in the constituent assembly because it was considered a red line that the Salafis, Al-Azhar, and a large section of the population were not willing to cross.

The new constitution undoubtedly represented significant gains in women's political, economic, and social rights. Yet these gains were not widely celebrated in civil and political society in Egypt because revolutionaries and feminists were divided on the question of the legitimacy of the new political order.

**Gendered Processes versus Outcomes**

Future challenges will be in the process of developing a gender policy in a bottom-up, inclusive, and accountable manner. The climate at the time of writing (May 2014) does not bode well for gender outcomes. The crackdown on civil activism under the rubric of "security concerns" and a new protest law that requires prior permit from the authorities before holding demonstrations, sit-ins, and the like, may undermine or altogether thwart the gender justice movements that emerged organically between 2012 and 2013. In a climate of heavy security surveillance, it will be impossible for informal youth-based initiatives to engage with crowds freely, draw graffiti on the walls, hold human chains in the streets, or hold rallies. If civil spaces continue to shrink and youth initiatives are either repressed or are allowed to degenerate, the loss of effective interventions pursued through gender justice movements will be immense. Moreover, prospects for collective action in highly inhibitive environments are limited. The possibilities of mobilization between and across different groups will be limited but not necessarily eliminated. The ability of initiatives to mobilize under Mubarak's regime suggests that even under authoritarianism, people circumvent systems, navigate politics, resist encroachments, and mobilize around worthwhile issues.

El-Sisi did not issue clear guidelines for his program of action should he come to power. He made gestures to indicate that women's equality would be on his agenda by meeting with members of the National Council for Women as part of his presidential election campaign in 2014 (Mossaad 2014). A top-down policy would inevitably bring the National Council for Women into greater alignment with the government. This would eliminate the prospects of having a truly independent national women's machinery, which was one of the aspirations of the feminist activists after the Egyptian revolution of 2011. It would also eliminate the prospects of having a structure that is downwardly accountable to gender justice movements, feminist initiatives, and Egyptian women more broadly. It is unlikely that state feminism under el-Sisi will be anything but top-down and paternalistic, but the question remains, what ideological kind of femocracy will it be? Will it be a variation of the first lady feminism witnessed under Mubarak or more of the state feminism witnessed under Abdel Nasser? That question is intrinsically associated with the kind of political economy choices that el-Sisi makes.

The decades-old youth political marginalization is a harsh reminder that those who instigated the ruptures have not assumed power. The youth revolutionaries have been sidelined time and time again from any nation-building project. Following the political settlement between the SCAF and the Muslim Brotherhood (from which they were excluded), the youth initiatives failed to gain any meaningful representation in any of the new nation-building processes, be it constitution writing, formation of parliament, or new government. The constitution of 2014 has set a quota for youth and women's representation in local councils, and if this is put into effect, it will be worthwhile to see if it has a transformative impact or if it reproduces patronage politics from above, but at the level below.

In 2012, when reflecting on the youth quota, one revolutionary female activist argued that "the only opportunity and way is for the youth to enter [into formal politics] from below. If we have tried to elicit change from above and it failed, then the local councils are the way to change from below" (interview by Mohamed Hussein, March 2012). In this statement, the activist was envisaging political participation in a postmilitary era. She had the SCAF in mind, but the ousting of Morsi via the intervention of the military has complicated the picture. Not all of the youth revolutionaries endorse the narrative of a military coup, but those who do are unlikely to opt for entry into formal politics from above or below. In the immediate future, the spaces for activism from below will be deeply constrained, though one cannot exclude the possibility of a break-out of mass protests if aspirations for better living conditions, more jobs, safe communities, and less injustice are not met. Likewise, one cannot exclude people's resourcefulness in finding innovative ways to mobilize collectively and effectively while circumventing risks to their political survival.

# 11

## GENDER, COLLECTIVE AGENCY,
## AND SHIFTING RED LINES

This book began with a vignette from the largest collective gathering led by Egyptian women since the uprising against British occupation in 1919. Women participated in overwhelmingly large numbers in the revolutions of January 2011 and June 2013. The events of December 2011 are distinct not only because of the size of the gathering but because they were initiated and led by women bearing an immensely subversive message regarding women's bodily integrity. Yet Egyptian women have had a long trajectory of public activism on gender-specific and other political causes.

One of the key messages behind many of the vignettes and case studies relayed in the previous chapters is that collective action can take many forms and comprise different actors with different political orientations, yet it remains powerful in its ability to challenge gender injustice initiated by state and nonstate actors. A modicum of unity in this diversity is necessary. When women and men rose against the army after the stripping of the young woman in Tahrir Square, the head of the SCAF was forced to issue a public apology to Egyptian citizens. When revolutionary youth forces and political parties formed alliances in celebration of International Women's Day in March 2012 they forged a collective front to deliver a message that could not be delivered just one year before.

Some of the most powerful examples of collective mobilization for gender justice come from the revolutionary phase of Egypt's modern history since the ousting of Mubarak. However, even in prerevolutionary times, there were junctures when mobilization for gender equality elicited powerful forms of mobilization. Though working behind unpredictable red lines, these initiatives created unity within concentric circles of different sizes: informal groups, campaigns, and larger coalitions.

The preceding chapters neither suggest that collective action is a panacea for redressing all forms of gender inequalities nor do they claim that it is the only pathway for addressing them. The gains made through collective action in terms of government recognition of inequality or policy-making do not always translate into a tangible impact on women's lives. Although collective action was critical for blocking reversals in a modicum of women's rights after Mubarak's ouster, the intensity of the backlash was acute, bringing to the fore the powerful role of counterforces in circumscribing the impact of collective action for gender justice.

In this book I have investigated what accounts for the emergence and sustenance of collective action around gender issues, as well as the forms, identities, strategies, and relationships that surround such collective action. I have explored the constellation of factors that enable or inhibit the achievement of the gender movements' goals. In this final chapter I revisit some of the main theoretical debates delineated in the introduction and empirically addressed in the chapters that followed. Although the approach I pursued was to recognize patterns, recurring themes, and underlying power dynamics, one can draw lessons from these items without assuming they have any predictive power. Their predictive power is limited because it is impossible to reproduce the same circumstances of a particular historical phase and the unintended consequences of unplanned actions. For example, at the time of the emergence of the FGM Taskforce and CEDAW Coalition, the member organizations were still nascent, and the level of professionalization had not become so entrenched (in terms of a focus on paid project work). Even though the taskforce worked behind harsh red lines, the competition over resources was not so acute and they were energized by the mobilizational power that the ICPD and the Beijing Conference had generated. Recreating these same conditions is almost impossible. Likewise, the revolutionary moment of 2011 was transformative but specific to that critical juncture. It unleashed energies and propelled organizations to engage in new kinds of activisms. Certainly, the emergence of informal youth-based collective actors had the unintended consequence of encouraging many organizations to think seriously about their constituency base.

## Collective Action: Contending Identities and Modalities

In examining the modalities of collective action that developed over the course of twenty years (1994–2014) I have argued that a number of internal and external factors have inhibited the emergence of a strong unified movement. Notwithstanding, people have been mobilizing through other modalities and under all kinds of identity banners. Building on the rich feminist scholarship that has analyzed collective action, I sought to expand the typology to examine identity and modality and encompass women's movements, women in movements, feminist and antifeminist movements, and gender justice movements. In applying them to the Egyptian context, I have challenged the pervading distinction between feminist as secular (the CEDAW being the only reference point) versus Muslim or Islamist (using religious frameworks in different ways). I argued that this distinction may have been the case in the 1980s and 1990s, but by the beginning of the twenty-first century, many feminists were increasingly resorting to the deployment of religious framings in their bid to influence spaces where religion had become particularly salient. This includes their engagement with society and, in some instances, the policy arena. At times this shift was pragmatic; they used appropriate messaging and framing to find common ground and appear nonthreatening. In other instances, it had deeper ideological significance, suggesting a personal transformation among some of the activists themselves. This book questioned and contested the association between feminism and secularity, suggesting that sometimes the relationship is a gray zone.

I have also questioned in previous chapters the notion that all expressions of women's agency are empowering. There are impressive models and examples of formidable women belonging to the Muslim Brotherhood and Salafi movements that illustrate strong personal agency and narratives of self-empowerment. However, the fact that these women advocate for agendas that not only seek to maintain patriarchal gender hierarchies, but to actually deepen and intensify them, merits careful assessment. The agendas that they espouse are antifeminist. Take, for example, the Muslim

Sisters' stances on revoking *khulʿ* and decriminalizing FGM, or the Salafi women's stance on prohibiting female representation in parliament. The intention here is not to suggest that they must meet some international yardstick for what constitutes rights. The threat lies in their revoking of the modicum of existing rights on the ground. Although not specific to Egypt, these forms of women's mobilization merit a distinct label. They do not fit the category of "women's movements," which may be patriarchal but would not have been established with the purpose of revoking women's rights. They are not simply "women in movement" because they hold their own distinct agenda around their identity as women, and they are neither gender justice nor feminist movements. Identification of such movements as antifeminist is intended to highlight the perceived outcome of their mobilization in a broader context.

The emergence of gender justice movements has also challenged the binary distinction between feminist and nonfeminist movements in the Egyptian context. This third way is neither strictly feminist nor women-centric insofar as it does not pursue a characteristically feminist agenda nor is its membership primarily or exclusively women (i.e., women's movements). The leadership of gender justice movements comprises men and women, and their agenda is not in conflict with feminism but is much broader and draws on humanism. Yet these movements are distinct from women in movement on account of the fact that they have a mandate that explicitly relates to challenging gender hierarchies.

Ultimately, the classification of these movements as "gender justice" is one that is used for analytical purposes. It shows how the composition of gender justice movements came to wield a new kind of collective struggle that was deeply gendered but not in the ways conventionally defined through women's movements, feminist movements, and women in movement. The aim is conceptual clarity rather than the establishment of a hierarchy within the typology. There are junctures in which feminists played a central role in the struggle for gender equality (in particular during the 1990s). At other times, women in movement were the most powerful at mobilizing, such as in workers' movements and revolutionary movements. Under Morsi's tenure, gender justice movements played a critical role in combination with other actors in challenging the status quo.

The second binary distinction contested from the literature is between movement and nonmovement. I argued that Egypt under Mubarak had witnessed many campaigns, coalitions, and networks around collective action. They lacked many of the elements that sustained a movement but they were often based on a pre-existing repertoire of social relations between individuals and groups. Based on Tilly's (2004) definition of the movement as having WUNC (worthiness, unity, numbers, and commitment), the worthiness of the cause is present in the level of gender inequality and how it plays out in daily life. However, there was never sufficient consensus on leadership and vision to allow for unity, and the numbers remained relatively small. The commitment to individual and organizational interests sometimes (not always) superseded a commitment to a movement requiring sustained collective action.

Perhaps the most common forms of collective action witnessed during Mubarak's era were campaigns that were often inspired by contextual triggers. As astutely observed by Magda Adley (see chapter 1), it is much easier to conjure collective work on short-term campaigns that do not require a substantial investment in time and effort than to work on causes that require a more sustained kind of collective action. There is another reason for the prevalence of campaigns under Mubarak: they were less likely to be seen as threatening by the security apparatus than if they were visible as a movement with significant mobilizational power.

One of the contributions to the literature on collective action that I sought to make in this book is to suggest that although the NGOization of feminist activism had a destructive impact on movement building, so too did the emergence of another equally obstructive phenomenon: that of collective action lite. Put simply, when modalities of collective action are engineered and tinkered with by external agents and run as if they are projects, they lack the inherent ingredients of making them sustainable and effective. It is collective action *lite* in that it is often affected by the epistemic power generated by donor policies and priorities. Collective action lite is associated with the enforcement of gender and development projects rather than political transformation. Its contentious powers vis-à-vis the state are often contained and controlled. Worse, it gives the semblance of being a collective initiative with all that collective action entails in terms of cohesion, consensus, and a political front. In reality, it is fragile and unsustainable with minimal levels of ownership.

This is not to suggest that the systemic problem is the presence or provision of Western funding itself. Both successful and unsuccessful forms of collective action have received Western funding. The CEDAW Coalition would not have emerged and thrived without the financial support of UNICEF, the European Union, and other donors. Likewise, the FGM Taskforce was supported through sustained funding from the Ford Foundation's regional office in Cairo. However, there is very limited evidence of the highly successful, informal youth-based initiatives receiving foreign funding (at the time of writing). Concurrently, the crackdown on NGOs was so insidious in 2011/2012 (see chapter 7) that feminist coalitions often had to make do without funding, though this did not affect their activism.

The issue is not the existence of foreign funding, but rather the circumstances under which it is introduced, the conditions that accompany it, and whether it is used to create enabling conditions for collective action. In practical terms, external support must not impinge on local ownership so that the collective actor can remain led and run by those who can claim it as their own.

**Sustained Collective Action in Unpredictable Environments**

Even in the midst of a highly inhibitive environment Egypt witnessed a number of effective forms of collective action that challenged the status quo in critical ways. The FGM Taskforce is one of the earliest contemporary attempts at building a collective front to deal with a deeply controversial and entrenched violation of girls' and women's bodily integrity. It succeeded on multiple levels: on a policy level through engaging with the government; on a grassroots level through a socially sensitive approach to changing community views and practices; and on an international level by drawing on transnational feminist solidarity while challenging stereotypes and reifications. The FGM Taskforce was also able to engage with opposition emanating from civil and political society actors that were inspired by religion or vested interests in maintaining the practice. The taskforce succeeded because it resisted NGOization; however, the absence of an institutionalized umbrella led to its failure to maintain a sustained collective front.

The other successful example of a collective actor during Mubarak's reign was the CEDAW Coalition—the longest surviving women's rights coalition during Mubarak's era. It succeeded in challenging the official narrative on gender equality in international spaces by exposing the scale and gravity of gender injustice, and it sought to hold the government accountable for its failures on the international stage.

As noted earlier, although networks play an important role in linking individuals and organizations, they do not necessarily have the leadership, cohesion, and consensus building around a common issue that allow them to mobilize the sum of all parts for a collective struggle. Campaigns can be highly effective methods of collective mobilization; however, issue and time sensitivity may undermine prospects of sustaining pressure. Coalitions, though they are rare, have emerged due to a constellation of factors. The first is the repertoire of social relations that exist between groups of people and organizations. In an environment in which personalized, informal networks are the basis for organizing, the selection of partners for collective action is primarily driven by pre-existing relations rather than common commitment to the same cause (although sometimes there is strong convergence between both factors). Hence when the NWRO sought to bring together NGOs that had the strongest track record in feminist activism rather than allow individuals to choose their partners, the efforts to build strong bridges were somewhat contrived. It is possible to identify the same repertoire of individuals and organizations in the FGM Taskforce, the CEDAW Coalition, the NWRO, and other collective fronts. The reproduction of the same repertoire in collective initiatives is not necessarily ideal because it creates a cliquish culture that prevents the growth of partners and the diversification of possible support bases. However, the repertoire of pre-existing relations continues to be an important ingredient for the catalysis of any collective initiative.

Another important factor in the emergence of coalitions is a meaningful cause that is seen as requiring a collective, rather than individual, response. Causes that are worthwhile but not deemed of sufficient priority for collective action (such as honor killings) have not led to sustained mobilization. What determines the significance of the cause (and conditions under which collective action emerges more generally) is the political moment. The political moment may comprise opportunities and/or threats. Opportunities may be associated with a favorable international environment, a sudden opening of political space locally or nationally, or new grant opportunities. Threats that catalyze collective mobilization include risk of reversibility of rights, the introduction of new policies, regulations, or laws that inhibit rights in significant ways, or a tragic event that makes people reach their tipping points. Many of these factors (opportunities, repertoires, and political moments) strongly resonate with the political sociological literature on social movements (e.g., Tilly, Tarrow, and McAdam 2001).

A combination of other factors enables the collective actor to build internal cohesion so as to maintain sustainability and increase effectiveness. Both the CEDAW Coalition and FGM Taskforce had an absolute lowest common denominator that bound their members together, irrespective of their ideological and political orientations or positioning in public life. Another important ingredient is leadership, which must be perceived in the eyes of participants as sufficiently legitimate. Operationally, legitimacy is the appearance of inclusivity, which allows members to claim ownership of the initiative. Legitimate leadership must also be organic, meaning that the person/group is not seen as external.

The leadership process is central to the success or failure of a coalition. Democratic representation and participation of all members of a coalition is not necessary for its success, but being able to create consensus among the steering/leading core group is absolutely essential. Leadership is also about recognizing the need for some level of centralized decision-making. Leadership in all of the successful coalitions was centralized and not loose as in networks. Coalitions need to be more than horizontal power-sharing structures; there needs to be internal cohesion, which is often facilitated by a select number of leaders that form the collective core.

The ability to establish alliances with sympathetic actors within and outside the state is another key element of coalitions. In the case of the FGM Taskforce, it actively sought to forge alliances with high-profile doctors, media personas, and religious figures to render legitimacy to its cause.

These alliances are important because they give a coalition the political weight it needs to influence and convince its members of the value of its collective endeavor. In the case of the CEDAW Coalition, it had not built up allies broadly in society, but it had earned the respect and recognition of key individuals within government and the National Council for Women (though there were times of extreme rivalry as well).

The successful feminist and gender justice coalitions that emerged in post-Mubarak Egypt had these same factors despite the different political context. From an agential point of view, they relied on networks with pre-existing repertoires of relations. Despite being horizontally structured, they had strong leadership in a core steering group that institutionalized a culture of consensus building and inclusiveness. In terms of structural factors, the political moment was a pending threat associated with the intensity of the backlash against women's rights and bodily integrity between 2011 and 2013. Simultaneously, it was a moment full of political opportunity manifest in the unfolding of a deeply mobilized citizenry committed to demanding and claiming their rights. Both feminist and gender justice initiatives owe much to this revolutionary moment in terms of their ability to maintain and sustain a collective front despite the volatile political context in which they operated. In addition, alliances were "make or break" factors for the success of collective actors after the Egyptian revolution. Feminists lacking the endorsement of the youth revolutionary forces and the political parties were extremely weak and their voices were easily sidelined. However, when feminists did forge alliances with these groups, their impact was quite powerful.

One characteristic of a successful coalition that is up for debate is its constituency, that is, individuals who are willing to stand up and say that the coalition represents them and their interests. This constituency could be from any class or background and can express its support in different forms (e.g., following a Facebook page so they can respond to calls for street action, participating at key events that endorse a cause, or signing a petition).

El Mahdi (2010) points out that Islamists and workers were able to build a constituency but feminist activists were not, even though all three thrived in a repressive environment. El Mahdi's explanation was that Islamists and workers were able to find socially appropriate entry points of engaging with people in a language and through a message that struck a chord, whereas the feminist language was elitist and disconnected from the grassroots. This is true to a certain extent: as suggested in chapter 1, feminist activists' focus on influencing policy detached them from engaging with politics from below. Even with security crackdowns that prevented direct street work, they still could have built a constituency via alliances with the workers' movement, in which women leaders were powerful and highly influential.

However, there are two important reflections on El Mahdi's argument. First, unlike workers and Islamists who faced opposition from the ruling powers, in the case of feminist activists, animosity toward their cause came not only from the government but also from large sections of the populace in civil and political society. Hence, they had to fight on multiple fronts, as the FGM Taskforce demonstrated. The second qualification is what it takes to build a bridge to forge constituencies. El Mahdi (2010) suggested that a narrative that is more religiously friendly would capitalize on the sentiment in society. However, the success of the gender justice initiatives (which did not use religious framings) shows that there is an alternative based on appealing to people's sense of humanity, fairness, and dignity.

Constituencies were important and influential because they could be translated into greater leverage in political bargaining processes. Informal youth-based initiatives with significant constituencies were more successful in gaining visibility and having their voices amplified than those that comprised a handful of friends. However, one of the key factors that allowed gender-just initiatives to build constituencies where feminist activists had failed is their choice of issue and how it was framed.

**Ruptures and Eruptions**

Egypt experienced two revolutions in thirty months. Although there has been much debate over whether the events of July 3rd amounted to a revolution or a coup, the stance I take in this book is that there is a need to disentangle the actual acts of mass uprisings from their outcomes. In the January 25th revolution, there were eighteen days of sustained citizen protests that at their peak numbered in the millions, yet the outcome was the takeover by the SCAF, who ruled for eighteen months. Nevertheless, there is consensus among many Egyptians of different political orientations (except pro-Morsi factions and some leftist parties) that January 25th was a revolution. It was not a revolution in the sense of replacing an authoritarian regime with a democratic one. However, it was a revolution in the sense of "rupture," the act of mass mobilization leading to the downfall of the status quo.

The nature of the power configurations in Egypt between January 2011 and December 2013 challenged much of the transitional literature that conceived of the overthrow of a regime as putting the country on the path to democratization. Chapters 6 and 7 exposed ways in which the discourse of a democratic transition was disconnected from the unfolding political situation on the ground after the ousting of Mubarak and up to the revolution of June 2013. This disjuncture between the literature/policy discourse and the unfolding political reality does not suggest Egyptian or Middle Eastern exceptionalism; instead it supports the growing literature that suggests that framings of democratic transition characterized by linearity and teleological pathways of change are highly problematic. Using a gender lens, the research has also exposed how external analyses' definition of civilian rule as being exclusively nonmilitary ignored the necessity of conceiving of it as nontheocratic. This also was reflected in feminist scholarship on regime type and gender outcomes. Building on the examples of Latin America and Eastern Europe, the focus in a lot of feminist literature was on the military regimes challenging the civilian nature of governance. However, when a government instates formally, and allows informally, special governance privileges to institutions and groups on account of their religious leadership, that too is a threat to civilian rule.

The errors of assuming that citizen voice can be captured solely through a ballotocracy have exposed the limits of liberal procedural democracy. This is not to suggest that elections are not important. Rather, it is to emphasize that when millions are participating in protests to express their rejection of a government, they cannot be ignored on account of having already expressed their voices through the ballot boxes.

At no point in time before or after the January revolution did the Egyptian authorities take genuine measures toward democratization (even though they did hold freer and fairer elections and were occasionally more tolerant of citizens' peaceful, public expression of dissent). Therefore, it is difficult to examine whether a change in regime type from authoritarian to democratic would make a genuine difference for gender justice. Nonetheless, the Egyptian case study bears a great deal of commonality with many Latin American countries after the overthrow of authoritarian regimes and in Eastern Europe with respect to resisting the backlash against women's rights.

Examination of the patterns of mobilization around women's rights before and after the January revolution echoes findings in feminist scholarship that the strength of cohesion of organized collective action around gender issues influences the reconfiguration of power in postrupture moments. The factors undermining prospects of engendering the new political order were numerous in Egypt because of hostility from the military, Islamists, and a broad section of Egyptian society, as well as the indifference of many non-Islamist political movements. However, there were key moments in which a strong movement could have made a political dent and secured some minimal gains (such as the reordering of the National Council for Women) had there been less fragmentation.

Three of the key factors that have enabled or inhibited the promotion of a gender-just agenda following the demise of the Mubarak regime are the role of external actors, alliance building, and ideology. External drivers and their role in influencing gender policy in moments of rupture is a factor that cannot be ignored. In countries such as Romania, leaders were compelled to actively engender processes of democratization in their transitions because of their desire to join the European Union. It did not matter that the regime in Romania was ultranationalist because the European Union carrot served as a central external factor in influencing policy choices more so than individual leaders' or party ideology (at least vis-à-vis laws and institutional policies). In Egypt, there was no such carrot. In fact, the Mubarak regime's desire to show progress on "the gender front" to the West as a sign of its prodemocracy nature was completely abandoned in postrevolutionary Egypt. As for foreign funding practices, although important, their impact on collective action and the gender agenda was minimal compared with the potential impact of foreign policy.

Most non-Islamist actors endorsing gender justice after the Egyptian revolution considered the role of Western actors to be particularly counterproductive. The Western rhetoric of insisting on Egypt's democratic transition meant that there was political omission of recognizing and engaging with the growing discontent expressed by large portions of the citizenry. Moreover, many foreign donors' insistence on feminist engagement with Islamists was seen as undermining the building of strong resistance movements.

Whereas the Western support for enabling local actors to challenge the regimes in power on gender policy waxed and waned during the three years after Mubarak's demise, according to many interviewees, the amount of funding coming from Gulf countries (such as Saudi Arabia, Qatar, and Kuwait) grew dramatically in that period. One of the gaps in this book is the inadequate coverage and analysis of Gulf funding to Islamist movements and how it influenced gender practices and policy projections. It is a real challenge to collect data on cash flow from overseas to Islamist partners in Egypt because of how opaque these processes are and the lack of strong evidence to examine their dynamics.

The important role of internal alliances and coalitions in enabling or constraining collective action is essential to understanding the underlying power dynamics at work, which are sometimes more informed by common political interests than an ideological agenda. Such alliances and coalitions force researchers to ask more politically strategic questions. How does endorsing or ignoring gender issues affect each party's negotiating powers? Do those who support gender justice bear any political weight, that is, what can they offer in return for the endorsement of their agenda? Whose interests do they have the power to block if their own gender agenda is blocked? These questions require dynamic analysis of ever-changing actors, agendas, interests, and networks.

## Islamists in Government and Coalitions:
## A Predictor of Gender Equality Outcomes?

One of the key themes explored in this book is the relationship between ideological orientation (Islamist/non-Islamist) and gender equality outcomes on the state level and in terms of collective action. By examining

nonstate collective action in previous chapters, I have shown how patriarchal values and practices have underpinned the actions of Islamist and
non-Islamist political actors in relation to women's political leadership in
post-Mubarak Egypt. For example, the vignettes in chapters 5–8 suggest
that when it came to affirmative action for women in the constitution and
electoral law, lines were not necessarily drawn along expected ideological
viewpoints. In 2011, when the election law was under review, youth revolutionary forces that defended women's rights to claim public space in ways
that Islamists and right-wing conservatives did not approve of (i.e., sleep-
ing overnight in Tahrir Square) were more vehement in their rejection
of the quota than the Muslim Brotherhood. In the constitutional debates
after the June 2013 revolution, so-called liberals and Nasserites who had
often paid lip service to gender equality were some of the fiercest opponents to the instatement of a woman's quota on a local or national level.
They thought that sharing power would detract from their own interest
groups (i.e., farmers, workers, youth, etc.).

The poor commitment (and indeed opposition) of the non-Islamist
parties to women's political leadership and power sharing suggests that
when it comes to gender quality, both camps (Islamist and non-Islamist)
are just as bad as each other (Abu-Lughod 2010). But the patterns of street-
and policy-level mobilization and advocacy that I present in previous
chapters suggest that a more nuanced reading is required. Islamists and
non-Islamists come in different shades, and as movements and parties they
are always changing, but there are some major differences with respect to
mobilization around gender justice issues. Although non-Islamists may be
gender blind, there is sufficient diversity in their stances on gender issues
that open opportunities for cross-alliance building. For example, some
right-wing conservative political parties remained silent during the backlash against women witnessed in post-2011 Egypt, but the popular leftist movement showed a consistent willingness to support women's issues
by opening critical reactionary discourses and actively participating in
marches, demonstrations, and sit-ins organized on gender justice issues.
Another example is the response of nonstate actors to the Commission on
the Status of Women's declaration on gender-based violence in 2012. Only
a few non-Islamist political figures and parties were willing to stand up

in the Shura Council and defend the declaration, but at least one leading liberal figure did as well (Amr Moussa, though some interviewees say that, on a personal ideology level, he is not what can be described as a feminist).

There was no such diversity in stances among Islamist political parties or any possibility of cross-alliances with them in 2011–13. Islamist parties consistently rejected measures or policies that fundamentally challenged gender hierarchies. Even political forces on the moderate/progressive side of the spectrum within Islamist movements, such as Abdel Moneim Abouel Fotouh of the Egypt Strong Party, who differed from the Freedom and Justice Party on many issues, endorsed the stance against the Commission on the Status of Women's declaration. Along the same lines, political figures from the Islamist movements never joined any of the marches or demonstrations on gender matters (as did some non-Islamist figures). Islamists generally were inclined to join forces against challenging gender hierarchies, at least in public space (not including members of Islamist movements who rebelled and exited). Hence, being part of an Islamist political party or movement is an important predictor of having an antithetical stance toward challenging gender hierarchies or at least of endorsing an Islamic bloc with a synchronized stance on maintaining the gender status quo. Being part of a non-Islamist political party/movement can go either way in terms of political stance and alliance building, depending on a number of agential factors.

There is also much debate regarding how regime type influences gender policy. Some feminist analysts have suggested that authoritarianism under Mubarak, Islamism under Morsi, and militarism under the SCAF with the interim government backed by el-Sisi are all faces of the same misogynist patriarchal ideology. Egyptian women under all three regime types were, for example, subjected to sexual violence: dissident women endured sexual torture under Mubarak, were stripped and raped (virginity tests) under the SCAF, and suffered politically motivated sexual assault under Morsi. Undoubtedly, all three regimes have deeply entrenched patriarchal underpinnings, a hatred of challenging gender hierarchies and roles, and a deeply disturbing commitment to hegemonic reactionary masculinities. The way these traits play out in public may differ, but ultimately there is a common set of normative values shared across regimes.

There are, however, some significant differences among these regimes in both gendered processes and gendered outcomes. Mubarak's first lady feminism was discriminatory toward poor women, dissident women, and those on the fringes of society. In tandem with liberal feminism, though, its reform of personal status law, nationality law, and a decree regarding women's mobility benefited women across different classes and ideological orientations. Even the reform of the personal status law affected poor women, who could now end their marriages arbitrarily through *khul'* (Al-Sharmani 2009).

In contrast, the Islamist version of empowering women was to recognize the rights of members of poor, female-headed households to medical insurance and social benefits, which they protected through a parliamentary law and in the constitution. If applied, such a law will make a difference in the well-being of marginalized women's lives. However, without downplaying the importance of this policy, its enactment did not challenge the gender hierarchy or division of labor in any fundamental way, unlike the reform of the Personal Status Law or women's newfound liberty to travel without their husbands' permission. The provision of charity or cash transfers via the state is commensurate with the idea of women being looked after while men's roles as heads of households remain intact. It is also commensurate with a neoliberal economic model in which the state provides a safety net for the "vulnerables" but is not obligated to play a central role in job creation or in the regulation of the private sector vis-à-vis its gendered labor practices. Such policy represents the complicity with which the Morsi regime tolerated the increasing power of Islamist movements and their role as guardians of morality. Many Islamist movements were emboldened to engage without restraint in anti–women's rights rhetoric and in some incidents incited assaults on women who did not conform to their ideas about proper attire and behavior. Against the backdrop of strong antifeminist mobilization, the backlash was intense though not uniformly so among all sections of the population. Poor Coptic women living in upper Egypt and in the squatter and populist settlements of big cities became particularly vulnerable targets.

Feminists had long lobbied for the laws passed under Mubarak, and revoking such laws would undermine Egyptian women's choice and agency on a large scale. When inequality on account of religious identity and class intersect, as in the case of poor Upper Egypt Coptic women, fate under the Muslim Brotherhood was far worse than under Mubarak or in the aftermath of the June 30th revolution. Such women were singled out not only on account of their gender but also as *kuffar* (infidels).

When the military enter into an alliance with Islamists, as they did in Egypt in 2011, a backlash against women is guaranteed. Neither the military's ideology nor its political priorities have any regard for securing inclusive citizenship for women or other excluded members of the population. During the military–Muslim Brotherhood entente in 2011, it was clear that the military and the Muslim Brotherhood had agreed to exclude women from power sharing at a macro level, and the military had no objections to the Islamists' control over women in public and private life.

On the level of nonstate actors, the evidence I examine in this book suggests that being a member of an organized Islamist political actor is a predictor of opposition to challenging gender hierarchies, especially in matters of sexuality and inequality. Coalitions involving Islamists tend to organize into blocs to limit or reverse women's equality outcomes. Non-Islamist political actors can also be supportive of circumscribing or negating gender equality; however, their positions tend to vary, with some endorsing the introduction of gender equality rights and others rejecting such rights. In the policy matters associated with challenging gender hierarchies (e.g., insurance for female-headed households, which is a great step forward but does not challenge the gender status quo), there are instances of some non-Islamist political movements endorsing specific measures (i.e., during the debates on the 2014 constitution). Conversely, there are no instances of organized collective Islamist actors supporting policies that redress gender inequalities.

On a state level, regime ideology does matter. All of the regimes in contemporary Egyptian history have been neoliberal in orientation, which has severely undermined social justice. All of them have been inherently patriarchal and authoritarian. However, the Islamist/non-Islamist ideological orientation of a regime, as witnessed in Egypt, was an important predictor of whether gender equality measures would be circumscribed.

This relationship is manifest in the different statuses of women in the Egyptian constitutions drawn under the leadership of Morsi and Adly Mansour. Although both the Islamist- and military-backed regimes are patriarchal, the gender equality outcomes of an Islamist regime are qualitatively worse for women. All shades of authoritarianism (theocratic and military) undermine gender justice, but ideological orientation is an important predictor of the extent of threats to gender equality outcomes.

**Reversion to the Old Red Lines?**

At the time of writing (May 2014) it is too early to determine whether el-Sisi's leadership will mean the pursuit of state feminism à la Mubarak or à la Nasser (see chapter 10). It remains to be seen whether the gains made in the constitution of 2014 will be enacted in terms of economic and political rights. The situation on the ground has somewhat improved insofar as the Islamists are no longer emboldened to control women's dress, behavior, and presence in public space as they did in many poor communities between 2011 and 2013. There is a systematic crackdown on the Muslim Sisters as well as on female dissidents who violate the new protest law (which requires permission from the authorities to protest), and this represents a genuine threat to women's political freedoms.

The grim reality is that the comparison that is being made here in relation to the gender agenda is between different kinds of undemocratic regimes (pre- and post-June 2013). The revolutionary cry of "bread, freedom, and social justice/dignity" is far from being achieved by the Egyptians who rose against the regimes and in particular the Egyptian women who expected recognition for their participation. In the following section I examine the scope of sustained struggles against red lines in the future.

The interface between a changing revolutionary context and gendered collective action has affected various groups and initiatives differently. Feminist initiatives, including NGOs and coalitions, engaged more politically with the explosion of citizen agency demanding their rights; however, there is a lot more room for transformation in terms of their language, strategies, and partners. Very little progress has been made in building constituencies, which has reproduced the old disjunctures on the street level.

For the Muslim Sisters, during the thirty months in which the Muslim Brotherhood was allowed to flourish politically, they too experienced political empowerment in pursuing their *da'wa* (proselytization), charity, and political mobilization activism freely. Analysis of the political trajectory of the Muslim Sisters after the ouster of Mubarak (presented in chapters 5–7) suggests that the assumption that they would undergo an internal reform process once the shackles of repression had been removed was misplaced. They continued to publicly advocate a patriarchal gender hierarchy that was premised on a gender division of labor. Muslim Sisters were the greatest champions of revoking laws in parliament and were behind the introduction of articles in the constitution that risked curbing women's rights by aligning them with conservative interpretations of the Shari'a. In short, they were key actors in the backlash against women's rights.

In terms of internal reform, if the Muslim Brothers had retained power for a longer period of time, they would have had more opportunities to recognize women's voices by placing women in the Shura Council and the Guidance Bureau and by assigning a leader among the sisters to give their division a higher status. However, for these actions to materialize, a more reformist-oriented leadership within the Muslim Brotherhood would have been necessary, in addition to strong advocates of the cause from within the Muslim Sisters. Because the Muslim Brothers have been ousted from office, there is no telling if, in a decade's time, the internal red lines for women's assumption of leadership roles in the movement will be challenged. For now, internal gender reform has been put on hold as broader struggles for survival take precedence.

In this book I focus more on the political role of the Muslim Brotherhood than the Salafis in relation to gendered collective action because the former was the most influential Islamist political movement in the period of study and its members were far more accessible than the Salafis. The same applies to the study of Salafi women. The Muslim Sisters are organized into an entity with a structure, linear flow of command, and a long history of institutionalized activism. Women in the Salafi movement do not have such an organizational or institutionalized structure, and therefore they must be studied as women in several movements (similar to women in revolutionary youth movements).

Because of the backlash that women experienced in the aftermath of Mubarak's ousting, and as a consequence of the revolution's release of citizen energy and transformation of political culture, a number of organic initiatives emerged that amounted to a nascent gender justice movement. The impact of these informal youth-based initiatives (see chapter 9) was to deghettoize women's equality by transforming sexual harassment from a women's issue/problem to that of the society and state. In the transformed society, harassers (not victims) are named and shamed, and the state is held accountable for making streets safe and for its role in perpetrating assault. Key to the success of the gender justice initiatives were their organic nature (no external engineering), cohesive structures, strong constituency, appropriate language, and their framing of issues without the gender and development lingo. Their street strategies have enabled these youth-based initiatives to gain credibility and visibility among a broad section of the Egyptian urban population. These strategies include security patrols and rescue operations, the use of graffiti, art, song, and catchy slogans, the use of human chains, male peer-to-peer community outreach, media engagement, and the use of social media to disseminate news and recruit new members.

Another central element of the success of these initiatives, and what distinguishes them from feminist or women's initiatives, is the high percentage of men in leadership and membership. Men's presence side by side with women increased the size and outreach of these initiatives. Men served as positive role models, challenging middle-class respectability that put the blame for sexual assault squarely on the shoulders of women as well as macho conceptions of acceptable and inacceptable behavior in relation to women's bodies. They have also contributed to the framing of issues in a way that speaks to the wider citizenry, in particular their fellow men. But men's involvement is not a magic ingredient for transforming gender relations. Although these young men were (for reasons highlighted in chapter 9) deeply moved to act on sexual harassment, it is unlikely that they will have a vested interest in mobilizing on gender inequalities that they do not experience firsthand, such as early marriage, sex trafficking, and female genital mutilation. This is not to suggest that these issues are yardsticks against which to measure commitment to gender equality, or that they are the most important issues, but rather to insist that unlike feminist movements, youth initiatives' commitment is to a particular type or manifestation of gender inequality rather than a broad gender agenda.

Many factors risk demobilizing these initiatives. The informal youth-based initiatives emerged because of a pending threat associated with the rise of politically motivated sexual assault in protest spaces such as Tahrir Square, which, for the youth who supported the revolution, was a sacrosanct space associated with the human struggle for liberation. Since these protest spaces have been vacated, many have raised questions as to whether their raison d'être still stands. Two of the initiatives examined in chapter 9 (Shoft Taharosh and Bassma) have already shifted their work toward other spaces where their interventions are needed: public transport, universities, and public gardens where crowds gather on holidays. The challenge will be for these initiatives to institutionalize without acquiring the ailments of the institutional culture of NGOs. One way forward for these initiatives is to avoid cocooning (turning inward) and instead forge alliances with other political forces that are committed to exposing and contesting patriarchy in all its forms (as suggested by Kandiyoti 2014).

Undoubtedly, the greatest two threats to these organic informal initiatives and to movement building more broadly in Egypt are the government's repression of civil spaces and the loss of a volunteer base. The return of the state security investigations apparatus in addition to a myriad set of military surveillance agencies means an extremely tight regulation of civil space. A high level of encroachment on civil space will kill the innovative forms of street activism that flourished during the revolutionary phase (graffiti, slogans, images, etc.). However, even under severe encroachments, some initiatives have shown resilience in surviving without being co-opted, changing the strategies of citizen engagement by shifting their work from the pavements to the transport system and from the squares to the universities.

The experience of the FGM Taskforce, which could not avoid NGOization or survive without a legal umbrella in an authoritarian context, may provide some insights into the kind of challenges that these youth-based initiatives might face in the future. In the long run, the government may seek to restrict the activities of initiatives that do not have a legal identity, in which case all of these initiatives would have to come under the fold of an existing organization, register with the authorities as a legal entity, or dissolve. As with the Taskforce, if they sustain their volunteer base, cohesive mode of governance and management, and protection of the safe space they preserve for their members, they can establish their niche and influence.

In addition to the individual survival of these initiatives, there is also the question of intragroup relations for movement building. One of the greatest challenges to sustaining a united collective front is the deep polarization between those who endorse the June 30th uprisings as a corrective revolution and those who regard it as a counterrevolution. There are two profound sources of polarization. The first emerged under SCAF rule and is between the Islamists and non-Islamists; it has become much deeper after the events of June 30th. The second source of fragmentation began between mostly non-Islamist movements with the removal of Morsi on July 3rd; it has created deep enmities within youth revolutionary movements, feminist NGO leaders and activists, and participants in gender justice initiatives.

The Egyptian nation needs healing before common fronts can emerge around common agendas. Or perhaps it is a common enemy or threat that will bring about restoration? As new red lines appear, it is likely that many individuals and groups will find ways of subverting, circumventing, and outmaneuvering any attempts to inhibit the revolutionary spirit. Even though spaces have closed, personal experiences have had a transformational impact on a cognitive level. But what kind of collective fronts will emerge next?

## Scenarios for the Future

Foresight into future power configurations and how they will affect gender equality, social justice, and well-being in Egypt is difficult to establish. The factors influencing political outcomes are as much about regional dynamics and international geostrategic interests as they are about domestic dynamics. A long-term perspective is necessary on women and men mobilizing behind red lines for gender justice and their relationship to broader struggles for emancipation from internal sources of oppression and external forces of domination. The two cannot be disentangled. Although women and men have mobilized behind shifting red lines as they have struggled under different types of authoritarian rule, it is difficult to replicate the same structure–agency configuration over and over again. The future of collective action will be shaped by the nature of regime, state ideology, regional and international dynamics, and the strength of intragroup and intergroup ties within existing collectives.

## Nature of Regime

The nature of the regime will greatly influence the prospects of successful mobilization around gender equality. The new agential dynamics and configuration of power on the ground mean that there can never be a replicable model of the past. Moreover, the notion of a "democratic path" in its linear teleological assumptions will never capture spaces where there are unusual and unexpected openings. To consider the future, we need to ask the following questions. Which freedoms will be tolerated, to what extent, and for whom? How do the different kinds of rights (social, economic, political) intersect in process and outcome?

The current projection for democratization in Egypt in the immediate future is extremely dim. It is likely that Egypt is entering a new phase of nondemocratic rule that is reconcilable with procedural democratic practices (holding regular elections, etc.). It is a phase without any meaningful opportunities for rotation of power or exercise of substantive rights, but it does differ from Mubarak's regime in that el-Sisi appears to have a strong populist appeal (at the time of writing in 2014). Moreover, it is likely that the war on terror in Egypt is going to be a prolonged one. Even if reconciliation occurred between the ruling order and the Muslim Brothers, the other militant groups still may not abandon their war against the Egyptian regime.

The implications are a society in which freedoms are severely circumscribed. The terms of political freedom afforded or denied will have a major impact on collective mobilization around gender equality. Restrictive legislation such as the current protest law and the proposed associational law will inhibit civic activism. The war on terror will mean an expansion of the spheres of influence of the secret political police. In effect, with the military intelligence and the secret political police both playing key governance roles, the country will be deeply securitized. This is likely to present survival challenges for the organic, informal street activism movements that emerged after the January 2011 revolution.

Beyond the general clampdown on civic expression, the political will of the regime could contract or expand spaces with respect to gender equality. If the government adopts a position of affirming women's rights (while ignoring other rights), it may afford formal and informal collective actors working on gender equality (depending on the issue) some contained space for engagement. It is possible that the regime will clamp down on activism on a number of human rights issues but assume an enabling policy toward political action on gender equality.

A likely scenario in the short term is for el-Sisi to pursue a policy of deploying his political clout to increase women's representation and participation in politics without strengthening the institutional mechanisms for policy enforcement. These actions will produce a new form of state feminism if women engage in a collective that can work with the political leadership to further women's rights. However, such actions can also produce a corps of ambitious women whose political survival in a highly patriarchal institutional context requires that they act in an entirely gender-blind manner.

The fate of the National Council for Women will play a central role in determining the extent to which collective actors working on gender equality issues have the space to hold the government accountable. As mentioned in the last chapter, the question of whether to engage the state has been highly divisive for collective actors who work on gender equality issues in Egypt. The National Council for Women requires a complete overhaul in its governance board. It needs greater representation from civil and political society (including Islamist groups). It should also include constituencies that are marginalized politically in Egypt, such as rural women, women from upper Egypt, and women younger than thirty. However, so far there is no indication that the state machinery will be accountable to anyone but the political leadership in the future.

Since the inception of the National Council for Women in Egypt, it was keen to engage with Western partners that presided in Egypt and in the United States and Europe. The fact that the NCW cared about its international image meant that nonstate actors could seek informal accountability via transnational spaces and actors. However, in the post-Mubarak phase, the prospects of influencing the state through transnational advocacy have greatly diminished. There is a stronger than usual anti-Western sentiment among the populace, and the Egyptian leadership does not seem to be as keen to win Western approval of its internal agendas. Hence, seeking transnational pathways for accountability does not seem, at this point in time, to provide much possibility for influence for gender justice or feminist activists.

Because gender justice can only be meaningful as part of a broader social justice agenda, the regime's orientation with respect to economic policies will have a significant impact on collective action around gender issues. If the regime espouses a state-centric model of economic development, one possible result is some type of state feminist orientation. If the regime adopts a neoliberal policy, then one option might be the reproduction of what Elsadda calls the "first lady syndrome" (see chapters 2 and 6). In such a scenario, the first lady assumes that gender matters are part of her realm and she represents herself as "the face of Egyptian women." Another possibility when a neoliberal model intersects with authoritarianism is the "benevolent dictator syndrome," in which the head of state takes particular actions or enacts policies in response to pleas for intervention from factions of the population. Regardless of how the pendulum swings it will almost certainly be influenced by the nature of state ideology.

## Nature of State Ideology

The future of collective action on gender equality and its effectiveness will be influenced by the ideological predisposition of the state. There are three critical questions surrounding state ideology. How does regime type intersect with prevalent ideologies? How are different ideologies intersecting with each other? How are they being negotiated via the nature of alliances and coalitions forged on a governance level?

With respect to intersecting ideologies, there is not always congruence between democracy and gender equality or authoritarianism and antifeminism. A majoritarian Islamist democracy circumscribed women's rights more than the authoritarianism of Mubarak. (The exception is the female leadership of Islamist movements, who would argue that they were able to express themselves in ways not possible under anti-Islamist authoritarianism.) The reality is that authoritarianism is bad for everyone except the ruling class. However, Islamist majoritarian democracy is especially bad for women, religious minorities, and dissenting groups who do not conform to the Islamist ideal (artists, musicians, atheists, and Muslims outside of the mainstream). Ideally, an inclusive democracy would secure the interests of groups on an intersecting basis (class, gender, religion, location, etc.).

The intensification of nationalism will entrench the idea that women's rights, minority rights, and the rights of workers and other interest groups should be sacrificed for the broader national project. The notion of "*tayha misr*" ("long live Egypt"), the motto of el-Sisi's presidential campaign, bears a strong resemblance to "Egypt above all else." One of its implications is the subordination of all citizen claims for the sake of the homeland. This brand of nationalism will not be ideologically inimical to collective action on gender equality in the same way that the Islamists' version of Islamism was in 2011–13. However, much depends on whether this brand of nationalism will be combined with non-Islamist or Islamist ideology. If combined with non-Islamist ideology, it is likely to be gender blind but far less damaging to gender equality in comparison to Islamist majoritarianism. In essence, it may not care for equality, but it is unlikely to be antifeminist (see chapter 2 for the definition of an antifeminist strand of Islamism). If nationalism is combined with strands of Islamism, the scenario for progressive gender equality agendas will be dire. Several factors will influence the nature of this ideological merger, the most important of which is the coalitional politics among those who rule Egypt.

The immediate future is contingent upon el-Sisi's coalitional strategy. El-Sisi has so far (up to 2014) been reluctant to establish his own political party. However, to avoid political isolation he is likely to engage in some version of coalition building or alliance making. Whom he aligns himself with will have major implications on the environment in which gender justice struggles unfold. It will either provide gender justice advocates with political allies who are sympathetic to their cause or political enemies who block and obstruct pathways for positive social change and progressive gender outcomes.

At the time of signing of the Roadmap in July 2013, the two obvious political contenders were the Salafis and the non-Islamist political forces represented in the person of Mohamed al-Baradie and by the Tamarod movement. Al-Baradie exited the political scene and left Egypt, and the Tamarod movement has split and does not have a strong constituency on the ground. The non-Islamist political parties and forces are weak, small, and fragmented. Some of them were established post-2011 and have not risen in politically enabling environments; others have existed for decades but suffer from a lack of constituency. Nevertheless, el-Sisi may wish to forge alliances with some of their leaders in light of their political visibility and influence.

The other key contenders are the ultraconservatives, the most visible of which are the Salafis. The presence of the Salafis in the Roadmap was critical for projecting the image of the post-Morsi order as inclusive of Islamist political parties and not a revolution against Islam. Their presence could have stirred a strong populist sentiment against the new order. The Salafis have deeply entrenched their power base in post-Morsi Egypt. They have lost several battles and had minimal influence on the Egyptian constitution of 2013 compared with 2012. The leadership of the Al-Nour Party, the key political platform of the Salafis, has come under fire for supporting a regime that the Islamist movements consider illegitimate for having overthrown an Islamist leader. Conversely, the government has given the Salafis significant reign to work on a grassroots level and to pursue their welfare work uninhibited (and to gather funds). In a context of extreme economic deprivation, they are now firmly positioned to build a constituency on the ground. Moreover, in view of the government's systematic repression of the Muslim Brotherhood and the uprooting of the Brotherhood's leadership and rank and file, some members who used to support the Muslim Brotherhood have since switched to supporting the Salafis. Even if they do not assume a visible formal presence in politics (at least during the early phases of el-Sisi's rule), they will still be able to advance their Salafi ideals from below.

If el-Sisi forges an alliance with the Salafis or other ultraconservative political forces or institutions, there would be dire consequences for the prospects of mobilizing collectively for gender justice and for the ability to elicit positive social change from the ground up on gender equality matters. The Salafis, as mentioned in chapter 1, are not gender blind or insensitive; they are antifeminist. They will obstruct the agendas of strong collective actors who advocate for any structural changes to the rigid patriarchal gender hierarchies in society. The deepening infiltration and consolidation of Salafis in Egypt on a grassroots level will present a major challenge to non-Islamist collective actors who wish to build a constituency for gender justice.

In the long term—whether el-Sisi stays in office or not—much will depend on the nature of coalitional politics. Egypt is not a case of an exclusively secular–Islamist ideological divide, but rather one of political interests and where they lie.

*Regional and International Dynamics*

In a highly turbulent Middle East, collective action on gender matters is directly affected by supranational dynamics, making issues of gender justice sensitive to foreign policy and security policies. The growth of the so-called Islamic State of Iraq and Syria (ISIS) and its enforcement of a highly reactionary brand of Islamism are generating waves of sympathy among radical Islamists in the Arab world and in Egypt as well as increased anxiety among women's civil society organizations and movements. If the reconfiguration of power enhances the position of Saudi Arabia, there could be a more insidious export of Wahabism in tandem with ISIS ideology. Similarly, an expansionist role for Qatar in foreign affairs would also lead to the export of highly conservative strands of Islamism. This would create a particularly challenging environment for advocates of gender justice; it would empower their opponents in the policy arena while diffusing reactionary views and practices about women in broader society.

In terms of stability, the disintegration of Syria, Libya, and Yemen will influence people's receptivity to dissent and engagement in unruly politics. The quest for stability may trump the quest for responsive government, which ultimately means that responsiveness to citizen engagement in contentious politics will be frowned upon if it is seen as undermining stability.

In Egypt in particular, since the ousting of Morsi in July 2013, relations with many Western countries have been tested. The Islamists and leftists had been the most outspoken political forces to oppose the West and Western aid in recent history. However, anti-Western sentiment now informs many officials' public rhetoric as well as that of a broader pool of the intelligentsia (including those independent of the state). Anti-Western sentiment will have a major impact on collective action on gender equality. Organizations that receive Western funding will be encroached upon, and opportunities to engage on gender equality in policy dialogues between Western and Egyptian counterparts will severely diminish.

Mubarak's regime was keen to give the West the semblance of a country committed to democracy, and its commitment to gender equality was a proxy for that democracy. The reverse is now true: the el-Sisi regime flourishes in showing indifference to the West. Hence, the prospects of collective action around gender bearing influence through supranational means in the near future will be closely tied to the nature of foreign relations between Egypt and the West.

If the scope of influence of Saudi Arabia and the Gulf countries continues to grow, it is likely that reactionary transnational Islamist networks will trump progressive, pro–gender equality international platforms.

## The Future of Collective Action

The strength of collective action around gender equality can only be examined in terms of its unfolding interactions with state and society. Much of the future of collective action will be contingent on the survival of the gender just movements that emerged organically and contributed so much innovation to making gender justice relevant to the public. Feminist organizations and coalitions also face a survival challenge. Deep polarization has ruptured relations and presents real hurdles for intragroup and intergroup healing.

Opportunities for influencing the agenda on gender equality will probably not be sufficient to elicit collective action. The constitution of 2013 could have brought together different actors supporting gender equality to jointly influence the unfolding process. However, the polarization in society regarding the legitimacy of the regime created a great schism that prevented collaborative work.

Gender identities will always intersect with political affiliations in a way that affects prospects of arriving at common denominators around a gender agenda. Divisions of political orientation mean that the essence of the disagreement is not necessarily around the gender matters in question but rather people's interpretations of the nature of the broader social and political order. Therefore, any future possibilities for collective mobilization are more likely to rely on perceived threats to gender equality than spaces for collaboration. When feminists organized to raise the banner of gender equality on International Women's Day in 2011, they were marginal. Yet the intensity of the backlash facing women's rights that unfolded over the course of that year propelled activists to respond to the threat. International Women's Day was marked by large collective mobilization bringing together initiatives from different political and civil affiliations. In other words, it is not the opportunities for influencing the regime behind the current red lines that will catalyze the joining of ranks among supporters of collective action. Rather, it is groups' *perceptions* of threats to women's equality as a consequence of the thickening or deepening of red lines that will propel collective action. Activists must pay careful attention to what may influence people's perceptions and the nature of the threat that may catalyze collective movement building. In the meantime, new modalities of resistance, subversion, compliance, and defiance will thrive under continuously shifting red lines.

# APPENDIX

◆

# GLOSSARY

◆

# WORKS CITED

◆

# INDEX

# APPENDIX

## Chapter 2 Interviewees

Interviewees in chapter 2 include: Marie Assaad, coordinator of the FGM Task-force; Aida Seif el Dawla, cofounder of the New Woman Foundation and the El Nadim Center for Rehabilitation of Victims of Torture and Trauma; Magdy Helmy, deputy coordinator of the FGM Taskforce; Nadia Wassef, feminist author and researcher; Amal Abd el Hady, leading researcher and board member of the New Woman Research Center; Seham Abd el Salam, pioneer of the campaign against male circumcision in Egypt; Yoanna Salib, director of the Coptic Associ-ation for Services and Training; the late Aziza Guindy, a leading figure in human development in the Arab world; Azza Soliman, head of CEWLA; Aziza Hussein, head of the National Commission on Population and Development; and Vivian Fouad, director of the Coptic Studies Center.

## Chapters 4 and 5 Interviewees

Hind Mahmoud interviewed the following people in July–August 2010 for research appearing in chapters 4 and 5: Amal Abd el Hady, member of the post-2011 feminist NGOs coalition and veteran feminist thinker and activist; Amal Mahmoud, feminist activist, member and founder of the Women and Develop-ment Forum, former coordinator of the CEDAW Coalition, and former infor-mal advisor to the Karama Coalition; Fareeda el Naqash, member of the NGO Forum for Women's Development (*Moultaqa al hay'at le tanmeyet al mar'a*) and its representative in the NWRO, as well as a leading intellectual who served on the editorial board of *Al-Ahali* newspaper; Afaf El Said, executive direc-tor of the Association for the Solidarity of Arab Women and member of the Karama Coalition; Lamia Lotfy, member of the New Woman Research Center, coordinator of the CEDAW Coalition, and former coordinator of the NWRO initiative; Abdel-Aal Mohamed, executive director of the Association for the

Enhancement of Sinai Women and Al-Arish coordinator for NWRO within the association; Mohamed Mahmoud Fahmy, executive director of Bader el Tawayel association for development in Sohag and coordinator for the NWRO project at the association; Dalia Zachary, executive director of the Gender Program at the Egyptian Association for Community Participation Enhancement (EACPE) and coordinator of the CEDAW Coalition's initiative at the association; Aida Nour el Din, head of the board of directors of the Women and Development Association (Alexandria) and member of the CEDAW Coalition, the NWRO initiative, and the Karama Coalition; Inas al Shafie, executive director of the Women's NGO Forum and formerly a coordinator of the CEDAW Coalition and the NWRO initiative in the forum; and Maher Bushra, head of the board of directors of Better Life Association in Minya and former member of the CEDAW Coalition and the NWRO initiative.

Hind and I both spoke to the late Afaf Mar'ie, vice head of the board of directors of the EACPE and coordinator (at the time) of the CEDAW Coalition; Mozn Hassan, executive director of the Nazra Center for Feminist Studies and member of the Karama Coalition; and Yousry Moustafa, the German International Development Agency executive director for the NWRO. The research also benefited from interviews I did with Mervat Abou Tieg, member of the CEDAW Coalition; Eman Mandour, member of the CEWLA and NWRO initiatives; Gaelle Le Maire, the officer responsible for overseeing the EACPE grant for the EU delegation for the CEDAW Coalition in Cairo; and Ineke Van De Pol, senior policy officer at the Dutch Ministry of Foreign Affairs who is responsible for oversight of the Dutch Fund for Millennium Development Goal 4 (MDG4; from which Karama–Egypt was funded).

In particular for chapters 4 and 5, I am grateful for interviews with Fatema Khafaga, formerly a member of the NWRO, whose breadth of knowledge on gender and development matters in Egypt never seizes to astound me. Many thanks are due for interviews granted to me by Margaret Sarofeem, head of gender work at the Coptic Evangelical Organization for Social Services and representative in the NWRO initiative; Seham Negm, member of the board of directors for the Women and Society Organization and the steering committee of the CEDAW Coalition (formerly a coordinator for CEDAW); Hala Abd el Kader, member of the board of directors of the Egyptian Foundation for Family Development and member of Karama and NWRO; Azza Kamel, board director of ACT and member of the Karama Coalition; Nehad Abou el Komsan, director of the Egyptian Center for Women's Rights and former member of Karama and the FGM

Taskforce; Hoda Badran, member of the board of directors for the Arab Alliance for Women and member of Karama and NWRO; Magda Adley, one of the founders of El Nadim Center for the Rehabilitation of Victims of Torture and Trauma and former member of the Karama Coalition; and Ashgan Farag, director of the Karama–Egypt. I also repeatedly interviewed Maya Morsi, Gielan el Messiri, and Yousry Moutapha, sometimes with them wearing their hats as Egyptian champions of gender equality and sometimes in their capacities working for donors.

## Chapters 6–8 Interviewees

Mohamed Hussein el Naggar interviewed the following people in April and May 2012 for research appearing in chapters 6–8: Dr. Amal Abd el Hady, member of the Revolutionary Feminist Coalition; Amira Abd el Fattah, head of programs for the educational component of CARE and member of NWRO and other coalitions; Azza Garaf, member of the 2012 parliament for the Freedom and Justice Party; Dalia Ziada, a women's rights activist and then director of the Ibn Khaldoun Center established by Saadeddin Ibrahim; Fareeda el Naqash, an activist involved in several coalitional efforts; Israa abd el Fattah, Sally Toma, and Samira Ibrahim, some of the iconic women figures of the 2011 Egyptian revolution; Nehad Abou el Komsan, the director of the Egyptian Center for Women's Rights and a seasoned women's rights activist; Niveen Mosaad, a professor at Cairo University who was also involved in several revolutionary coalitions; Reham Sabry, the media spokesperson for *Islah wal Tanmeya* (Reform and Development), a right-of-center political party; Rabha Fathi, head of the Association of Egyptian Female Lawyers; Nancy Okail, then director of Freedom House in Egypt.

Mohamed Hussein performed another set of interviews in July 2012 with Azza Soliman, a core member of several revolutionary coalitions; Hala Kamal, a leading figure of the Women and Memory Forum and member of the coalition of feminist NGOs; Iman Hassan, an activist with a long history of collective engagement; Ayman Abd el Wahab, head of the civil society department at the Ahram Center for Political and Strategic Studies who was appointed to the National Council of Women; Hafez Abou Seda, the secretary general of the Egyptian Organization for Human Rights; Zeinab Afifi, the head of El Etehad al Nabawy for Orphans and head of the Pears of Charity and two other associations in Menoufiyya and Tanta; Aida Nour el Din (see profile above); Margaret Sarofeem (see profile above); Nevine Ebeid, professor of political science at Cairo University, member of the New Woman Foundation, and member of the coalition of feminist NGOs; Hala Kamel, professor of English literature at Cairo University, member of the Woman and Memory Forum, and member of the coalition of feminist NGOs.

Robeir el Fares performed in-depth interviews with Mahmoud Ghozlan, a senior member of the Guidance Bureau of the Muslim Brotherhood; Suzie Adly, who was nominated by the Protestant Church in Egypt and replaced Manal el Tibi when she resigned; Manal el Tibi, human rights activist who was renowned for defending the rights of Nubians; Judge Abd el Fattah el Husseiny, secretary general of the proposals committee in the constituent assembly and member of the Shura Council; Amany Abou el Fadl, an Islamist activist; Tarek Abd el Hameed, member of the Shura Council and leading member of the Freedom and Justice Party; Omayma Kamel, the political counselor to President Morsi; Ahmed Maher, a leader of the April 6th youth movement; Mohamed Mohie El-Din, member of the Ghad al-Thawra Party; Ashraf Abd el Ghafour, secretary general of the arts syndicate in the constituent assembly; Judge Edward Ghaleb, a representative of the Coptic Orthodox Church; and Professor Huda Ghaniyya, an Islamist.

# GLOSSARY

*al bayʿa* **(pledge of allegiance):** Homage, pledge of allegiance. A pledge of obedience given by the citizens to their imam (Muslim ruler).

*ʿabayya:* Thick, loose robe often in black that covers the entire body down to one's ankles.

*ʿawra* **(shame, depravity):** Women's and men's private parts, which must be covered. There is consensus in Islamic *fiqh* that a man's *ʿawra* constitute the part of his body below the naval. Muslim jurists have differed on which parts of a woman's body constitute *ʿawra*. Some have argued that it is all of her body except her face and hands; hardliners such as the Salafis consider even her voice a source of *ʿawra*.

*ʿbadat* **(devotions, worship):** Devotions, devotional acts, or acts of worship. Islamic jurisprudence is divided into two parts: the jurisprudence of worship/devotions (*ʿbadat*) and jurisprudence of transactions. *ʿBadat* include five main areas: prayer, purity, *zakat*, fasting, and pilgrimage. Each of these main areas covers many other details.

**Caliphate:** Successor, vicegerent. The word is used in the Qur'an for Adam as the vicegerent of the Almighty on earth. In Islam it is the title given to the successor of Prophet Mohamed, who is vested with absolute authority in all matters of state, both civil and religious, as long as he rule in conformity with the law of the Qur'an and *hadith* (sayings of the Prophet). It is absolutely necessary that the Caliphate be a free man, an adult, a sane person, a person learned in divine matters, a powerful ruler, and a just person.

*daʿwa:* call to Islam.

*ʿeid* **(the feast):** In Arabic Islamic society there are two main feasts: *ʿeid al-Feter* and *ʿeid al-Adha*. *ʿEid al-Feter* is celebrated as the end of the month of fasting (Ramadan). *ʿEid al-Adha* is celebrated as the sacrifice of an animal. Each feast lasts for a few days (average of four), and they are generally nationwide holidays. Each feast holiday starts with special prayer, followed by official and popular celebrations.

*farida*: Duty, obligation, task. An enjoined duty, religious duty, or ordinance.

*feloul* (remnants): In classical Arabic, the remnants of the murderers and criminals after they have been defeated. In Egyptian society, this term emerged in February 2011 to describe the remnants of former President Hosni Mubarak's regime. In 2011, it had negative connotations and was intended to discredit anyone associated with the regime. However, as the political situation changed, the term began to refer to influential political forces from the former Mubarak regime who openly challenged the 2011 revolution.

*fiqh* (jurisprudence): the theology of Islam. The scholars of Islamic thought define *fiqh* as the science of studying the Islamic legal rulings based on scientific evidence. The main purpose of the *fiqh* is to answer people's questions about daily life in the light of Shari'a and to help people arrive at the right judgement. Scholars of the *fiqh* are called *al-Foqahaa* (singular is *al-Faqih*).

*hisba*: Enjoining what is right and forbidding what is wrong.

*huddud*: Prescribed punishments; the limits that prevent something (also translated as "borders"). In Islamic law *huddud* are punishments used to prevent the commission of certain acts. They are considered God's sanctions. Not all punishments can be considered *huddud*. The six main *huddud* are adultery, drinking alcohol, false accusation, theft, robbery, and highway robbery.

*ijma'a* (consensus): A unanimous agreement on something among a group of people. In Islamic jurisprudence *ijma'a* is the agreement or the consensus of the main Islamic *'ulama* (*Ahl el-Hel wa el-Aked*) on an issue. *Ijma'a* is the third source of Islamic jurisprudence (after the Qur'an and sunna). *Ijma'a* can be done by either words or actions.

*ijtehad*: An independent judgment in a legal question, based on the interpretation and application of the four foundations (*'usul*) as opposed to individual judgement (*taqleed*).

*jihad* (exertion, striving): Struggle for the sake of God, whether for self-discipline or self-purification. "Jihad for the sake of God" comprises all acts and statements made to spread or defend Islam. It also extends to self-jihad; a Muslim can strive in different ways, including giving of self, effort, money, providing assistance, or any other form of contribution.

*kufr* (infidelity): That which covers the truth. *Kufr* means disbelief in any of the articles of Islamic faith: to believe in Allah (God), his angels, his messengers, his revealed books, the day of resurrection, and *Al-Qadar* (i.e., divine preor-dainments; whatever Allah has ordained must come to pass). *Kufr* consists of rejection of the divine guidance communicated through the prophets and messengers of Allah. *Kuffar* is the plural of *kafer*, meaning infidel.

*marja'iyya*: Reference or framework. In Islamic and Arabic thought, it is used to refer to the epistemic basis or reference framing upon which ideas and issues are weighed and analyzed (i.e., Islamic reference or human rights reference, etc.).

*millioniyya*: A term coined during the uprisings of the Egyptian people against Mubarak to indicate the attempted mobilization of more than one million citizens. The call for a *millioniyya* to voice various demands and agendas was made by the civil political forces and the Islamists in the months and years following Mubarak's demise.

*mosheer* (field marshal): In Egypt, the highest rank in an army. Usually only one person can be appointed to it.

*moubadarat*: Plural for *moubadra*, meaning initiative.

"*mousharaka la moughalaba*" ("participation not domination"): A political slogan used by the Muslim Brotherhood in April 2011 before the parliamen-tary election to encourage political party activism. It was meant as a state-ment of the position of the Muslim Brothers in that they intend to participate in rather than dominate the political science. In 2014, the Al-Nour Party raised the same banner, "*mousharaka la moughalaba*," in preparation for the coming Egyptian parliamentary election.

*niqab* (Islamic face covering): The *niqab* is a type of clothing that covers the face of women in full, except the eyes. There is debate among Islamic jurists as to whether wearing the *niqab* is the proper Islamic attire or whether other forms of veiling that reveal the face are what is mandated.

*safka*: Conclusion of a contract, deal, bargain, or transaction.

*Shari'a*: Islamic canonical law based on the teachings of the Qur'an and the tra-ditions of the Prophet (*hadith* and sunna), prescribing both religious and secular duties and sometimes retributive penalties for breaking the law.

*shar'yya*: Legitimacy, legitimate.

*shura*: The consultation; from the Qur'an, "and consult them in affaires (of moment)."

*tafsir* (interpretation): The explanation and clarification of texts. It is one of the main Islamic sciences that endeavors to contribute to the full understanding of the Qur'an and the clarification of its meaning.

*tanzeem* (**organization**): An organization of a formal or informal nature; a group of people working together to achieve a specific goal. Usually members of a *tanzeem* follow a clear command of orders in a hierarchical structure with a strong leadership.

*'ulama* (**Islamic scholars**): The term is used as the title of learned teachers in Islam and jurisprudence. This term usually includes all religious teachers, such as *imams* (clergy leaders/rulers), *muftis* (authoritative persons issuing a *fatwa* or religious opinion), and *qadi* (judges).

*ummah* (**the nation**): A people, nation, or race. The word occurs approximately forty times in the Qur'an. *Ummah* is a term for a group of people associated with certain ties such as language, history, sex, and/or religion. The nation is considered a larger entity than the state. In Arabic and Islamic culture, the nation is a gathering of people with one religion (Islam). It includes groups of different governments and different generations (past, present, and future).

# WORKS CITED

Abasi, Eid. 2002. *Al-Da'wa al-salafiya wa mokefha men al-harakat al-okhra.* Alexandria: Dar al-Iman.

Abd el 'Al, Ali. 2012. "Al salafeyoon fi misr." In *Wak'e wa moustaqbal al harakat al salafiyya fi misr,* edited by Ahmed Ban, 25–31. Cairo: Markaz al Neel lil Derasat al Iqtesadeya wal Istratejiyah.

Abd el Fattah, Wael. 2015. "Bi mounasabet zhouhorha al ka'eeb." *Al-Tahrir,* January 20. http://www.tahrirnews.com/posts/138918.

Abdel Hadi, Amal. 2006. "A Community of Women Empowered: The Story of Deir El Barsha." In *Female Circumcision: Multicultural Perspectives,* edited by Rogaia Mustafa Abusharaf, 104–24. Philadelphia: Univ. of Pennsylvania Press.

Abd el Hady, Fatema. 2011. *Rehlati ma'a al akhawat min imam Hassan al Banna 'ila sogoon Abd el Nasser.* Cairo: Dar el Shorouk.

Abdel-Latif, Omayma. 2008. *In the Shadow of the Brothers: The Women of the Egyptian Muslim Brotherhood.* Washington, DC: Carnegie Endowment for International Peace.

Abd el Salam, Seham. 1999. "A Comprehensive Approach for Communication about Female Genital Mutilation in Egypt." In *Male and Female Circumcision,* edited by George C. Denniston, Frederick Mansfield Hodges, and Marilyn Fayre Milos, 317–30. New York: Kluwer Academic/Plenum.

Abd el Wahab, Ayman. 2012. "The January 25th Uprisings: Through or in Spite of Civil Society?" *IDS Bulletin* 43 (1): 71–77.

Abou el Fadl, Reem. 2013. "Sectarianism and Counter-Revolution in Egypt: Not a Family Affair." *Jadaliyya,* July 2. http://www.jadaliyya.com/pages /index/12581/sectarianism-and-counter-revolution-in-egypt_not-a.

Abouelnaga, Sherine. 2015. "Reconstructing Gender in Post-revolution Egypt." In *Rethinking Gender in Revolutions and Resistance,* edited by Maha el Said, Lena Meari, and Nicola Pratt, 35–58. London: Zed.

Abu-Lughod, Lila. 2010. "The Active Social Life of Muslim Women's Rights: A Plea for Ethnography, Not Polemic, with Cases from Egypt and Palestine." *Middle East Women's Studies* 6 (1): 1–45.

Abu-Lughod, Lila, and Rabab El-Mahdi. 2011. "Beyond the Woman Question in the Egyptian Revolution." *Feminist Studies* 37 (3): 683–91.

Agouz, Fadwa el. 2012. "The Formation of the National Council of Women: What the Fuloul Want!" *Ikhwan Online*, February 20. Accessed February 22, 2012. http://ikhwanonline.com/print.aspx?ArtID=101785&SecID=323 (site discontinued).

Ahmed, Leila. 1992. *Women and Gender in Islam: Historical Roots of a Modern Debate*. New Haven and London: Yale Univ. Press.

*Akhbar al-Youm.* 2012. "The Presidential Programme for Dr. Mohamed Morsi: The Renaissance Project." May 16. http://www.masress.com/akhbarelyom gate/33481.

Akram, Alfi. 2013. "Youth, Demographics, and Violence." Unpublished manuscript, presented to the Institute of Development Studies.

Ali, Nadje Al-. 2000. *Secularism, Gender and the State in the Middle East: The Egyptian Women's Movement*. Cambridge, UK: Cambridge Univ. Press.

———. 2014. "Reflections on (Counter) Revolutionary Processes in Egypt." *Feminist Review* 106: 122–28.

Ali, Khalid. 2012. "Precursors of the Egyptian Revolution in the Pulse of Egypt's Revolt." *IDS Bulletin* 43 (1): 16–25.

*Al Jazeera.* 2012. "Egypt's Morsi Stands by Decree." November 26. http://www .aljazeera.com/news/middleeast/2012/11/2012112520126225396.html.

Alvarez, Sonia E. 1999. "Advocating Feminism: The Latin American Feminist NGO Boom." *International Feminist Journal of Politics* 1 (2): 181–209.

Amar, Paul. 2011. "Turning the Gender Politics of the Security State Inside Out?" *International Journal of Feminist Politics* 13 (3): 299–328.

———. 2013. *The Security Archipelago: Human-Security States, Sexuality Politics, and the End of Neoliberalism*. London: Duke Univ. Press.

*The American Heritage Student Science Dictionary.* 2014. 2nd ed. Boston: Houghton Mifflin.

Amnesty International. 2011. "Egypt's Military Pledges to Stop Forced 'Virginity Tests.'" Press release, June 27. http://www.amnestyusa.org/news /press-releases/egypt-military-pledges-to-stop-forced-%E2%80%98virginity -tests.

―――. 2013. "An Alarming Statement by the Muslim Brotherhood on Egypt." *Women's Action Network* (Amnesty International UK blog), March 16. http://www.amnesty.org.uk/blogs/womens-action-network-blog/alarming -statement-muslimbrotherhood-eygpt-cedaw-calling-it-against.

Ashraf, Fady. 2013. "Constituent Assembly Member Names Announced." *Daily News Egypt*, September 1. http://www.dailynewsegypt.com/2013/09/01 /constituent-assembly-member-names-out/.

Bachelet, Michelle. 2011. "Pathways of Democratic Transitions: Reflections on the Chilean Experience." *UN Women*, June 5. http://www.unwomen.org/en /news/stories/2011/6/pathways-of-democratic-transitions-reflections-on-the -chilean-experience.

Badran, Margot. 1995. *Feminists, Islam, and Nation: Gender and the Making of Modern Egypt*. Princeton, NJ: Princeton Univ. Press.

Badry, Yusuf El-. 2007. "Sahefat al da'wa lel ta'n 'ala karar hazr khtan al-inath wa al-hokm al-sader feh." http://www.mohamoon-montada.com/default.aspx ?Action=Display&ID=85358&Type=3.

Bakr, Alaa. 2011. *Malameh raesiya lel manhag al-salafy*. Alexandria: al-Dar al-Salafiya lel nashr wel tawzee'.

Bakry, Mustafa. 2011. *Al Gaysh wal thawra Kesset al ayam al 'akheirah*. Cairo: Akhbar al-Youm.

Baldez, Lisa. 2002. *Why Women Protest: Women's Movements in Chile*. Cambridge, UK: Cambridge Univ. Press.

Banna, Gamal El. 2005. *Khetan al-banat layes sonna wala makrama laken jarima*. Cairo: Dar el-Fikr al-Islamy.

Barkati, Mohammed al-. 2003. *Al Ta'reefat al fiqheya: Moajam Yashrah al alfaz al-Mustalah aliyha bayn al-fuqahaa' wa al-osoliyeen*. Beirut: Dar el Kitab al 'lmeya.

Barker, Gary, Manuel Contreras, Brian Heilman, Ajay Singh, Ravi Verma, and Marcos Nascimento. 2011. "Evolving Men: Initial Results from the International Men and Gender Equality Survey (IMAGES)." Washington, DC and Rio de Janeiro: International Center for Research on Women (ICRW) and Instituto Promundo. http://www.icrw.org/publications/evolving-men.

Barker, Gary, Christine Ricardo, and Marcos Nascimento. 2007. "Engaging Men and Boys in Changing Gender-Based Inequity in Health: Evidence from Programme Interventions." Geneva: World Health Organization. http:// www.who.int/gender/documents/Engaging_men_boys.pdf.

Basu, Amrits, ed. 2013. *Women's Movements in the Global Era: The Power of Local Feminisms*. Boulder, CO: Westview.

Batliwala, Srilatha. 2007. "Putting Power Back into Empowerment." *OpenDemocracy*, July 30. http://www.opendemocracy.net/article/putting_power_back _into_empowerment_0.

———. 2008. *Changing Their World: Concepts and Practices of Women's Movements*. Toronto, ON: Association for Women's Rights in Development.

———. 2012. *Changing Their World: Concepts and Practices of Women's Movements*. 2nd ed. Toronto, ON: Association for Women's Rights in Development. http://www.awid.org/sites/default/files/atoms/files/changing_their_world _2ed_full_eng.pdf.

Batliwala, Srilatha, and Alexandra Pittman. 2010. *Capturing Change in Women's Realities: A Critical Overview of Current Monitoring and Evaluation Frameworks and Approaches*. Toronto, ON: Association for Women's Rights in Development. http://www.awid.org/publications/capturing-change-womens -realities.

Bayard de Volo, Lorraine. 2003. "Analyzing Politics and Change in Women's Organizations." *International Feminist Journal of Politics* 5 (1): 92–115.

Beckwith, Kate. 2007. "Mapping Strategic Engagements: Women's Movements and the State." *International Feminist Journal of Politics* 9 (3): 312–38.

———. 2013. "The Comparative Study of Women's Movements." In *The Oxford Handbook of Gender and Politics*, edited by Georgina Waylen, Karen Celis, Johanna Kantola, and S. Laurel Weldon, 411–36. New York: Oxford Univ. Press.

Beinin, Joel, and Frédéric Vairel. 2011. *Social Movements, Mobilization, and Contestation in the Middle East and North Africa*. Stanford, CA: Stanford Univ. Press.

Bobo, Kimberley A., Jackie Kendall, and Steve Max. 1991. *Organizing for Social Change: A Manual for Activists in the 1990s*. Santa Ana, CA: Seven Locks.

Bobo, Kimberley A., Jackie Kendall, Steve Max, and Midwest Academy. 2001. *Organizing for Social Change: Midwest Academy Manual for Activists*. Santa Ana, CA: Seven Locks.

Boyle, Elizabeth Heger. 2002. *Female Genital Cutting: Cultural Conflict in the Global Community*. Baltimore, MD: Johns Hopkins Univ. Press.

Brody, Alyson. 2009. *Gender and Governance: Overview Report*. Brighton, UK: Institute of Development Studies.

Carothers, Thomas. 2002. "The End of the Transition Paradigm." *Journal of Democracy* 13 (1): 5–21.

Choudry, Aziz, and Dip Kapoor. 2013. *NGO-ization: Complicity, Contradictions and Prospects*. London: Zed.

Cooke, Miriam. 2001. *Women Claim Islam*. Oxford, UK: Routledge.

Dabh, Basil El-. 2013. "99.3% of Egyptian Women Experience Sexual Harassment: Report." *Daily News Egypt*, April 28. http://www.dailynewsegypt .com/2013/04/28/99-3-of-egyptian-women-experienced-sexual-harassment -report/.

Dakhakhni, Fatheya Al-. 2006. "Hosni: Al-hejab awdah lilwaraa . . . wa asbahna nastame' elaa fatawi bethalath mleem." *Al Masry Al Youm*, November 16.

Daly, Sunny. 2012. "Young Women as Activists in Contemporary Egypt: Anxiety, Leadership, and the Next Generation." *Journal of Middle East Women's Studies* 6 (2): 59–85.

Dar al-Eftaa' al-Masriya. 2010. *Al-Fatawi al-Islamiya men Dar al-Eftaa' al-Masriya*. 2nd ed., vol. 9. Cairo: Supreme Council of Islamic Affairs.

Diaa, Mohamed. 2013. "The Status of Egyptian Women in 2012." *Egyptian Center for Women's Rights* (blog), January 22. http://ecwronline.org/?p=1743.

Dion, Karen Gardiner. 2012. "Justice Remains Elusive for Victims of Egypt's Virginity Testing." *Women Under Siege* (blog), May 24. http://www.women undersiegeproject.org/blog/entry/justice-remains-elusive-for-victims-of -egypts-virginity-testing.

Diop, Nafissatou, and Ian Askew. "The Effectiveness of a Community-Based Education Program on Abandoning Female Genital Mutilation/Cutting in Senegal." *Studies in Family Planning* 40 (4): 307–18.

Easton, Peter, Karen Monkman, and Rebecca Miles. 2003. "Social Policy from the Bottom Up: Abandoning FGC in Sub-Saharan Africa." *Development in Practice* 13 (5): 445–58.

"Egypt." 2007. *Coalition Equality without Reservation* (blog), April 10. https:// cedaw.wordpress.com/2007/04/10/egypt-reservations-to-cedaw/.

Egypt's Revolutionary Women's Coalition. Facebook page. Accessed August 13, 2013. https://www.facebook.com/RevolutionaryWomensCoalition (site discontinued).

Elsadda, Hoda. 2011. "Egypt: The Battle over Hope and Morale." *OpenDemocracy*, November 2. https://www.opendemocracy.net/5050/hoda-elsadda/egypt -battle-over-hope-and-morale.

————. 2012. "Women's Rights Activism in Post-Jan25 Egypt: Combating the Shadow of the First Lady Syndrome in the Arab World." *Middle East Law and Governance* 3 (1–2): 84–93.

Esplen, Emily. 2006. *Engaging Men in Gender Equality: Positive Strategies and Approaches*. Brighton, UK: Institute of Development Studies. http://www.bridge.ids.ac.uk/reports/BB15Masculinities.pdf.

Essam El-Din, Gamal. 2012. "Islamists Tighten Grip on Egypt's Shura Council." *Al-Ahram Online*, December 25. http://english.ahram.org.eg/NewsContent/1/64/61266/Egypt/Politics-/Islamsits-tighten-grip-on-Egypts-Shura-Council.aspx.

European Neighbourhood Info Centre. 2012. "Ashton in Cairo Ahead of EU-Egypt Taskforce: EU Pledge to Help Economy." News release, November 12. http://www.enpi-info.eu/medportal/news/latest/30999/Ashton-in-Cairo-ahead-of-EU-Egypt-Task-Force:EU-pledge-to-help-economy.

Eyben, Rosalind, and Laura Turquet, eds. 2013. *Feminists in Development Organizations: Change from the Margins*. London: Practical Action.

Ezbawy, Yusry Ahmed. 2012. "The Role of the Youth's New Protest Movements in the January 25th Revolution." *IDS Bulletin* 43 (1): 99–109.

Fitzsimmons, Tracy. 2000. "A Monstrous Regiment of Women? State, Regime, and Women's Political Organizing in Latin America." *Latin American Research Review* 35 (2): 216–29.

Fleishman, Jeffrey. 2012. "After Revolution in Egypt, Women's Taste of Equality Fades." *Los Angeles Times*, February 15.

Fowler, Alan. 1997. *Striking a Balance*. London: Earthscan.

Gad, Ibrahim. 2014. *Tamarod wal tareeq ela 30 Junio*. Cairo: Dar El Mahrousah.

Gaventa, John. 2008. *Building Responsive States: Citizen Action and National Policy Change*. Brighton, UK: Institute of Development Studies.

Gerges, Fawaz. 2013. "Egypt Coup: The Military Has Not Just Ousted Morsi. It Has Ousted Democracy." *Guardian*, July 14. http://www.theguardian.com/commentisfree/2013/jul/04/egypt-coup-military-morsi-democracy.

Gibaly, Omaima El-, Barbara Ibrahim, Barbara S. Mensch, and Wesley Clark. 2002. "The Decline of Female Circumcision in Egypt: Evidence and Interpretation." *Social Science & Medicine* 54 (2): 205–20.

Gilbert, Leah, and Payam Mohseni. 2011. "Beyond Authoritarianism: The Conceptualization of Hybrid Regimes." *Studies in Comparative International Development* 46 (3): 270–97.

Gladwell, Malcolm. 2010. "Small Change: Why the Revolution Will Not Be Tweeted." *New Yorker*, October 4. http://www.newyorker.com/reporting /2010/10/04/101004fa_fact_gladwell?currentPage=5.

Goetz, Anne Marie. 2007. "Gender Justice, Citizenship and Entitlements: Core Concepts, Central Debates and New Directions for Research." In Gender Justice, Citizenship and Development, edited by Maitrayee Mukhopadhyay and Navsharan Singh, 15–57. Delhi: Zubaan.

———. 2008. *Governing Women: Women's Political Effectiveness in Contexts of Democratization and Governance Reform*. Oxford, UK: Routledge.

Goetz, Anne Marie, and Shireen Hassim, eds. 2003. *No Shortcuts to Power: African Women in Politics and Policy Making*. London: Zed.

Guenena, Naema, and Nadia Wassef. 1999. *Unfulfilled Promises: Women's Rights*. Cairo: Population Council, West Asia and North Africa Office.

Hafez, Sherine. 2001. "The Terms of Empowerment: Islamic Women Activists in Egypt." *Cairo Papers in Social Science* 24 (4): 1–114.

———. 2012. "No Longer a Bargain: Women, Masculinity, and the Egyptian Uprising." *American Ethnologist* 39 (1): 37–42.

———. 2014. "The Revolution Shall Not Pass through Women's Bodies: Egypt, Uprisings and Gender Politics." *The Journal of North African Studies* 19 (2): 172–85.

Hagras, Hanan. 2014. "Hewar ma' Farkhonda Hassan." *El Mogaz*, March 14. http://www.elmogaz.com/node/141651.

Haj, Samira. 1992. "Palestinian Women and Patriarchal Relations." *Signs* 17 (4): 761–78.

Hallez, Kristina. 2012. "Changing Focus: Exploring Images of Women and Empowerment in Egypt." *IDS Bulletin* 34 (5): 104–9.

Haney, Lynne. 1994. "From Proud Worker to Good Mother: Women, the State, and Regime Change in Hungary." *Journal of Women Studies* 14 (3): 113–50.

Hassim, Sherin. 2004. "Voices, Hierarchies and Spaces: Reconfiguring the Women's Movement in Democratic South Africa." *Politikon: South African Journal of Political Studies* 32 (2): 175–95.

Hatem, Mervat. 1986. "The Enduring Alliance of Nationalism and Patriarchy in Muslim Personal Status Laws: The Case of Modern Egypt." *Feminist Issues* 6 (1): 19–43.

———. 1994. "Egyptian Discourses on Gender and Political Liberalization: Do Secularist and Islamist Views Really Differ?" *Middle East Journal* 6 (1): 661–76.

————. 2013. "Gender and Counterrevolution in Egypt." *Middle East Report* 268: 10–17.

Helgesen, Vidar. 2011. "Pathways for Women in Democratic Transitions: International Experiences and Lessons Learned." Keynote address, International IDEA, June 2. http://www.idea.int/gender/women-transitions.cfm.

Hellal, Amira. 2013. "Mervat Tallawy: Lam nazhab lilomam al mutaheda lilnail min somet Misr." *Al-Ahram*, March 18. http://www.ahram.org.eg /NewsQ/137178.aspx.

Helmy, Mustapha. 1976. *Qawaed al-manhag al-Salafy.* Cairo: Dar al-Ansaar.

Hendy, Mariam. n.d. "Khetan el-Enath bayn olmaa al-Shareaa wa al-atebaa." Accessed August 22, 2013. http://www.saaid.net/book/open.php?cat=4& book=2504.

Hesham Mubarak Law Center (HMLC). 2013. *Destour 2012 Derasah Tahleeliyah Tashri'e mejalet al siyassat al tashri'eyah.* Cairo: Author.

Higgins, Tracy E. 1997. "Democracy and Feminism." *Harvard Law Review* 110 (8): 1657–703.

Hogg, Steve, and Adrian Leftwich. 2007. *Leaders, Elites and Coalitions: The Case for Leadership and the Primacy of Politics in Building Effective States, Institutions and Governance for Sustainable Growth and Social Development.* London: Developmental Leadership Programme.

Horn, Jessica. 2013. *Gender and Social Movements: Overview Report.* Brighton, UK: Institute of Development Studies. http://docs.bridge.ids.ac.uk/vfile /upload/4/document/1310/FULL%20REPORT.pdf.

Hussein, Abdel-Rahman. 2012. "Muslim Brotherhood Supporters Protest Military Power Grab." *Guardian*, June 19. http://www.theguardian.com/world /2012/jun/19/muslim-brotherhood-supporters-protest-military.

Ivekovic, Rada. 2011. "Arab Insurgencies, Women in Transition." *OpenDemocracy*, March 8. http://www.opendemocracy.net/rada-ivekovic/arab-insurgencies -women-in-transition.

Jad, Islah. 2004. "The NGO-isation of Arab Women's Movements." *IDS Bulletin* 35 (4): 34–42.

Jaquette, Jane S., and Sharon L. Wolchik. 1998. "Women and Democratisation in Latin America and Central and Eastern Europe: A Comparative Introduction." In *Women and Democracy: Latin America and Central and Eastern Europe*, 1–28. Baltimore, MD: Johns Hopkins Univ. Press.

Joseph, Suad, ed. 2013. *Women and Islamic Cultures: Disciplinary Paradigms and Approaches.* Leiden, UK: Brill.

Kabeer, Naila. 1999. "Resources, Agency, Achievements: Reflections on the Measurement of Women's Empowerment." *Development and Change* 30 (3): 435–64.

Kandeel, Hesham. 2014. *Soldiers, Spies, and Statesmen: Egypt's Road to Revolt.* London: Verso.

Kandiyoti, Deniz. 2013. "Fear and Fury: Women and Post-revolutionary Violence." *OpenDemocracy*, January 10. http://www.opendemocracy.net/5050/deniz-kandiyoti/fear-and-fury-women-and-post-revolutionary-violence.

———. 2014. "Contesting Patriarchy-as-Governance: Lessons from Youth-Led Activism." *OpenDemocracy*, March 7. http://www.opendemocracy.net/5050/deniz-kandiyoti/contesting-patriarchy-as-governance-lessons-from-youth-led-activism.

Karam, Azza. 1997. "Women, Islamisms and the State." In *Muslim Women and the Politics of Participation*, edited by Mahnaz Afkhami and Erika Friedl, 18–28. Syracuse, NY: Syracuse Univ. Press.

———. 1998. *Women, Islamisms and the State: Contemporary Feminisms in Egypt.* London and New York: Macmillan and St. Martin's.

Katz, Nancy, David Lazer, Holly Arrow, and Noshir Contractor. 2004. "Network Theory and Small Groups." *Small Group Research* 35 (3): 307–32.

Khafagy, Fatema. 2007. *Assessment of National Machineries in Egypt.* Cairo: Euromed Role of Women in Economic Life Programme.

Khalaf, Abdel-Wahab. 1956. *'elm osoul al fiqh.* Cairo: Maktabet al da'wa al islamiyya.

Khattab, Moushira, Vivian Fouad, and Magdy Helmy. 2004. *Khitan al inath, ila mattah?* Cairo: Majles al Qawmi lil Omoumah Wal Toufoulah.

Kingsley, Patrick. 2012. "Mohamed Morsi's Last Interview as President of Egypt." *Guardian*, July 14. http://www.theguardian.com/world/video/2013/jul/04/mohammed-morsi-last-interview-egypt-president-video.

Kinoti, Kathambi. 2011. "The Centrality of Investing in Women's Rights Organizations and Leadership: The Launch of the Dutch FLOW Fund." *AWID News and Analysis*, June 24. http://www.awid.org/news-and-analysis/centrality-investing-womens-rights-organizations-and-leadership-launch-dutch-flow.

Kittleson, Shelly. 2014. "Egyptian Regime 'Going After Youth and Rights Organizations': Anti-torture Center Co-founder Discusses Women and Military Rule." *ANSA Med*, January 22. http://www.ansamed.info/ansamed/en/news/sections/politics/2014/01/21/Egyptian-regime-going-youth-rights-organizations-_9938085.html?idPhoto=1.

Kortam, Hend. 2013. "HarassMap: More Than Half of Sexual Harassment Takes the Form of Groping." *Daily News Egypt*, April 1. http://www.dailynews egypt.com/2013/04/01/harassmap-more-than-half-of-sexual-harassment -takes-the-form-of-groping/.

Kretschmer, Kelsy, and David Meyer. 2013. "Organizing around Gender Identities." In *The Oxford Handbook of Gender and Politics*, edited by Georgina Waylen, Karen Celis, Johanna Kantola, and S. Laurel Weldon, 390–410. New York: Oxford Univ. Press.

Kuumba, Bahati. 2001. *Gender and Social Movements*. Walnut Creek, CA: Alta Mira.

Lazreg, Marnia. 2002. "Development: Feminist Theory's Cul-de-Sac." In *Feminist Post-development Thought: Rethinking Modernity, Post-colonialism and Representation*, edited by Kriemild Saunders, 123–45. London: Zed.

Legal and Human Rights Centre. 2004. *The Legal Process: Can It Save Girls from FGM? A Case of Three Maasai Girls in Morogoro. A Report on the Enforcement of the FGM Law*. Dar es Salaam, Tanzania: Author.

Lewis, Pauline. 2007. "Zainab Al-Ghazali: Pioneer of Islamic Feminism." *Michigan Journal of History* 4 (27): 1–47.

Longbottom, Wil, and Hugo Gye. 2011. "Thousands of Women Brave Brutal Police in Tahrir Square." *Daily Mail*, December 21. http://www.dailymail .co.uk/news/article-2076547/Egypt-protests-Thousands-women-march-mis treatment-TahrirSquare.html.

Mahdi, Rabab El. 2010. "Does Political Islam Impede Gender-Based Mobilization? The Case of Egypt." *Totalitarian Movements and Political Religions* 11 (3–4): 379–96.

Mahmood, Saba. 2008. "Feminist Theory, Embodiment, and the Docile Agent: Some Reflections on the Egyptian Islamic." *Cultural Anthropology* 16 (2): 202–36.

Mahmoud, Abdel-Haleem. 1988. *Kittab al jihad*. Cairo: Dar al maʿaref.

Masriya, Amina, al-. 2013. "Not Your Booty." YouTube video, posted March 8. https://www.youtube.com/watch?v=0DkdYPs_qfE.

McAdam, Doug. 1995. "Initiator and Spin-Off Movements: Diffusion Processes in Protest Cycles." In *Repertoires and Cycles of Collective Action*, edited by M. Traugott, 217–40. Durham, NC: Duke Univ. Press.

McAdam, Doug, John D. McCarthy, and Mayer N. Zald. 1996. *Comparative Perspectives on Social Movements: Political Opportunities, Mobilizing Structures, and Cultural Framings*. Cambridge, UK: Cambridge Univ. Press.

Meyer, David S. 2004. "Protest and Political Opportunities." *Annual Review of Sociology* 20 (1): 125–45.

Meyer, David S., and Sidney Tarrow, eds. 1998. *The Social Movement Society.* Oxford, UK: Rowman & Littlefield.

Miller, Laurel E., Jeffrey Martini, F. Stephen Larrabee, Angel Rabasa, Stephanie Pezard, Julie E. Taylor, and Tewodaj Mengistu. 2012. *Democratization in the Arab World: Prospects and Lessons from around the Globe.* Santa Monica, CA: RAND Corporation. http://www.rand.org/content/dam/rand/pubs /monographs/2012/RAND_MG1192.pdf#page=47&zoom=150,0,74.

Mohamud, Asha, Samson Radeny, and Karin Ringheim. 2006. "Community-Based Efforts to End Female Genital Mutilation in Kenya: Raising Awareness and Organizing Alternative Rites of Passage." In *Female Circumcision: Multicultural Perspectives,* edited by Rogaia Mustafa Abusharaf, 75–103. Philadelphia: Univ. of Pennsylvania Press.

Molyneux, Maxine. 1985. "Mobilisation without Emancipation? Women's Interests, State and Revolution in Nicaragua." In *New Social Movements and the State in Latin America,* edited by David Slater, 233–59. Amsterdam: CEDLA.

———. 1998. "Analyzing Women's Movements." *Development and Change* 29 (2): 219–45.

———. 2006. *Women's Movements in International Perspective: Latin America and Beyond.* London: Institute of Latin American Studies.

Moncrieffe, Joy. 2006. "The Power of Stigma: Encounters with 'Street Children' and 'Restavecs' in Haiti." *IDS Bulletin* 37 (6): 34–46.

Moncrieffe, Joy, and Rosalind Eyben. 2007. *The Power of Labelling: How People Are Categorized and Why It Matters.* London: Earthscan.

Moser, Caroline. 2001. "The Gendered Continuum of Violence and Conflict: An Operational Framework." In *Victims, Perpetrators or Actors? Gender, Armed Conflict and Political Violence,* edited by Caroline Moser and Fiona Clark, 30–51. New York: Zed.

Mossaad, Nevine. 2014. "Molahazat ala leqaa el-Sisi." *El-Shorouk,* April 17. http://www.shorouknews.com/columns/view.aspx?cdate=17042014&id=7a9 cd443-c4e7-407e-a816-bc4571bba1bf.

Mostafa, S. R., N. A. El Zeiny, S. E. Tayel, and E. I. Moubarak. 2006. "What Do Medical Students in Alexandria Know about Female Genital Mutilation?" *Eastern Mediterranean Health Journal* 12 (2): 578–92.

Moubasher, Bahaa. 2013. "Al-Shura eataber watheqat al-maraa' hadman lekyan al-asrah." *Al-Ahram*, March 18. http://www.ahram.org.eg/NewsQ/137149 .aspx.

Muslim Brotherhood. 2006. "Al Mubadara." Accessed September 5, 2010. http:// ikhwanweb.com/home (site discontinued).

Mussalam, Mahmoud, and Mona Yasin. 2006. "Al-Ikhwan utaleboon raees al-gomhoriya beazl Farouk Hosni." *Al Masry Al Youm*, November 18.

Mustafa, Hala, Abd al-Ghaffar Shukor, and Amre Hashem Rabi'. 2005. *Building Democracy in Egypt: Women's Political Participation, Political Party Life, and Democratic Elections*. Stockholm: International Institute for Democracy and Electoral Assistance and the Arab NGO Network for Development.

Mustapha, Yousry. 2012. "Donors' Responses to Arab Uprisings: Old Medicine in New Bottles?" *IDS Bulletin* 43 (1): 99–109.

Nabil, Walaa. 2009. "Safwat Hegazy Moharedan." *Al Masry Al Youm*, October 13. http://today.almasryalyoum.com/article2.aspx?ArticleID=229113.

Naggar, Ahmed Al-Sayied El. 2010. *Al-inheyar al-eqtesady fi asr Mubarak: Haqaeq al-fasad wa al-betalah we al-ghalaa' wa al-rekood*. Cairo: Dar Merit.

Namla, Abdel-kareem, al-. 2009. *Al Shamel fi hodoud wa ta'reefat mostalahat 'lm osoul al fiqh wa sharh sahehoh*. 2 vols. Riyadh: Maktabet Al Roshd.

Nasr, Nahed. 2009. "Nawal el-Sa'adawi: Harabt 60 Aam deda el-khetan wa faqat wazefaty wa somaaty wa endama sadar el-kanon nasaboo al-fadl lezawgat el-raees." *Alyaum Alsabee*, October 8. http://bit.ly/1PxHcUF.

Nazneen, Sohela, and Maheen Sultan, eds. 2014. *Voicing Demands: Feminist Activism in Transitional Contexts*. London: Zed.

Nazra for Feminist Studies. 2013. "Brutal Sexual Assaults in the Vicinity of Tahrir Square and an Unprecedentedly Shameful Reaction from the Egyptian Authorities: 101 Incidents of Sexual Assaults during the Events of June 30th 2013." Joint statement, July 3. http://nazra.org/en/node/244.

Nechemias, Carol, and Kathleen Kuehnast. 2004. *Post-Soviet Women Encountering Transition: Nation Building, Economic Survival, and Civic Activism*. Washington, DC: Woodrow Wilson Center Press.

Obermeyer, Carla Makhlouf. 1999. "Female Genital Surgeries: The Known, the Unknown and the Unknowable." *Medical Anthropology Quarterly*, 13 (1): 79–116.

Osanloo, Arzoo. 2008. "Whence the Law: The Politics of Women's Rights, Regime Change, and the Vestiges of Reform in the Islamic Republic of Iran." *Radical History Review* 101: 42–58.

Osman, Ghada. 2003. "Back to Basics: The Discourse of Muslim Feminism in Contemporary Egypt." *Women and Language* 26 (1): 73–78.

Othman, Mahmoud Hamed. 2002. *Al kamous al mabyan fi istelahat al osoleyeen.* Riyadh: Dar Al Zeham lel Nashr wal Tawz'eih.

Othman, Mohammed Fathi. 1981. *Al-salafiya fe al-mogtama'at al-moasera.* Kuwait City: Dar al-Qalam.

Ottaway, Marina. 2004. *Women's Rights and Democracy in the Arab World.* Washington, DC: Carnegie Endowment for International Peace. http://carnegie endowment.org/files/CarnegiePaper42.pdf.

Pascall, Gillian, and Kwak Anna. 2005. *Gender Regimes in Transition in Central and Eastern Europe.* Bristol, UK: Policy Press.

Pathways of Women's Empowerment. 2012. *Empowerment: A Journey Not a Destination.* Brighton, UK: Author. https://www.ids.ac.uk/files/dmfile/Synthesis Report12DecR.pdf.

Phillips, Anne. 2010. *Gender and Culture.* Cambridge, UK: Polity.

Pittman, Alexandra, and Rabéa Naciri. 2013. "Voicing Autonomy through Citizenship: The Regional Nationality Campaign and Morocco." In *Voicing Demands: Feminist Activism in Transitional Contexts,* edited by Maheen Sultan and Sohela Nazneen, 118–51. London: Zed.

Population Council. 2011. *Survey of Young People in Egypt.* Cairo: Population Council, West Asia and North Africa Office. http://www.popcouncil.org /uploads/pdfs/2010PGY_SYPEFinalReport.pdf.

Rabie, Amr Hashem, ed. 2012a. *Daleel Al Nokhba Al Barlamaneya al Misriyya.* Cairo: Al Ahram Center for Political and Strategic Studies.

———, ed. 2012b. *Intekhabat majles al sha'ab 2011/2012.* Cairo: Al Ahram Center for Political and Strategic Studies.

Rahman, Anika, and Nahid Toubia. 2000. *Female Genital Mutilation: A Guide to Laws and Policies Worldwide.* London: Zed.

Rai, Shirin, ed. 2000. *International Perspectives on Gender and Democratisation.* London: Macmillan.

Rashed, Dena. 2009. "Strike for Now." *Al-Ahram Weekly,* April 9.

Rashwan, Diaa. 2009. "Hawla malameh el-zahera el-Islamiya fe Misr." *Al-Shorouk,* November 17. http://www.shorouknews.com/Columns/Column .aspx?id=155466 (site discontinued).

Rashwan, Hoda. 2008. "Moagahat al-asela al-ashra ben Askar wa Moshira hawl khetan al-enath." *Al Masry Al Youm,* August 10. http://today.almasryal youm.com/article2.aspx?ArticleID=116696.

Rashwan, Hoda, and Mamdouh Thabet. 2007. "Thalathet a'laf moaten erfaoon sorat al-shaheda Bedoor fe maserah did khetan al-enath be Asiut." *Al Masry Al Youm*, July 6. http://today.almasryalyoum.com/article2.aspx?ArticleID =67538.

Ray, Raka, and Anna Korteweg. 1999. "Women's Movements in the Third World: Identity, Mobilization, and Autonomy." *Annual Review of Sociology* 25: 47–71.

Razavi, Shahrashoub. 2000. *Women in Contemporary Democratization*. Geneva: United Nations Research Institute for Social Development.

Regan, Colm. 2012. "Women, Citizenship and Change: The Role of the Women's Movement in the Arab World." In *Change and Opportunities in the Emerging Mediterranean*, edited by Stephen Calleya and Monika Wohlfeld, 234–51. Msida, Malta: Univ. of Malta.

Reilly, Niamh. 2009. *Women's Human Rights: Seeking Gender Justice in a Globalizing Age*. Cambridge, UK: Polity.

*Reuters*. 2013. "Egypt Courts Hands Jail Terms to 43 NGO Workers, including 15 US Citizens." June 4. http://rt.com/news/egypt-ngo-workers-jail-227/.

Ricardo, Christine, Marci Eads, and Gary Barker. 2011. *Engaging Boys and Young Men in the Prevention of Sexual Violence: A Systematic and Global Review of Evaluated Interventions*. Pretoria, South Africa: Promundo.

Rousseau, Stephanie. 2006. "Women's Citizenship and Neopopulism: Peru under the Fujimori Regime." *Latin American Politics and Society* 48 (1): 117–41.

Rowbotham, Sheila. 1992. *Women in Movement: Feminism and Social Action*. Oxford, UK: Routledge.

Rustow, Dankwart. 1970. "Transitions to Democracy." *Comparative Politics* 2 (3): 337–63.

Safa, Helen Icken. 1990. "Women's Social Movements in Latin America." *Gender and Society* 3 (3): 354–69.

Sampanis, Maria, ed. 2003. *Preserving Power through Coalitions: Comparing the Grand Strategy of Great Britain and the United States*. Santa Barbara, CA: Praeger.

Schirmer, Jennifer. 1989. "Those Who Died for Life Cannot Be Called Dead: Women and Human Rights Protest in Latin America." *Feminist Review* 32: 3–29.

Seif el Dawla, Aida. 1999. "The Political and Legal Struggle over Female Genital Mutilation in Egypt: Five Years Since the ICPD." *Reproductive Health Matters* 7 (13): 128–36.

Shakʿa, Mustapha Al. 1994. *Islam bela mazahip.* Cairo: Egyptian Lebanese Dar.

Sharmani, Mulki Al-. 2009. "Egyptian Family Courts: A Pathway of Women's Empowerment?" *Hawwa* 7 (2): 89–119.

Shash, Farah. 2013. "Uncovering Stories of Sexual Assault in the Shadow of The Brothers." *Pathways of Women's Empowerment,* June. http://s3-eu-west-1 .amazonaws.com/pathwaysofempowerment-org-production/downloads /uncovering_stories_of_sexual_assault_original12854b8f7935685e52600b d699fe8c15.pdf.

Shell-Duncan, Bettina, and Ylva Hernlund. 2001. *Female Circumcision in Africa: Culture, Controversy and Change.* Boulder, CO: Lynne Rienner.

Sholkamy, Hania. 2011. "From Tahrir Square to My Kitchen." *OpenDemocracy,* March 14. https://www.opendemocracy.net/5050/hania-sholkamy/from -tahrir-square-to-my-kitchen.

———. 2012. "The Jaded Gender and Development Paradigm of Egypt." *IDS Bulletin* 43 (1): 94–98.

Singerman, Diane. 2013. "Youth, Gender, and Dignity in the Egyptian Uprising." *Journal of Middle East Women's Studies* 9 (3): 1–27.

Soliman, Samer. 2006. *Al-nezam al-qawi wa al-dawlah al-daeefa: Edaret al-azmah al-maliya wa al-tagheer al-siyasi fi ahd Mubarak.* 2nd ed. Cairo: Al-Dar Lilnashr wa al-Tawze'e.

Sternbach, Nancy Saporta, Marysa Navarro-Aranguren, Patricia Chuchryk, and Sonia E. Alvarez. 1992. "Feminisms in Latin America: From Bogotá to San Bernardo." *Signs: Journal of Women, Culture and Society* 17 (2): 393–434.

Tadros, Mariz. 2000. "Hadithi, Breaking the Silence: An Egyptian Experience." *Rainbo Publications* 2: 1–35.

———. 2010a. "Between the Elusive and the Illusionary: Donors' Empowerment Agendas in the Middle East in Perspective." *Comparative Studies of South Asia, Africa and the Middle East* 30 (2): 224–37.

———. 2010b. "Quotas: A Highway to Power in Egypt . . . but for Which Women?" *IDS Bulletin* 41 (5): 89–99.

———. 2011a. "The Securitisation of Civil Society: A Case Study of NGOs–State Security Investigations (SSI) Relations in Egypt." *Journal of Security, Conflict and Development* 11 (1): 79–103.

———. 2011b. "We, the Women Who Revolt." *Participation, Power and Social Change* (blog), December 21. https://participationpower.wordpress.com/2011 /12/21/we-the-women-who-revolt/.

———. 2011c. *Working Politically behind Red Lines: Structure and Agency in a Comparative Study of Women's Coalitions in Egypt and Jordan.* London: Developmental Leadership Programme.

———. 2012a. *Battling with Increased Gender-Based Violence in Egypt's Transition: Report on the Scoping Workshop Held in Cairo, November 2012.* Brighton, UK: Institute of Development Studies. https://www.ids.ac.uk/pub lication/battling-with-increased-gender-based-violence-in-egypt-s-transi tion-report-on-the-scoping-workshop-held-in-cairo-november-2012.

———. 2012b. "Egyptian Women Have Had Enough of Being Told to Cover Up." *Guardian*, May 29. http://www.guardian.co.uk/commentisfree/2012 /may/29/egypt-women-cover-up-coptic.

———. 2012c. "Introduction: The Pulse of Egypt's Revolt." *IDS Bulletin* 43 (1): 1–15.

———. 2012d. "The Islamization of State Policy." *OpenDemocracy*, January 8. http://www.opendemocracy.net/5050/mariz-tadros/egypt-islamization-of -state-policy.

———. 2012e. *Muslim Brotherhood in Contemporary Egypt: Democracy Redefined or Confined.* Oxford, UK: Routledge.

———. 2012f. "The Perilous Slide: Towards an Islamist Dictatorship in Egypt?" *OpenDemocracy*, November 26. http://www.opendemocracy.net/5050/mariz -tadros/perilous-slide-towards-islamist-dictatorship-in-egypt.

———. 2013a. *Database of Collective Actors Involving Men Tackling Gender-Based Violence in Public Space in Post-Mubarak Egypt.* Brighton, UK: Institute of Development Studies. http://www.ids.ac.uk/publication/database -of-collective-actors-involving-men-tackling-gender-based-violence-in -public-space-in-post-mubarak-egypt.

———. 2013b. *Egypt's Unfinished Transition or Unfinished Revolution? Unruly Politics and Capturing the Pulses of the Street.* Brighton, UK: Institute of Development Studies. http://www.ids.ac.uk/publication/egypt-s-unfinished -transition-or-unfinished-revolution-unruly-politics-and-capturing-the -pulses-of-the-street.

———. 2013c. "Missing the Pulse of Egypt's Citizens?" *Power and Social Change* (blog), July 4. https://participationpower.wordpress.com/2013/07/04 /missing-the-pulse-of-egypts-citizens/.

———. 2013d. *Politically Motivated Sexual Assault and the Law in Violent Transitions: A Case Study from Egypt.* Brighton, UK: Institute of Development

Studies. http://www.ids.ac.uk/publication/politically-motivated-sexual-assault
-and-the-law-in-violent-transitions-a-case-study-from-egypt.

———. 2013e. "Understanding the Politics and Pulse of Egypt's Protests." *Institute of Development Studies News*, August 15. http://www.ids.ac.uk/news
/understanding-the-politics-and-pulse-of-egypt-s-protests.

———. 2014. "Ejecting Women from Formal Politics in the Old-New Egypt." In *Women in Politics: Gender, Power and Development*, 101–34. London: Zed.

———. 2015. "Understanding Politically Motivated Sexual Assault in Protest Spaces: Evidence from Egypt (March 2011 to June 2013)." *Journal of Social and Legal Studies*, March 30. http://sls.sagepub.com/content/early/2015/03/2
6/0964663915578187.full.pdf+html.

———. 2015. *Mobilizing against Sexual Harassment in Public Space in Egypt: From Blaming "Open Cans of Tuna" to "the Harasser is a Criminal."* Brighton, UK: Institute of Development Studies. http://opendocs.ids.ac.uk/opendocs
/handle/123456789/7109#.VpKBYVJlz6k.

Taha, Rana. 2013. "Constitutional Amendments Mostly Criticised." *Daily News Egypt*, August 27. http://www.dailynewsegypt.com/2013/08/27/constitutional
-amendments-mostly-criticised/.

Tahir, Nadia. 2012. "'We Are Not Women, We Are Egyptians': Spaces of Protest and Representation." *OpenDemocracy*, April 6. https://www.opendemocracy
.net/5050/nadia-taher/we-are-not-women-we-are-egyptians-spaces-of-pro
test-and-representation.

Talhami, Ghada. 1996. *The Mobilization of Muslim Women in Egypt*. Gainesville: Univ. Press of Florida.

Tarrow, Sidney. 2011. *Power in Movement: Social Movements and Contentious Politics*. Cambridge, UK: Cambridge Univ. Press.

Tilly, Charles. 2004. *Social Movements, 1768–2004*. Boulder, CO: Paradigm.

Tilly, Charles, and Sidney Tarrow. 2007. *Contentious Politics*. Boulder, CO: Paradigm.

Tilly, Charles, Sidney Tarrow, and Doug McAdam. 2001. *Dynamics of Contention*. Cambridge, UK: Cambridge Univ. Press.

Tolmany, Susan. 2013. "A Step Forward Amid Strong Opposition to Women's Human Rights at this Year's 57th Commission on the Status of Women." *AWID News and Analysis*, March 22. http://www.awid.org/news-and-analysis
/step-forward-amid-strong-opposition-womens-human-rights-years-57th
-commission#sthash.6P4HtgrR.dpuf.

V-Day. 2005. "V-Day Announces Launch of the Karama Program and the Opening of Bayat Hawa, the First Safe House for Women in Cairo." Press release, August 17. http://www.vday.org/node/1406.html#.Vm-wJ8rR9wg.

Viterna, Jocelyn, and Kathleen Fallon. 2008. "Democratization, Women's Movements and Gender Equitable States: A Framework for Comparison." *American Sociological Review* 73: 668–89.

Wasserman, Stanley, and Katherine Faust. 1994. *Social Network Analysis: Methods and Applications (Structural Analysis in the Social Sciences)*. Cambridge, UK: Cambridge Univ. Press.

Waylen, Georgina. 1994a. *What Can the South African Transition Tell Us about Gender and Democratization?* Belfast: Centre for Advancement of Women in Politics, Queens Univ.

———. 1994b. "Women and Democratization: Conceptualizing Gender Relations in Transition Politics." *World Politics* 46 (3): 327–54.

———. 2007. *Engendering Transitions: Women's Mobilization, Institutions and Gender Outcomes*. Oxford and New York: Oxford Univ. Press.

Weldon, Laurel, and Mala Htun. 2013. "Feminist Mobilisation and Progressive Policy Change: Why Governments Take Action to Combat Violence against Women." *Gender and Development* 21 (2): 231–47.

Win, Everjoice J. 2004. "When Sharing Female Identity Is Not Enough: Coalition Building in the Midst of Political Polarisation in Zimbabwe." *Gender and Development* 12 (1): 19–27.

World Health Organization. 2014. "Female Genital Mutilation." Factsheet, last updated February. http://www.who.int/mediacentre/factsheets/fs241/en/.

Zanaty, Fatma El-, Enas M. Hussein, Gihan A. Shawky, Ann Way, and Sunita Kishor. 1996. "Egypt Demographic and Health Survey 1995." Calverton, MD: National Population Council (Arab Republic of Egypt) and Macro International Inc.

Zanaty, Fatma El-, and Ann A. Way. 2004. "2003 Egypt Interim Demographic and Health Survey." Cairo: Ministry of Health and Population, National Population Council, El-Zanaty and Associates, and ORC Macro.

Zeheily, Wahba el. 2010. *Maw'sou'et al fiqh al Islami wal qadayah al mou'asrah*. 3 vols. Damascus: Dar el Fekr.

Zulu, Lindiwe. 2000. "Institutionalizing Change: South African Women's Participation in the Transition to Democracy." In *International Perspectives on Gender and Democratisation*, edited by Shirin Rai, 166–81. Basingstoke, UK: Palgrave Macmillan.

# INDEX

**Mariz Tadros** is the co-leader of the Power and Popular Politics research cluster at the Institute of Development Studies, University of Sussex, UK. She is the editor of *Women in Politics: Gender, Power and Development* (2014) and the author of *The Muslim Brotherhood in Contemporary Egypt: Democracy Redefined or Confined?* (2012) and *Copts at the Crossroads: The Challenges of Building Inclusive Democracy in Egypt* (2013). Tadros edited "The Pulse of Egypt's Revolt" (*IDS Bulletin* 43.1, 2011) and "Religion, Rights and Gender at the Crossroads" (*IDS Bulletin* 42.1, 2010), and she co-edited "Quotas: Add Women and Stir?" (*IDS Bulletin* 41.5, 2010) with Analice Costa. She has led several multidiscipline, multicountry research initiatives, and she currently writes about religion and development, gender and security, and civil and political action. Before joining the Institute of Development Studies, Tadros was an assistant professor of political science at the American University in Cairo. For almost ten years, she worked as a journalist for *Al-Ahram Weekly* newspaper, where she contributed more than three hundred articles on women's rights, civil society, developmental issues, and social issues.